The Zucchini Festival

Written by Ed Cho
Illustrated by Lee Cherolis

with

Cover Colors by Sara Gross
Book Layout by Samantha Kyle

This volume collects stories from the *Little Guardians* website originally published online from June 2011 through March 2012.

www.littleguardianscomic.com

Second edition June 2013

When I first met Lee I knew immediately I wanted to work with him. His line work and art style were amazing, and best of all he was a cool guy that I knew I could get along with. Once it was decided, yes, we should work on a comic together, we then had to sit down and figure out what that comic was going to be. I did not have scripts in my back pocket, waiting for an amazing artist to come along. After much brainstorming and colluding, the initial concepts for Little Guardians were born.

We had the makings of a pretty cool fantasy, adventure comic; my job being to write the scripts, which included dialogue, scenes, specific events, etc. The only problem was I didn't have a lot of background in the fantasy genre. (I've only read Lord of the Rings once!) I instead drew upon my video game knowledge, specifically Japanese RPG games to which I owe a lot of the writing of this story. These games include Shining Force 1 and 2, Phantasy Star 4, the Final Fantasy series (From a narrative perspective FF 9 is my favorite), Lunar, Breath of Fire 2 and 3, Azure Dreams, and many more great games. I could not have written Little Guardians if I hadn't hacked 'n slashed my way through all those experience giving baddies.

We of course have to thank the ladies in our lives. Sam was instrumental in the making of our website, critiquing the art, and helping with the layout of this book. I am so grateful to my wife, Nancy, for putting up with me going over to Lee's house to work on comic book stuff while we had a crying baby at home.

Hope you enjoy the book and thanks for reading.

-Ed

I've never had more fun working on a comic or really any other project and I could not ask for a better partner to share the experience with.

-Lee

Prologue

The Birth

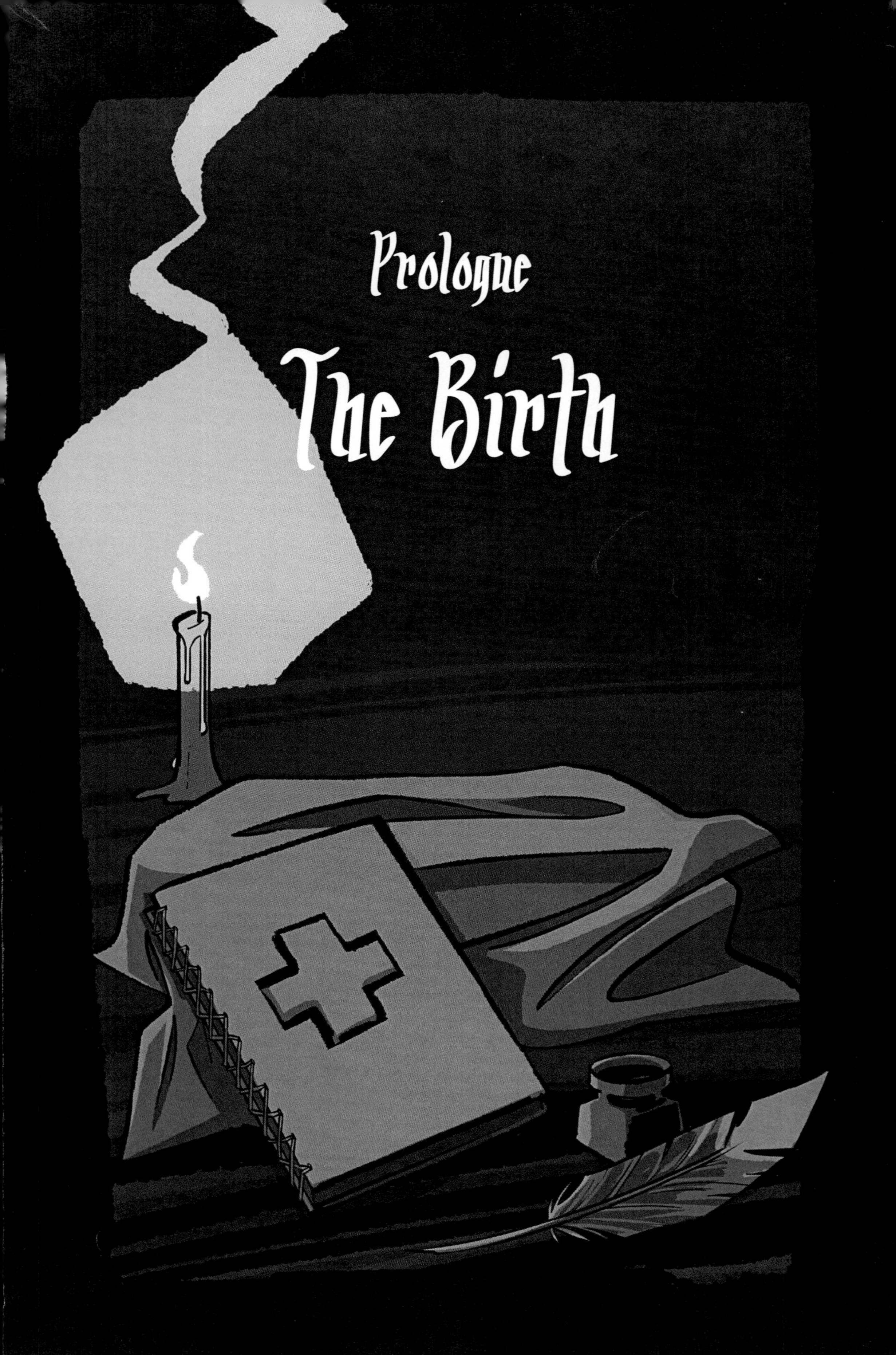

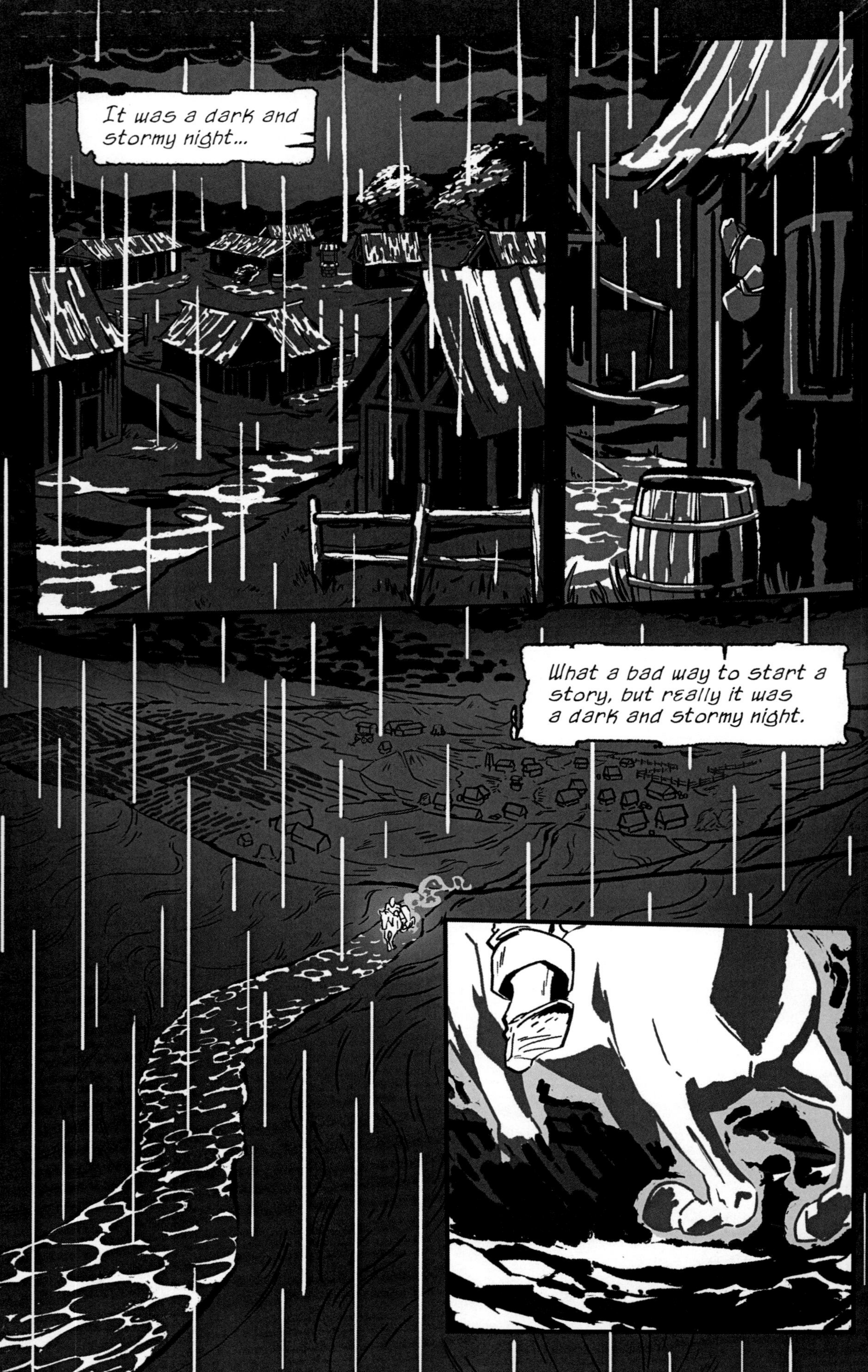
It was a dark and stormy night...
What a bad way to start a story, but really it was a dark and stormy night.

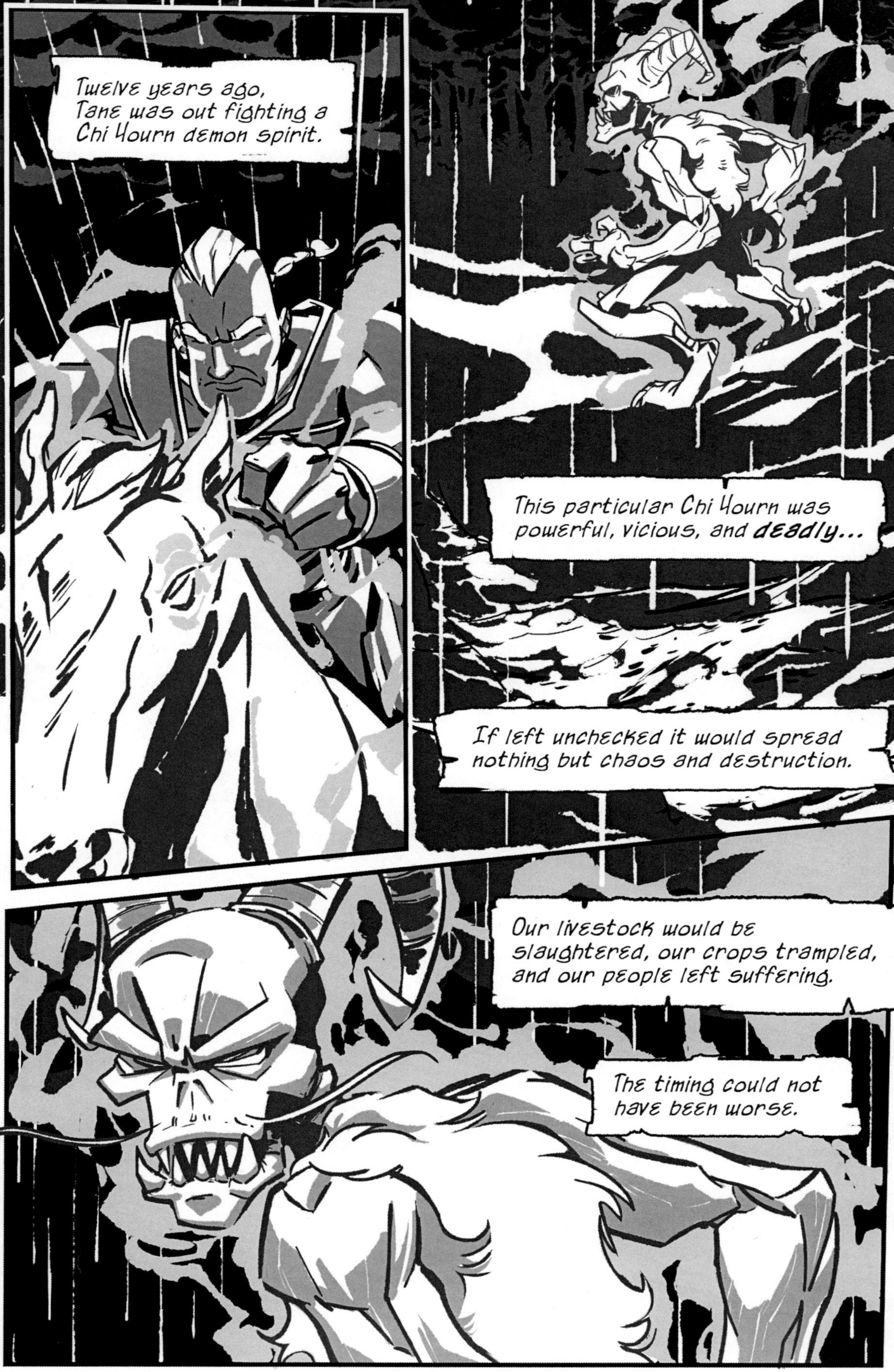
Twelve years ago, Tane was out fighting a Chi Yourn demon spirit.
This particular Chi Yourn was powerful, vicious, and **deadly...**
If left unchecked it would spread nothing but chaos and destruction.
Our livestock would be slaughtered, our crops trampled, and our people left suffering.
The timing could not have been worse.

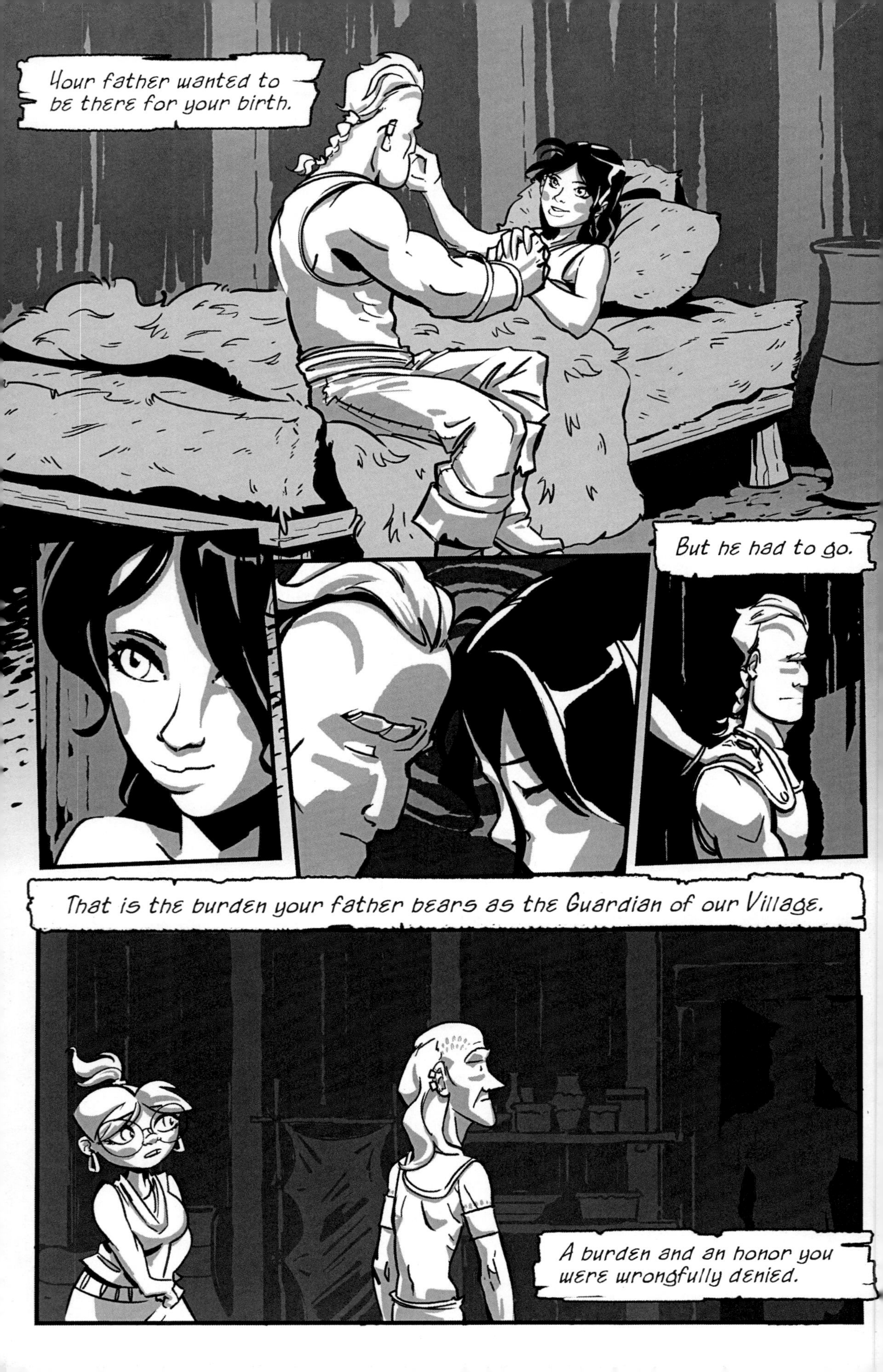
Your father wanted to be there for your birth.
But he had to go.
That is the burden your father bears as the Guardian of our Village.
A burden and an honor you were wrongfully denied.

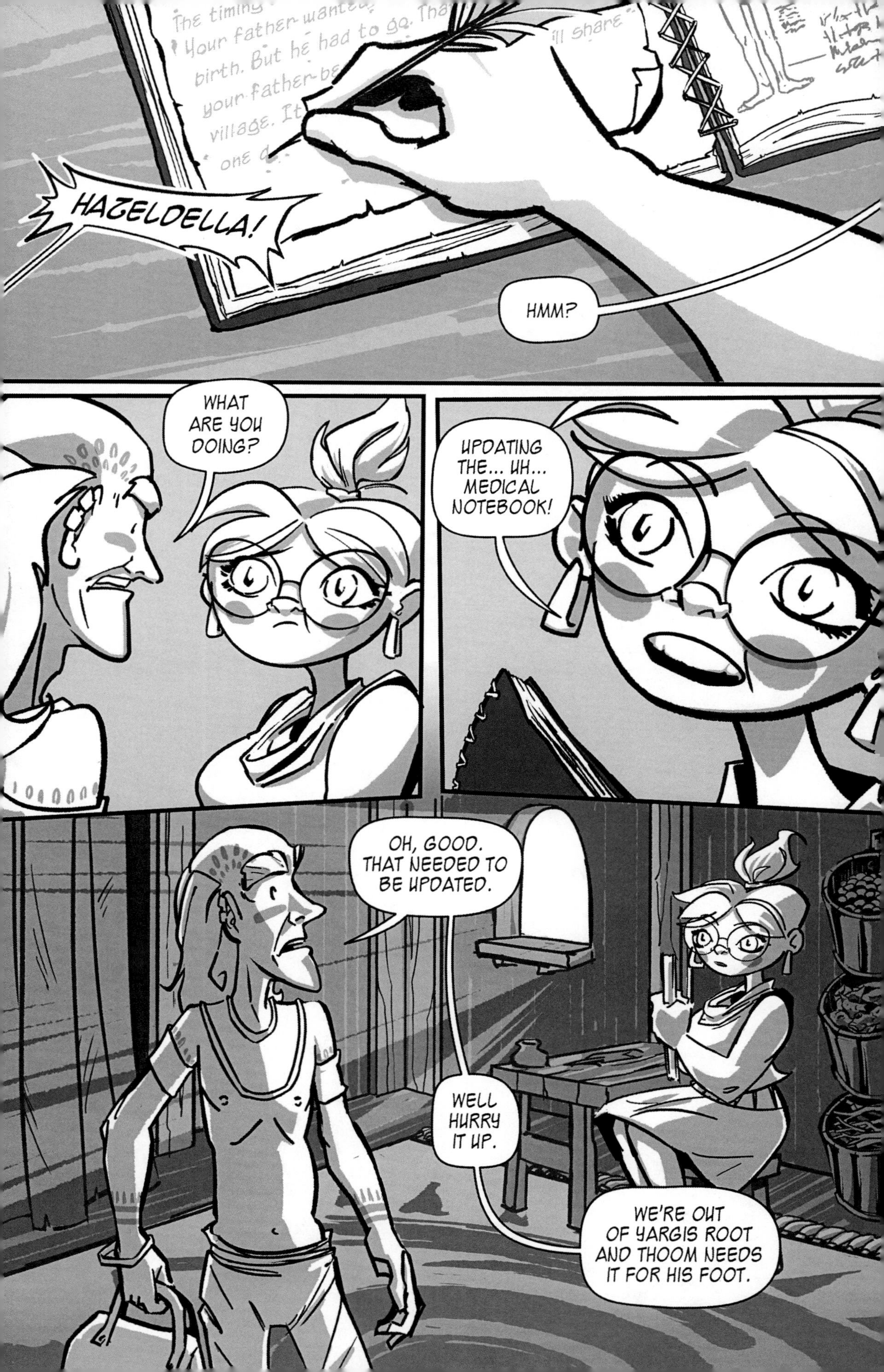
HAZELDELLA!
HMM?
WHAT ARE YOU DOING?
UPDATING THE... UH... MEDICAL NOTEBOOK!
OH, GOOD. THAT NEEDED TO BE UPDATED.
WELL HURRY IT UP.
WE'RE OUT OF YARGIS ROOT AND THOOM NEEDS IT FOR HIS FOOT.

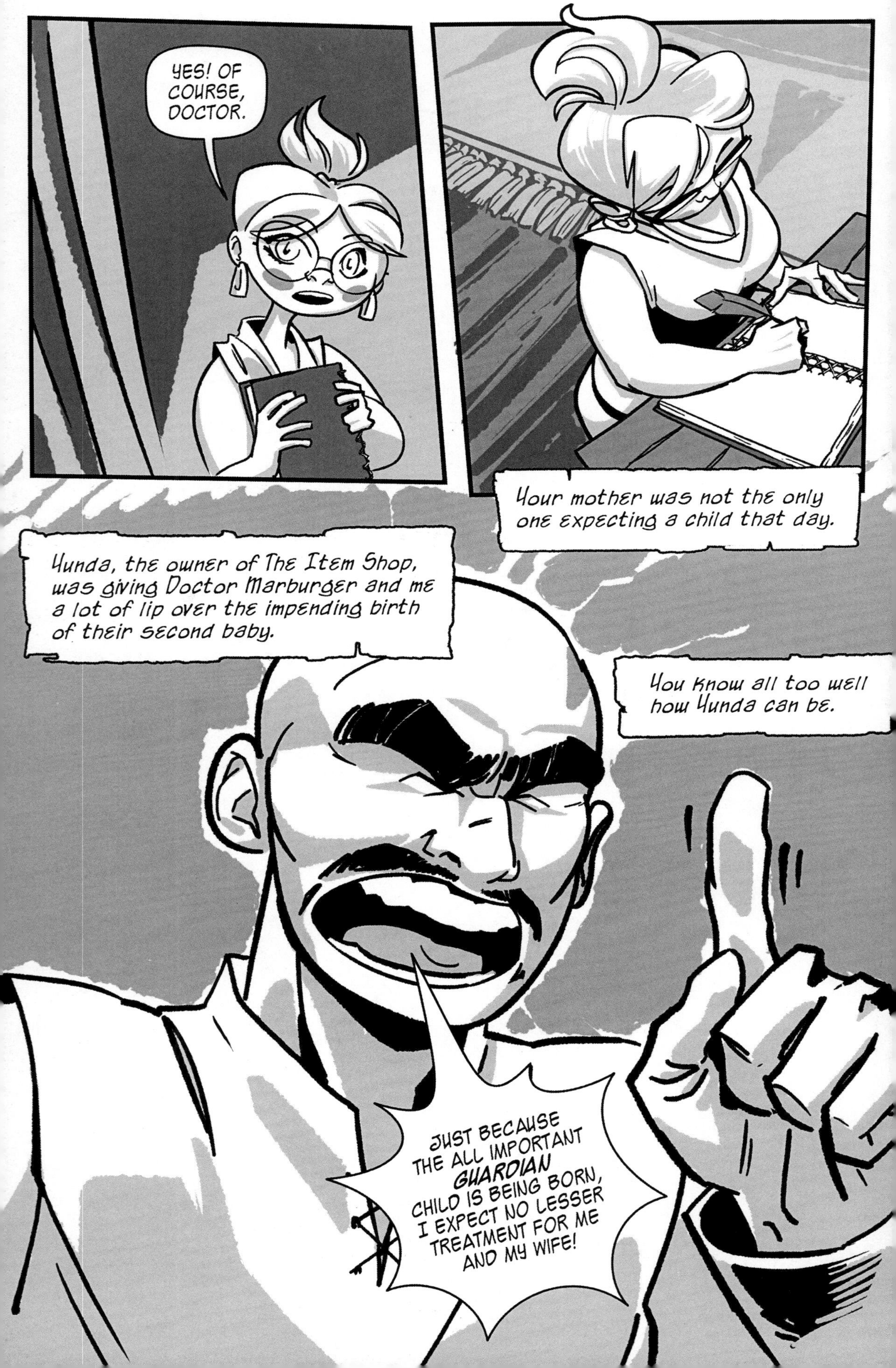
YES! OF COURSE, DOCTOR.
Your mother was not the only one expecting a child that day.
Yunda, the owner of The Item Shop, was giving Doctor Marburger and me a lot of lip over the impending birth of their second baby.
You know all too well how Yunda can be.
JUST BECAUSE THE ALL IMPORTANT GUARDIAN CHILD IS BEING BORN, I EXPECT NO LESSER TREATMENT FOR ME AND MY WIFE!

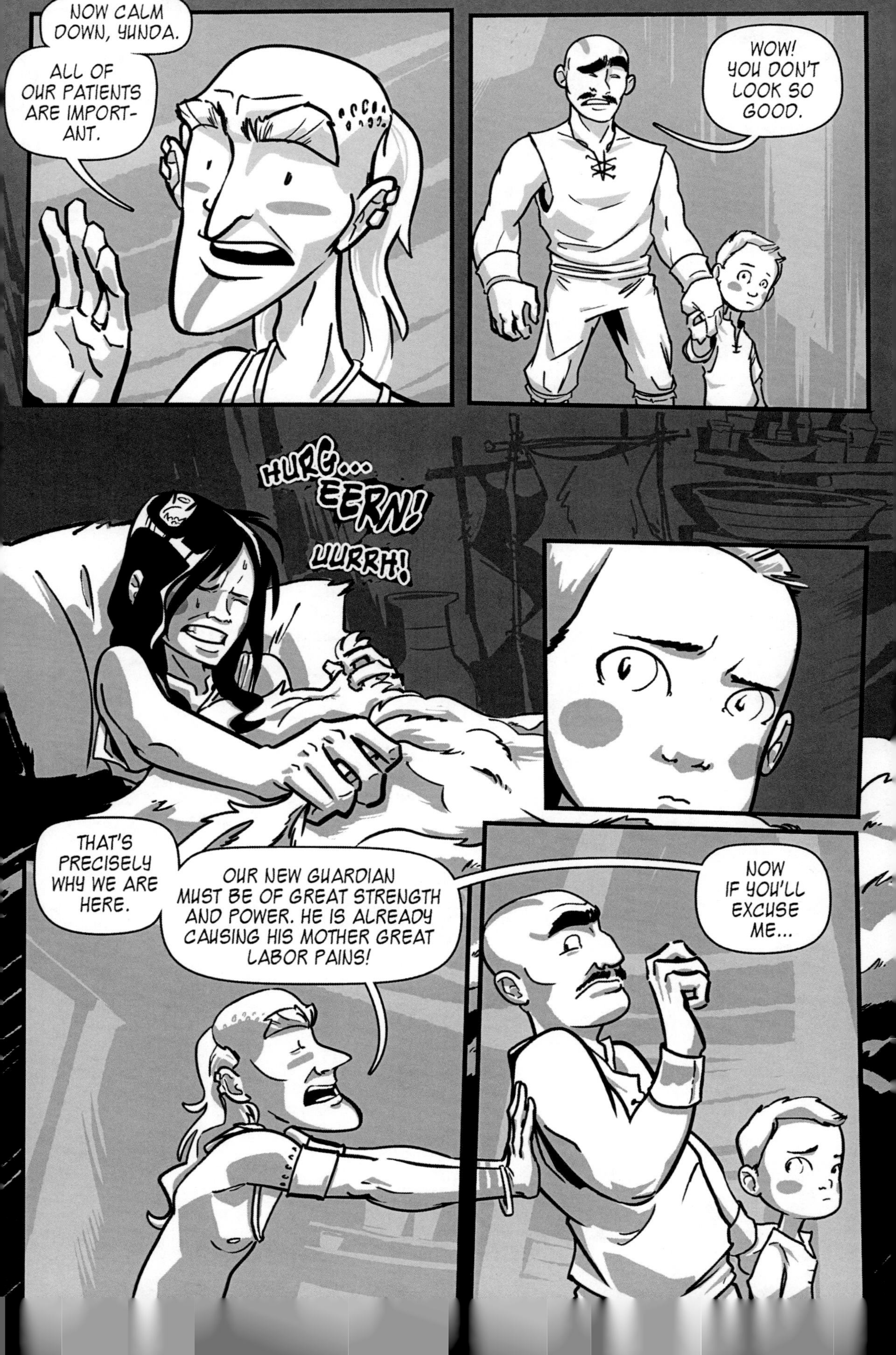
NOW CALM DOWN, YUNDA.
ALL OF OUR PATIENTS ARE IMPORT-ANT.
WOW! YOU DON'T LOOK SO GOOD.
HURG... EERN!
UURRH!
THAT'S PRECISELY WHY WE ARE HERE.
OUR NEW GUARDIAN MUST BE OF GREAT STRENGTH AND POWER. HE IS ALREADY CAUSING HIS MOTHER GREAT LABOR PAINS!
NOW IF YOU'LL EXCUSE ME...

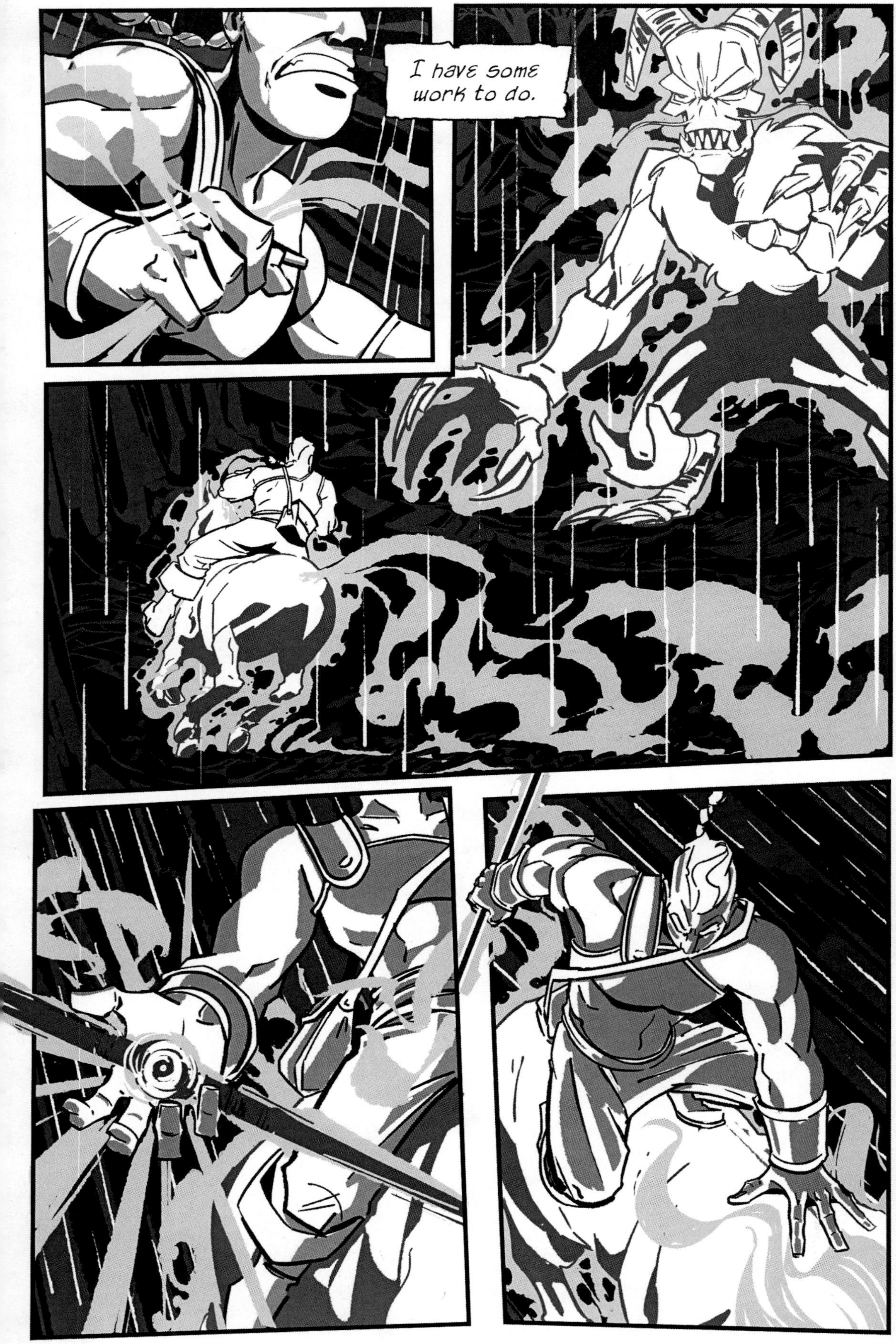
I have some work to do.

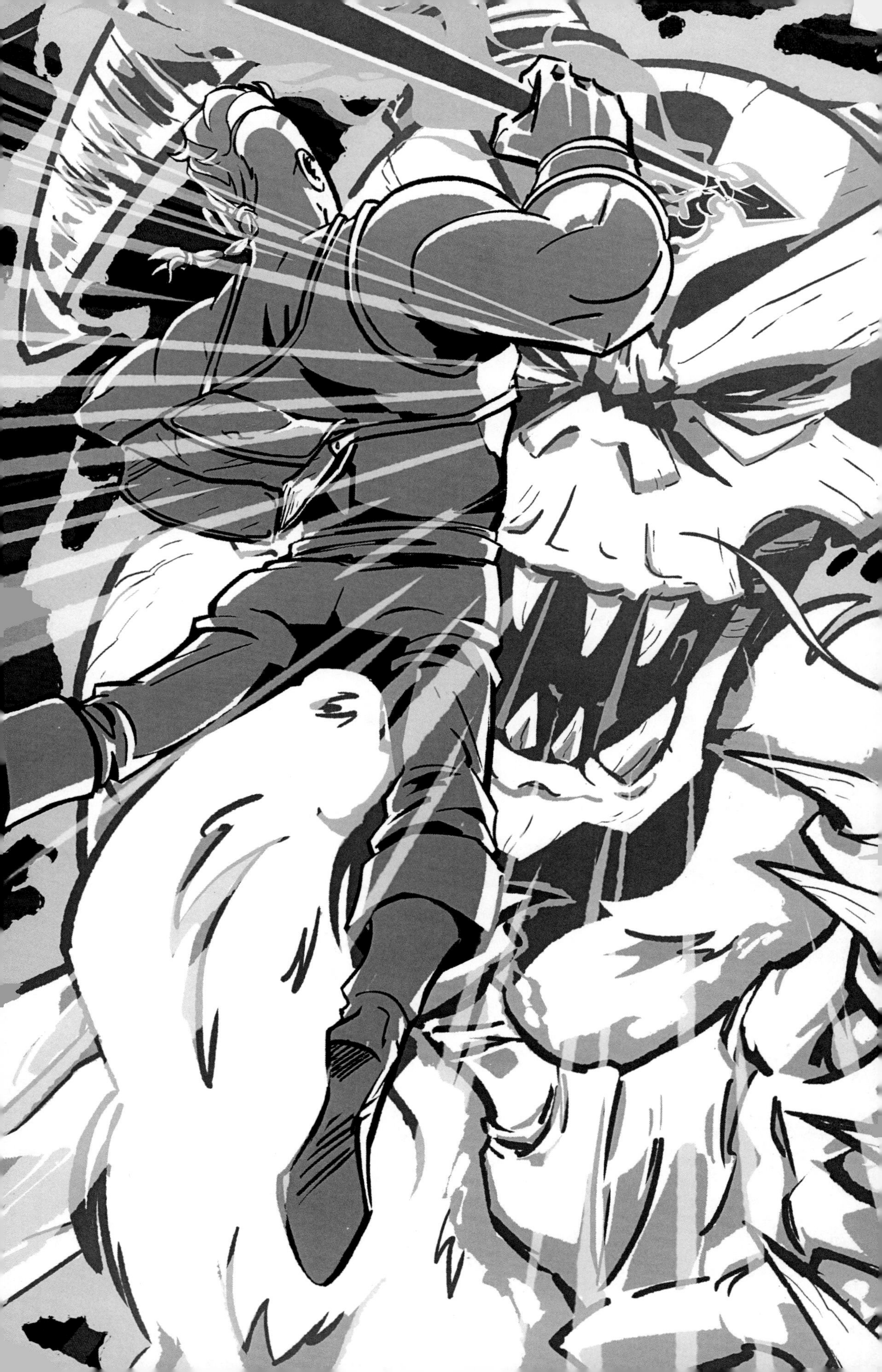

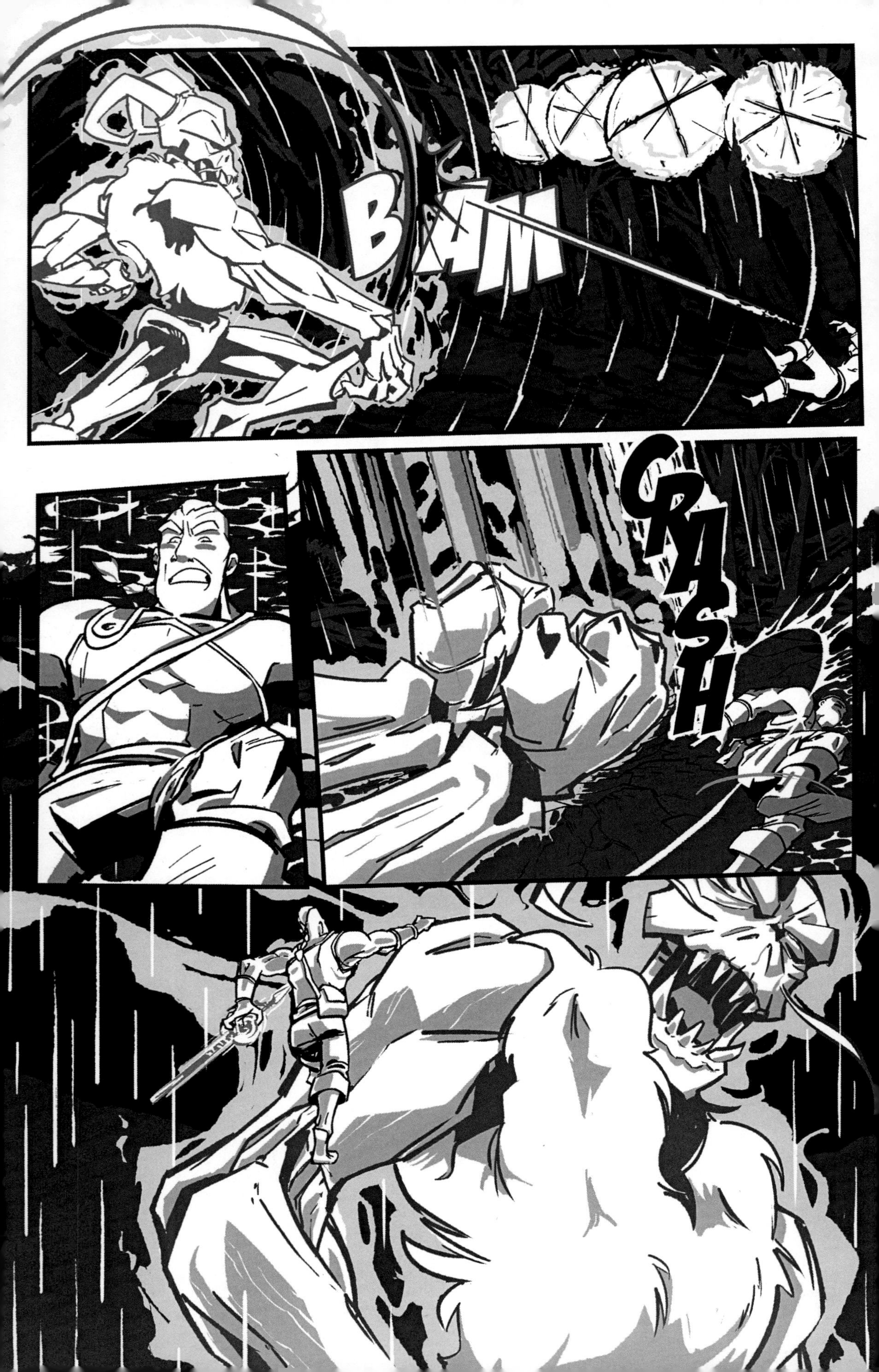

BAM
CRASH

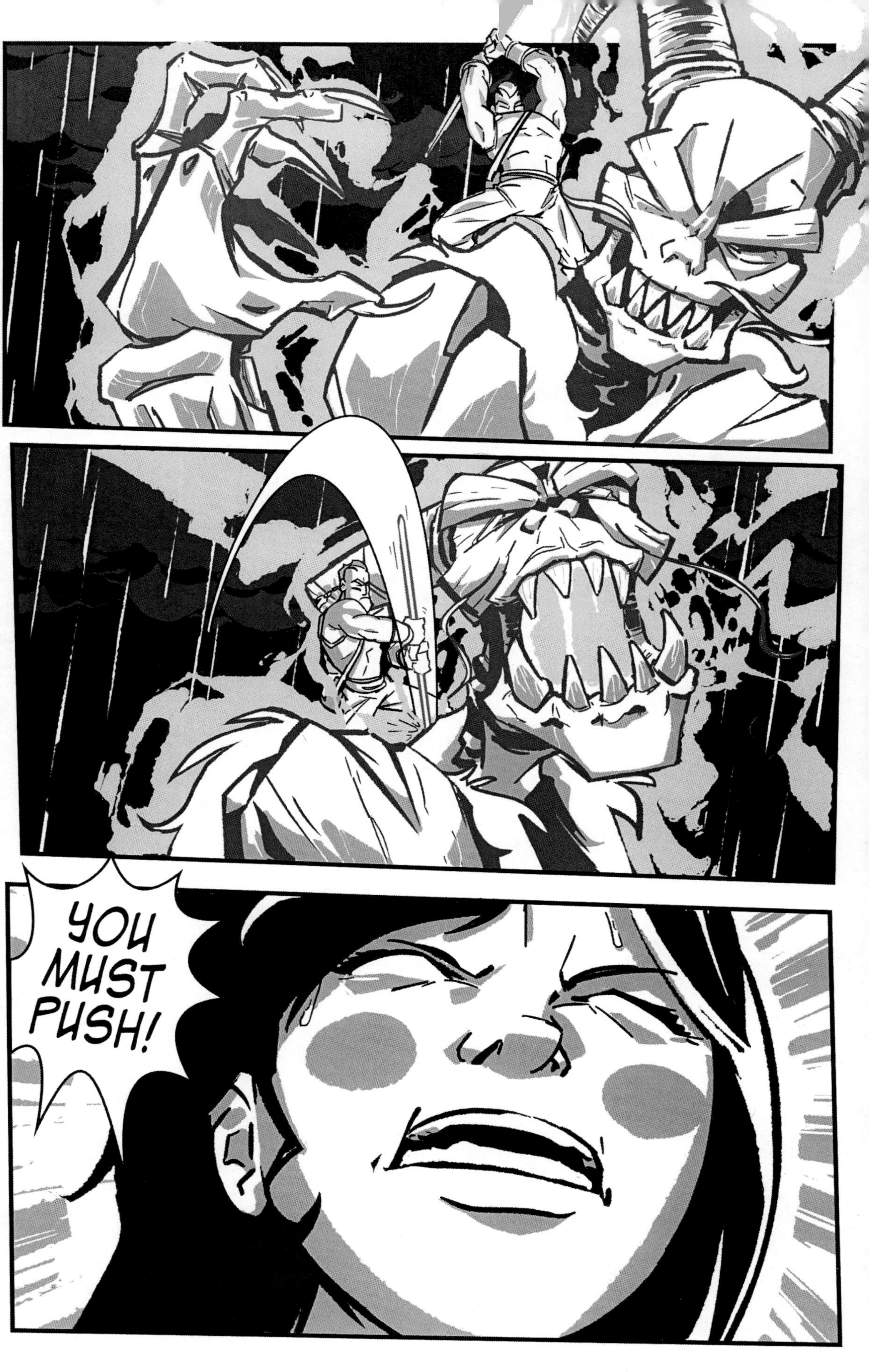
YOU MUST PUSH!

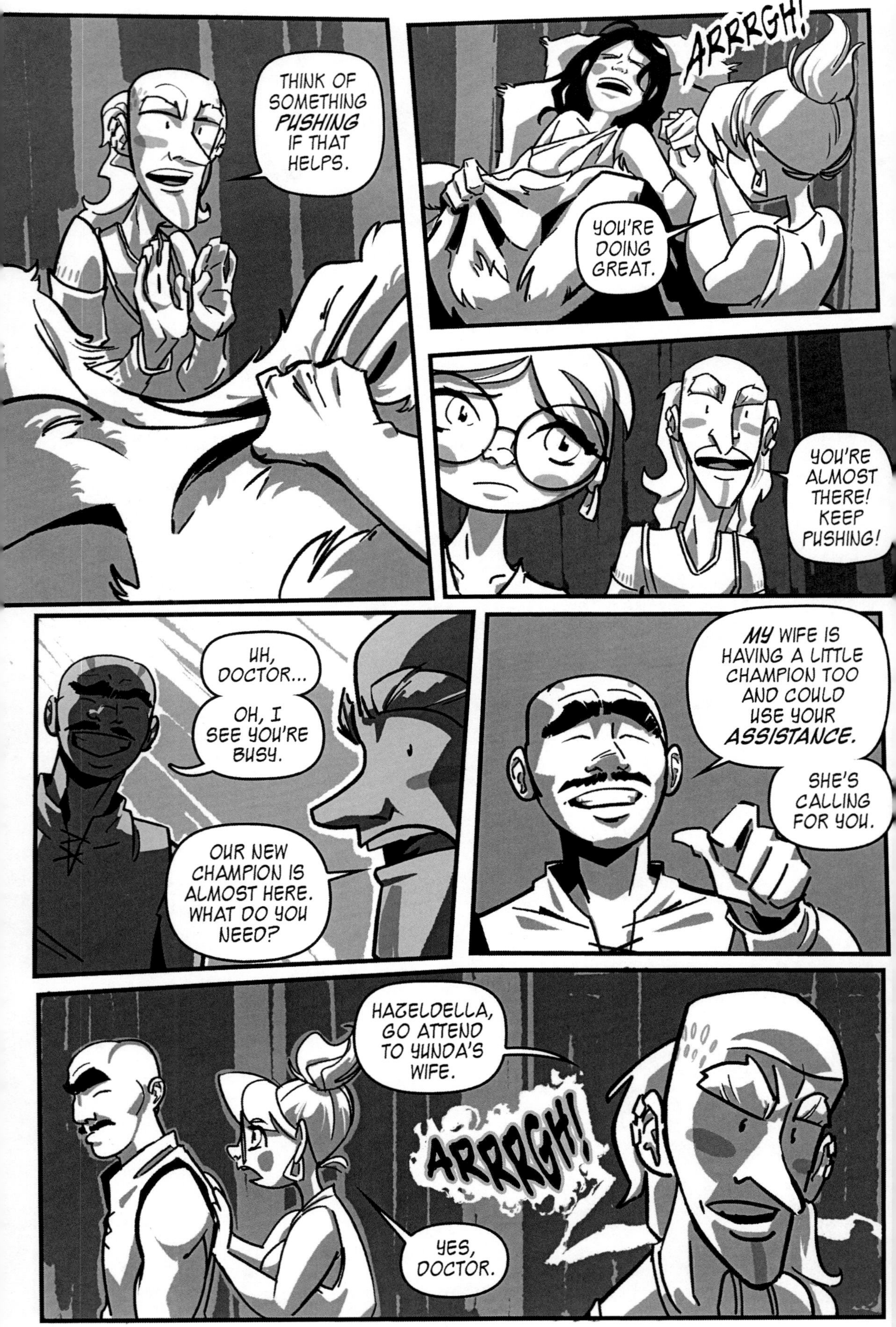
THINK OF SOMETHING *PUSHING* IF THAT HELPS.
ARRRGH!
YOU'RE DOING GREAT.
YOU'RE ALMOST THERE! KEEP PUSHING!
UH, DOCTOR...
OH, I SEE YOU'RE BUSY.
OUR NEW CHAMPION IS ALMOST HERE. WHAT DO YOU NEED?
MY WIFE IS HAVING A LITTLE CHAMPION TOO AND COULD USE YOUR *ASSISTANCE.*
SHE'S CALLING FOR YOU.
HAZELDELLA, GO ATTEND TO YUNDA'S WIFE.
ARRRGH!
YES, DOCTOR.

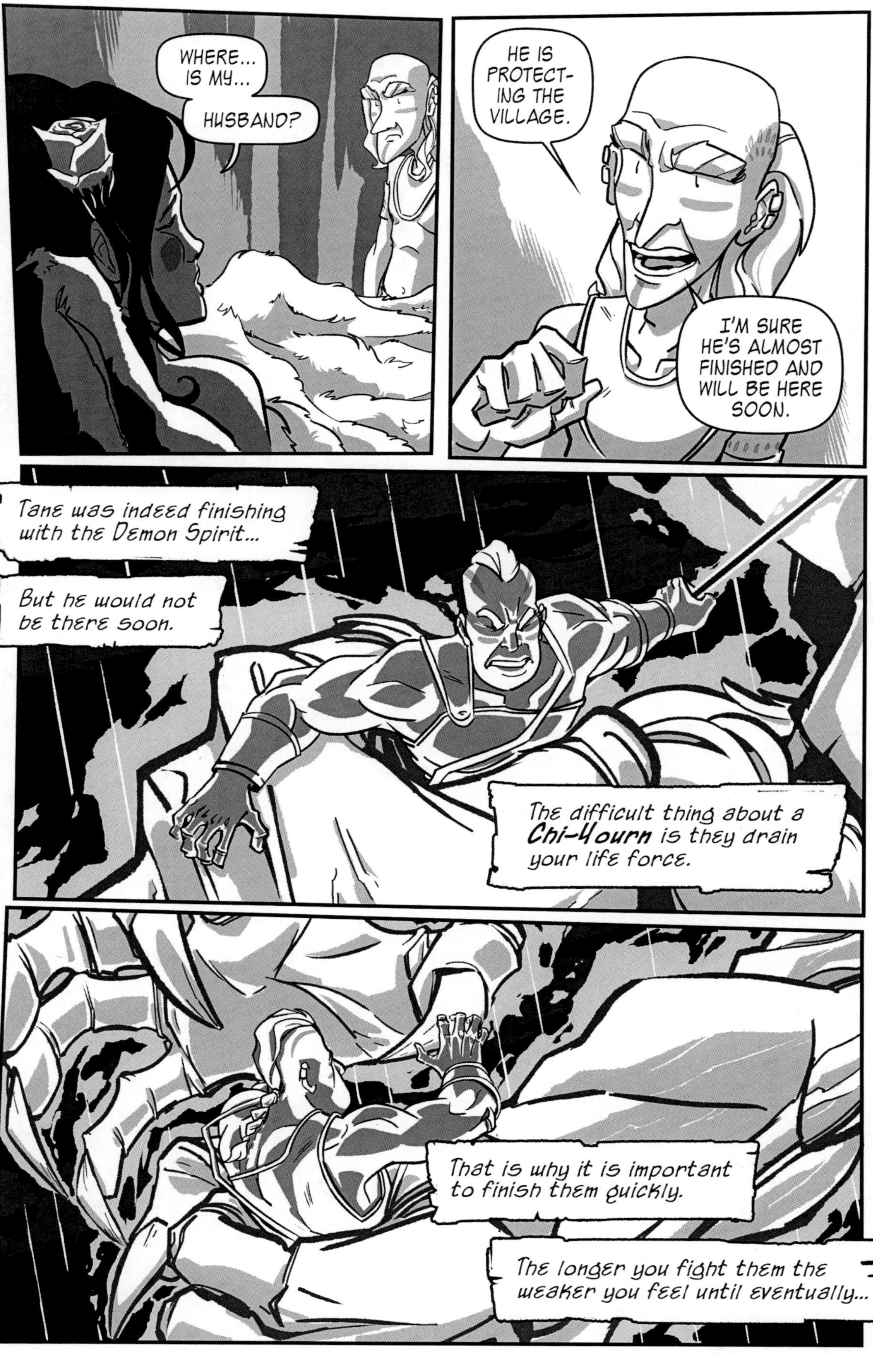
WHERE... IS MY...
HUSBAND?
HE IS PROTECTING THE VILLAGE.
I'M SURE HE'S ALMOST FINISHED AND WILL BE HERE SOON.
Tane was indeed finishing with the Demon Spirit...
But he would not be there soon.
The difficult thing about a Chi-Yourn is they drain your life force.
That is why it is important to finish them quickly.
The longer you fight them the weaker you feel until eventually...

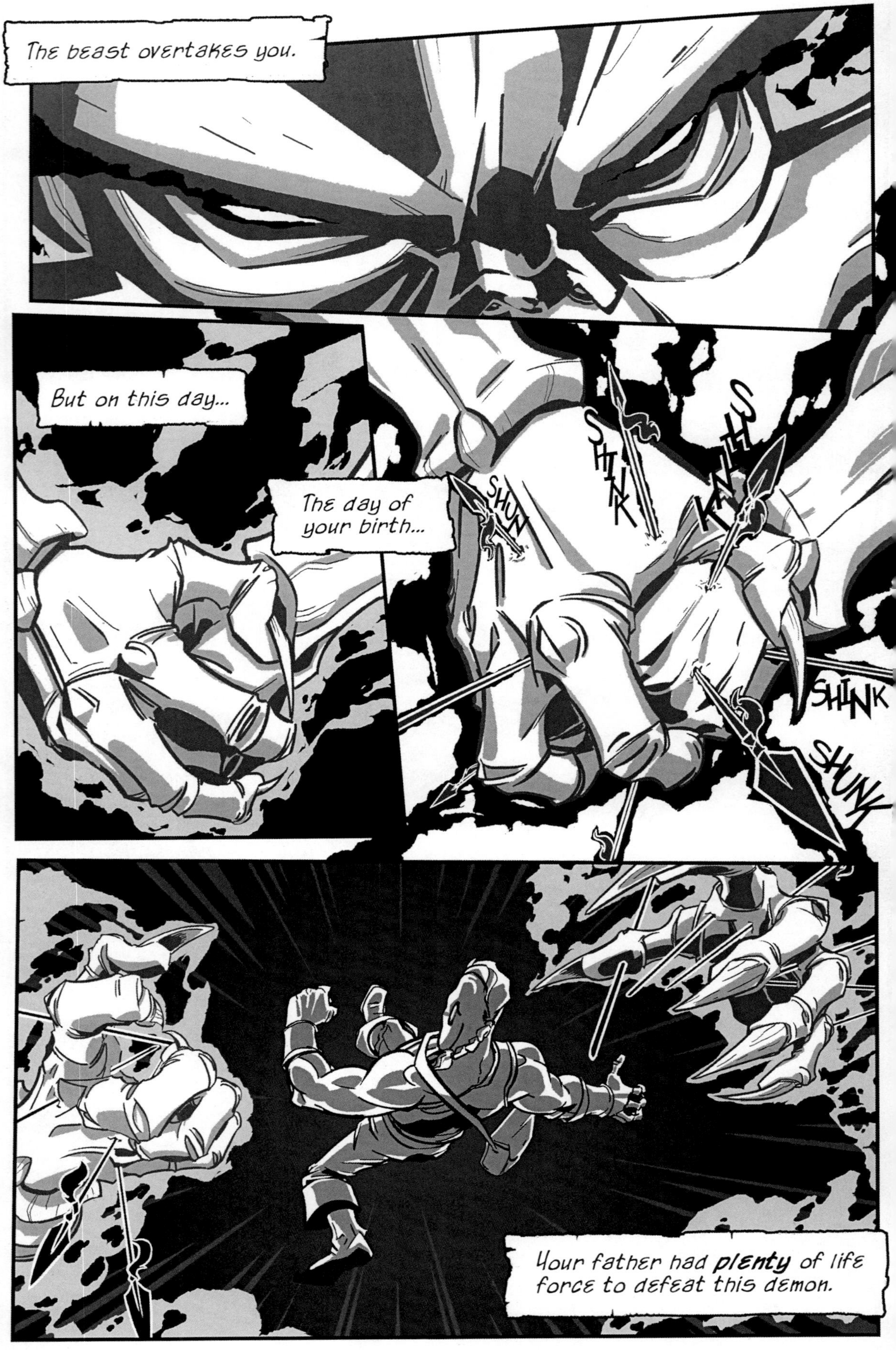
The beast overtakes you.
But on this day...
The day of your birth...
SHUN
SHINK
SHINK
SHINK
SHUNK
Your father had **plenty** of life force to defeat this demon.

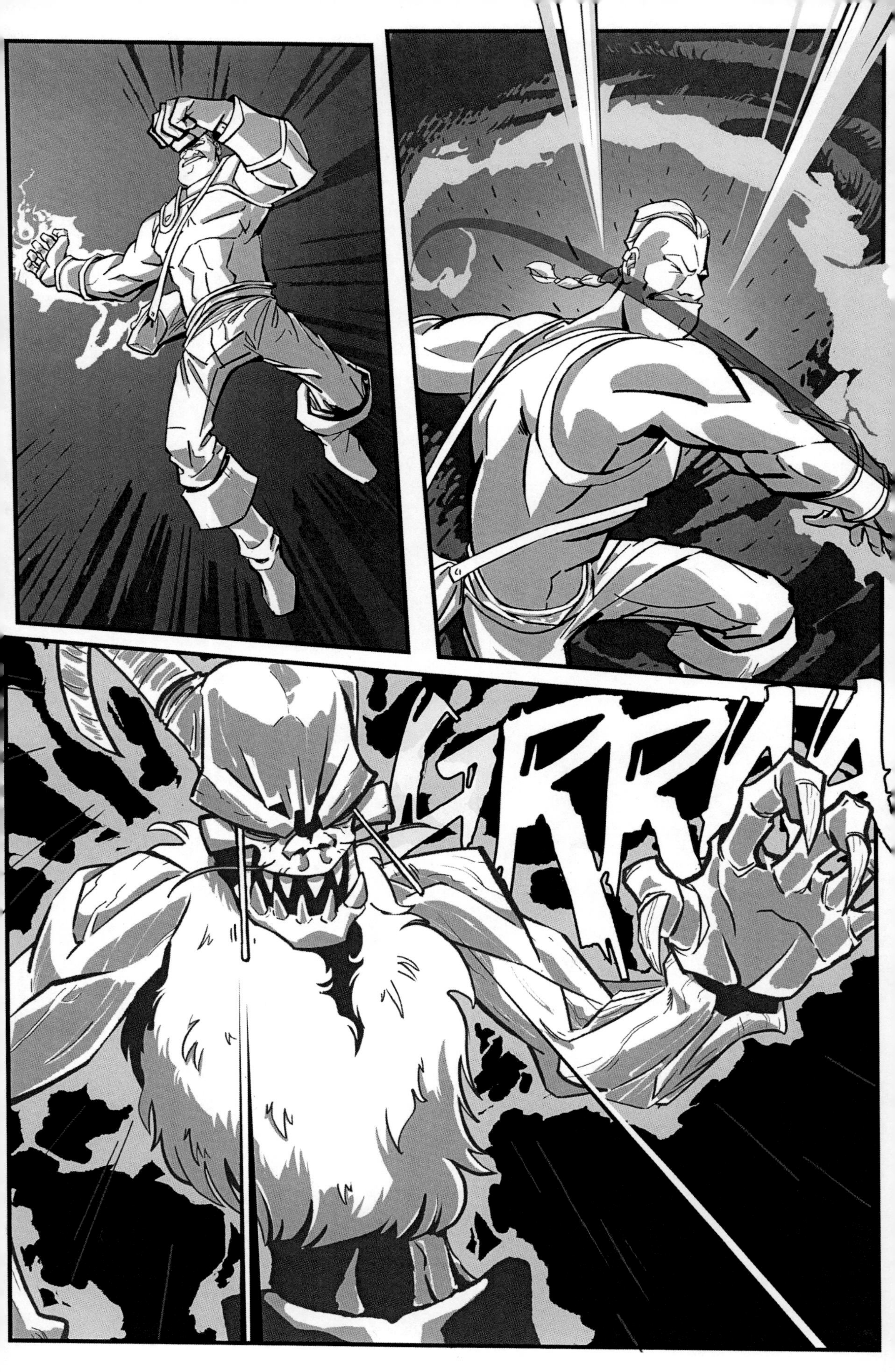
GRRA

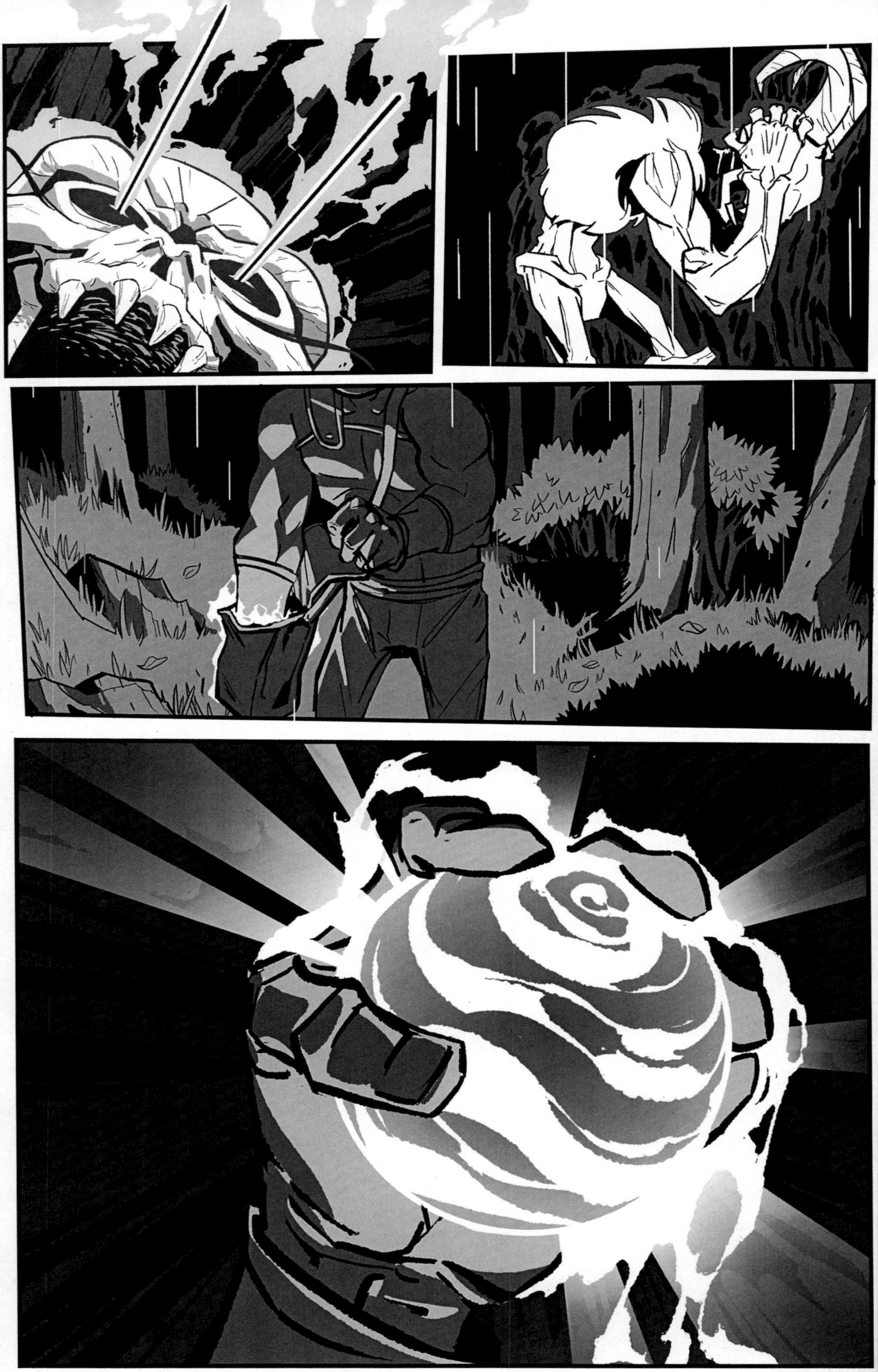

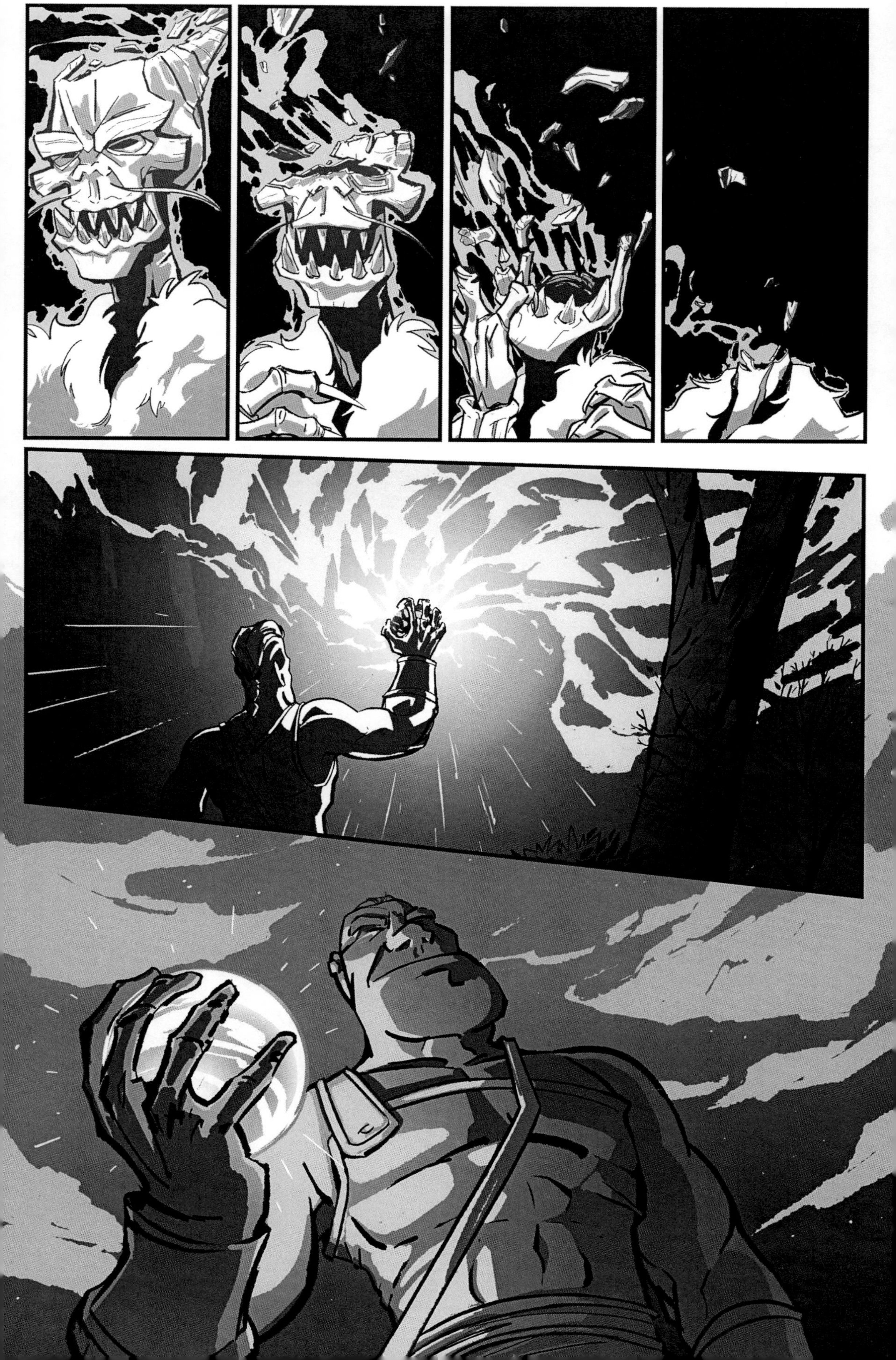

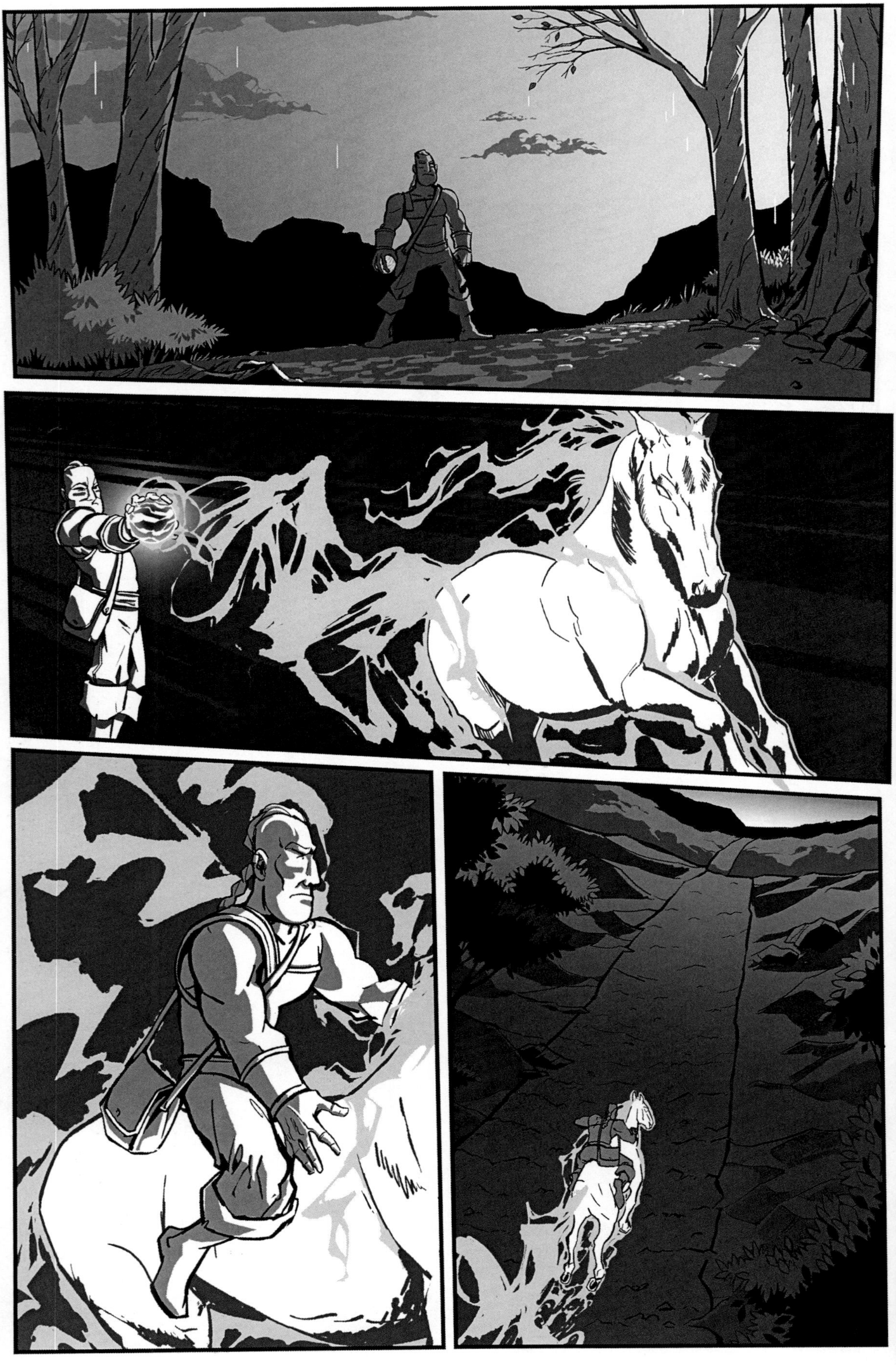

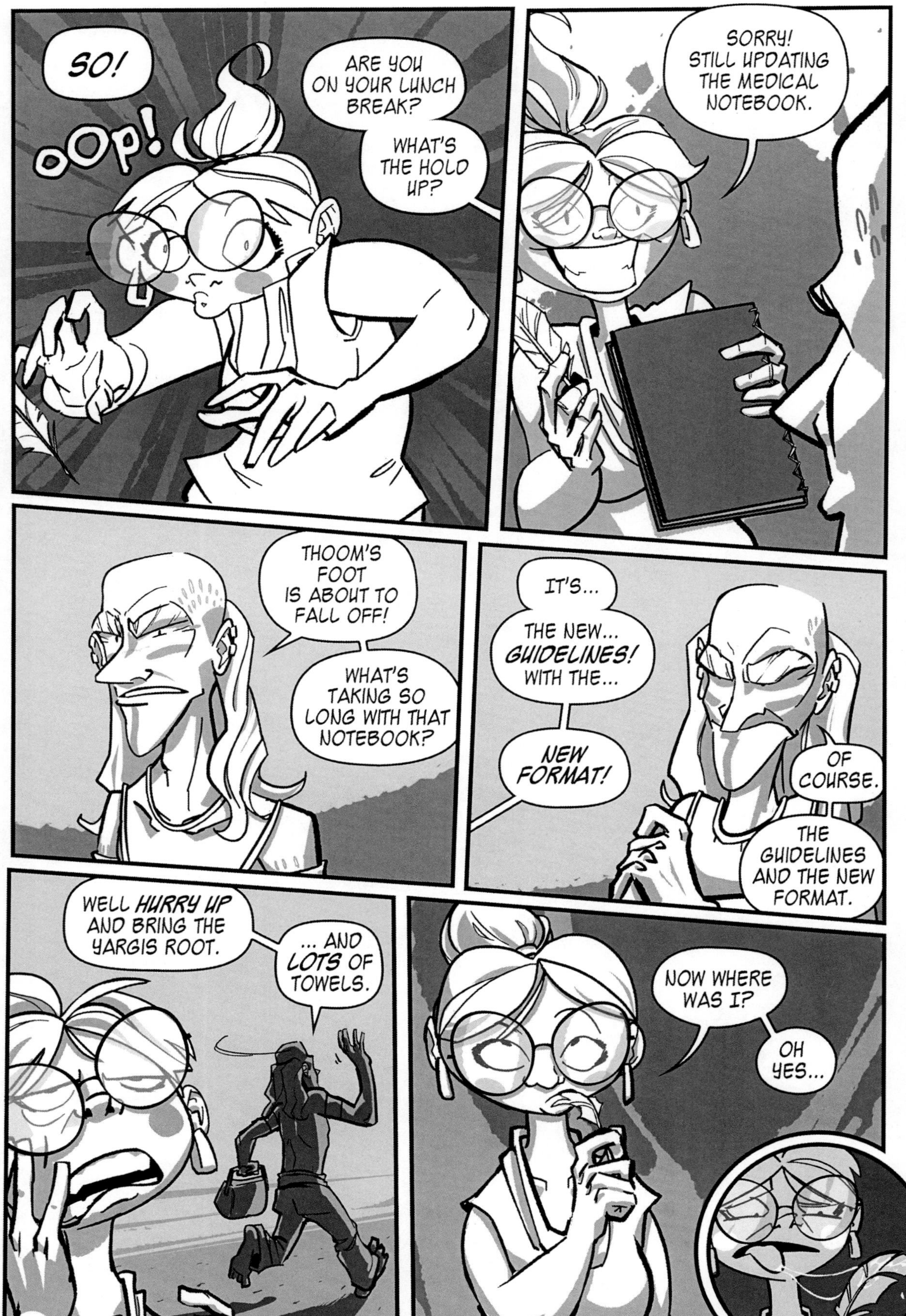
SO!
oOp!
ARE YOU ON YOUR LUNCH BREAK?
WHAT'S THE HOLD UP?
SORRY! STILL UPDATING THE MEDICAL NOTEBOOK.
THOOM'S FOOT IS ABOUT TO FALL OFF!
WHAT'S TAKING SO LONG WITH THAT NOTEBOOK?
IT'S...
THE NEW... GUIDELINES! WITH THE...
NEW FORMAT!
OF COURSE.
THE GUIDELINES AND THE NEW FORMAT.
WELL HURRY UP AND BRING THE YARGIS ROOT.
... AND LOTS OF TOWELS.
NOW WHERE WAS I?
OH YES...

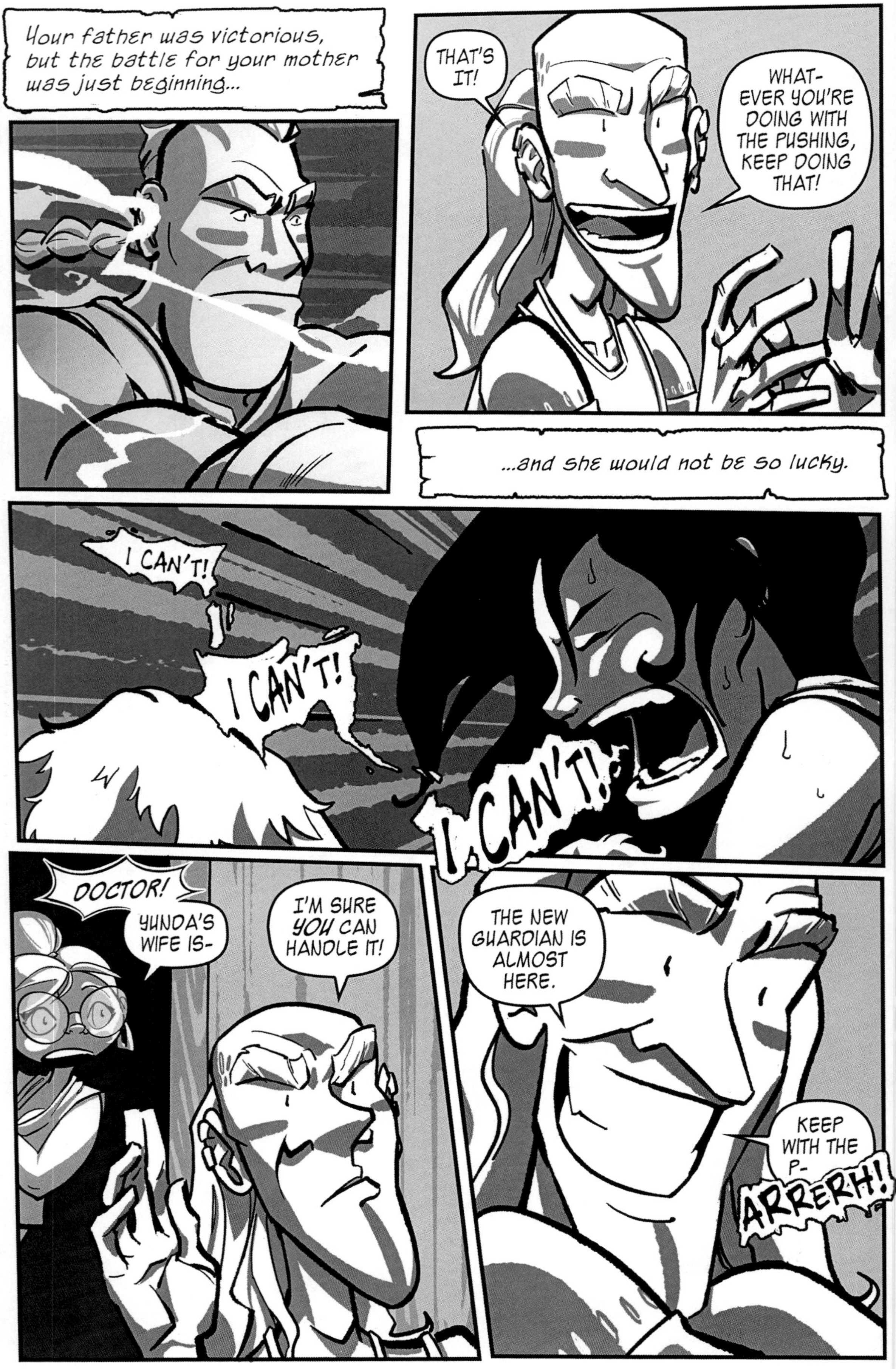
Your father was victorious, but the battle for your mother was just beginning...
THAT'S IT!
WHAT-EVER YOU'RE DOING WITH THE PUSHING, KEEP DOING THAT!
...and she would not be so lucky.
I CAN'T!
I CAN'T!
I CAN'T!
DOCTOR!
YUNDA'S WIFE IS-
I'M SURE YOU CAN HANDLE IT!
THE NEW GUARDIAN IS ALMOST HERE.
KEEP WITH THE P-
ARRERH!

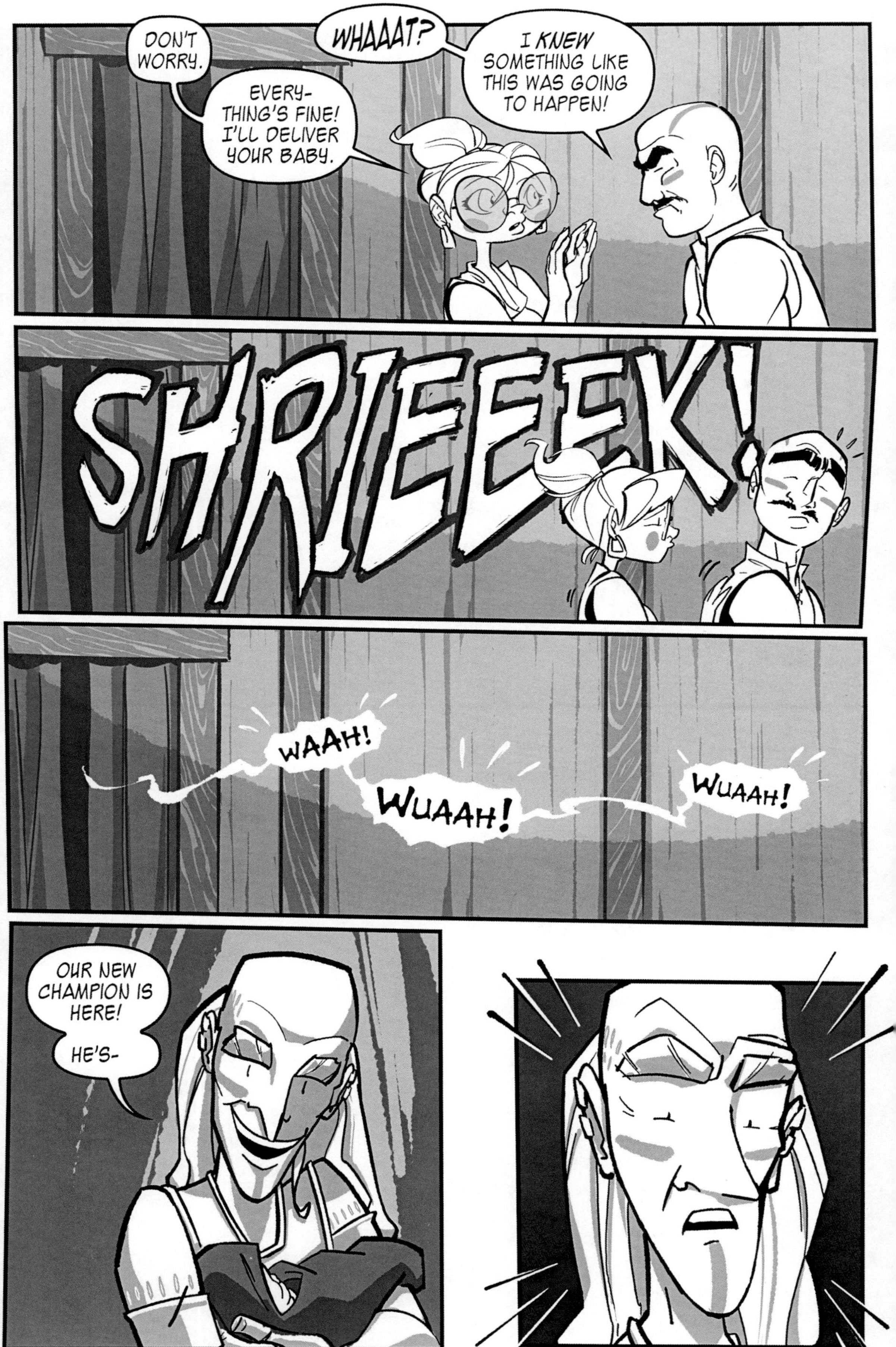
DON'T WORRY.
EVERY-THING'S FINE! I'LL DELIVER YOUR BABY.
WHAAAT?
I KNEW SOMETHING LIKE THIS WAS GOING TO HAPPEN!
SHRIEEEK!
WAAH!
WUAAH!
WUAAH!
OUR NEW CHAMPION IS HERE!
HE'S-

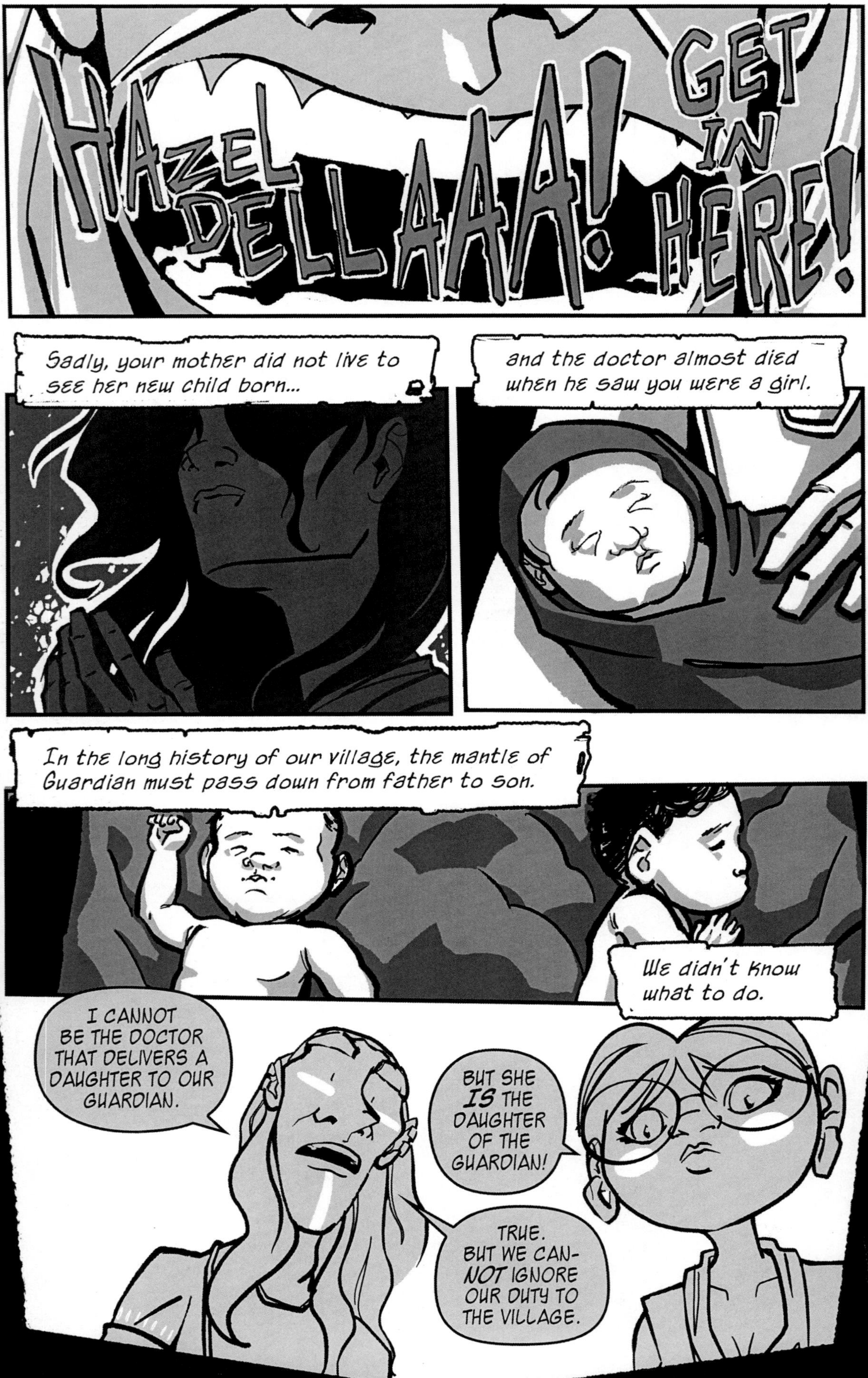
HAZEL DELLAAA! GET IN HERE!
Sadly, your mother did not live to see her new child born...
and the doctor almost died when he saw you were a girl.
In the long history of our village, the mantle of Guardian must pass down from father to son.
We didn't know what to do.
I CANNOT BE THE DOCTOR THAT DELIVERS A DAUGHTER TO OUR GUARDIAN.
BUT SHE *IS* THE DAUGHTER OF THE GUARDIAN!
TRUE. BUT WE CAN-*NOT* IGNORE OUR DUTY TO THE VILLAGE.

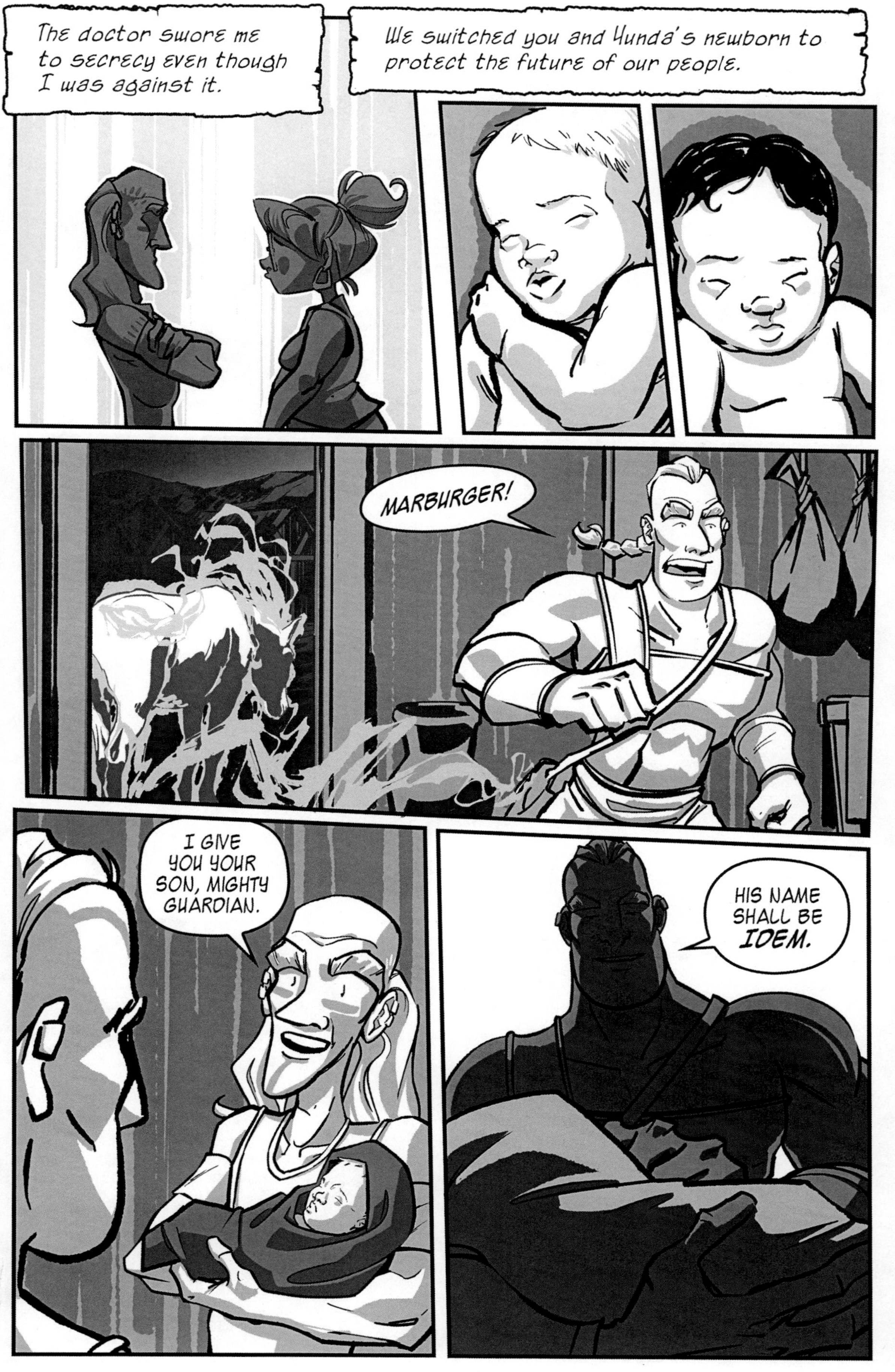
The doctor swore me to secrecy even though I was against it.
We switched you and Yunda's newborn to protect the future of our people.
MARBURGER!
I GIVE YOU YOUR SON, MIGHTY GUARDIAN.
HIS NAME SHALL BE IDEM.

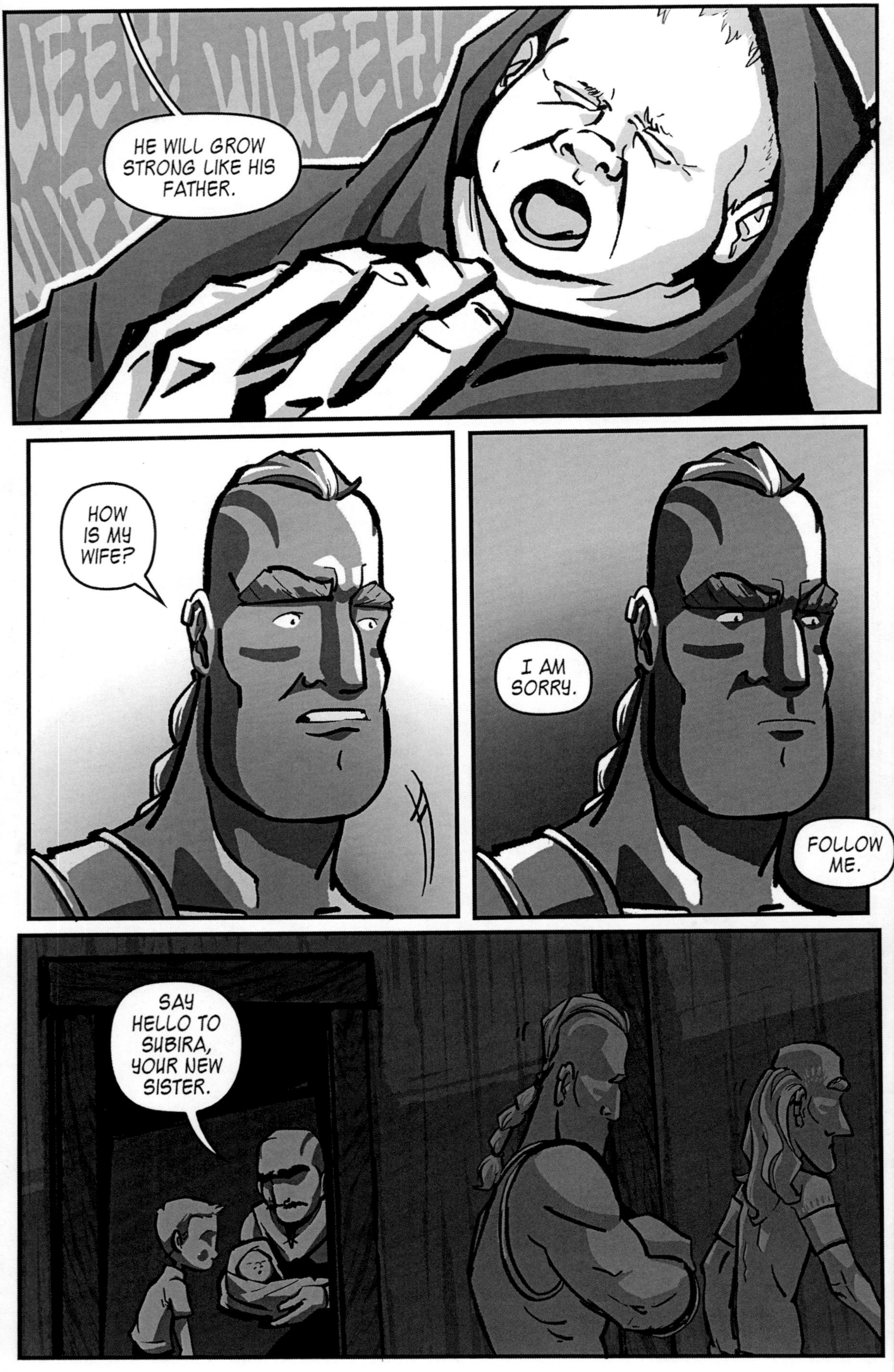
WEEH! WEEH! WUEEH!
HE WILL GROW STRONG LIKE HIS FATHER.
HOW IS MY WIFE?
I AM SORRY.
FOLLOW ME.
SAY HELLO TO SUBIRA, YOUR NEW SISTER.

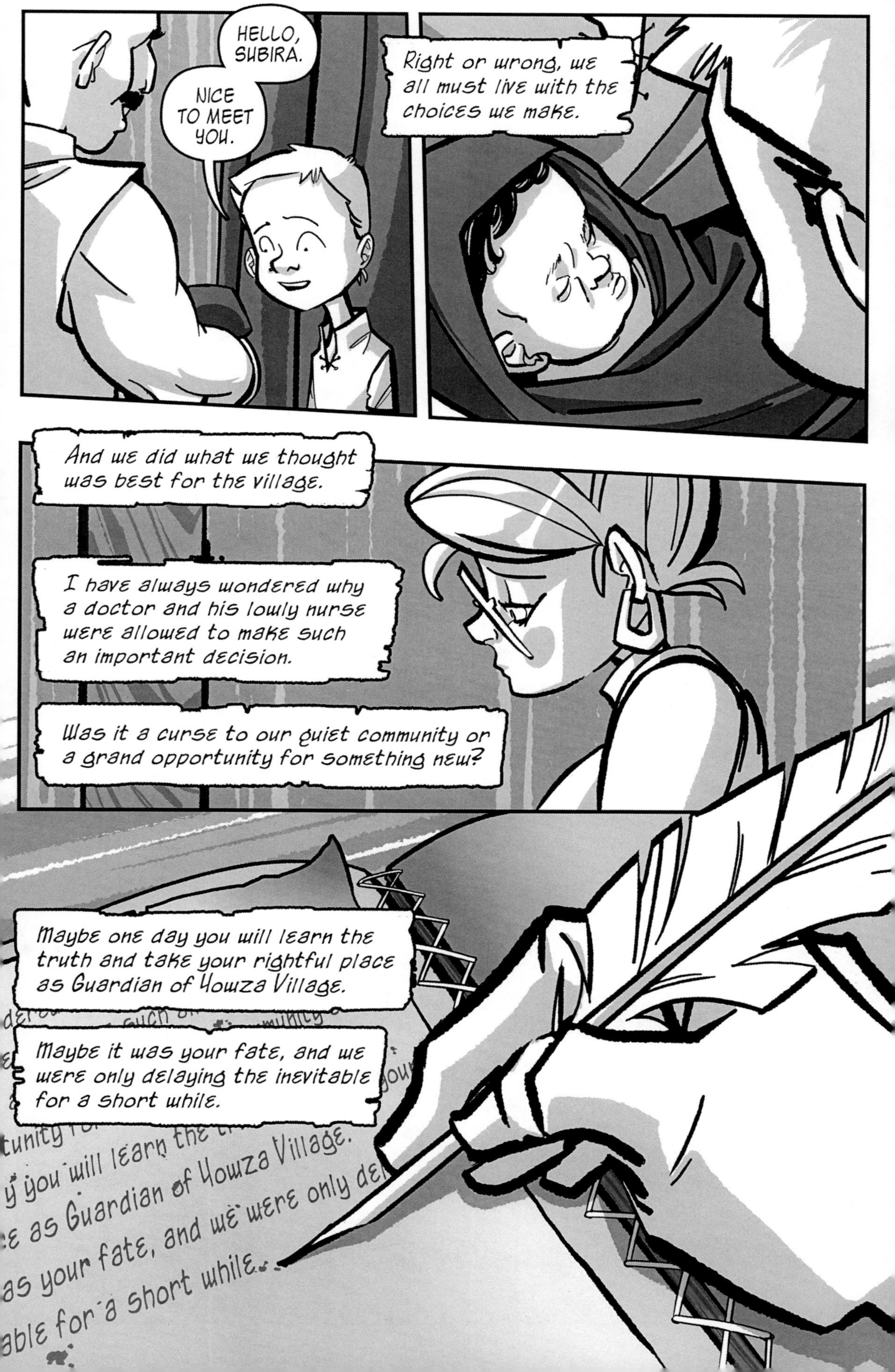
HELLO, SUBIRA.
NICE TO MEET YOU.
Right or wrong, we all must live with the choices we make.
And we did what we thought was best for the village.
I have always wondered why a doctor and his lowly nurse were allowed to make such an important decision.
Was it a curse to our quiet community or a grand opportunity for something new?
Maybe one day you will learn the truth and take your rightful place as Guardian of Yowza Village.
Maybe it was your fate, and we were only delaying the inevitable for a short while.
as Guardian of Yowza Village.
as your fate, and we were only
for a short while.

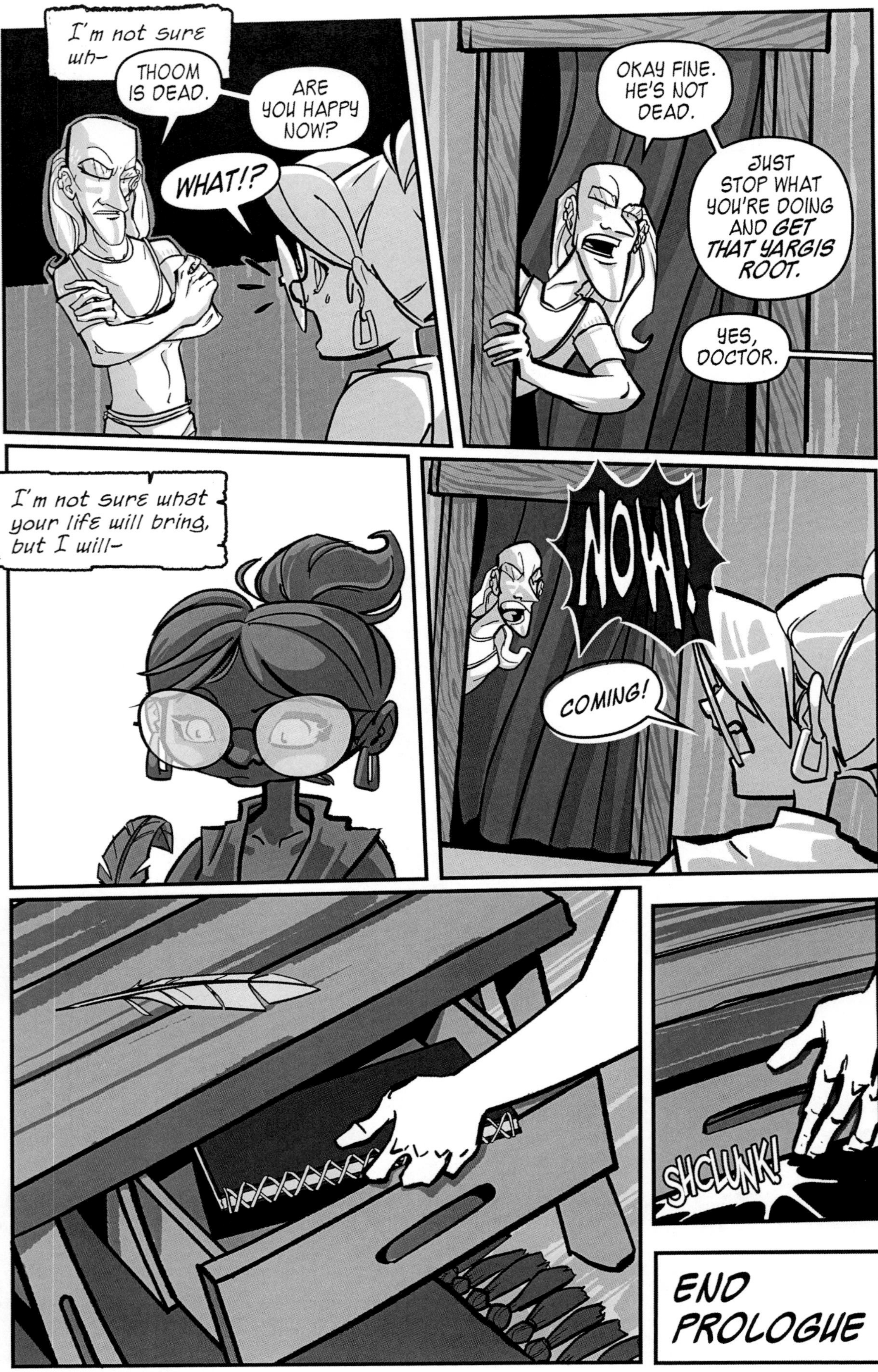
I'm not sure wh-
THOOM IS DEAD.
ARE YOU HAPPY NOW?
WHAT!?
OKAY FINE. HE'S NOT DEAD.
JUST STOP WHAT YOU'RE DOING AND GET THAT YARGIS ROOT.
YES, DOCTOR.
I'm not sure what your life will bring, but I will-
NOW!
COMING!
SHCLUNK!
END PROLOGUE

Chapter 1
The Zucchini Festival

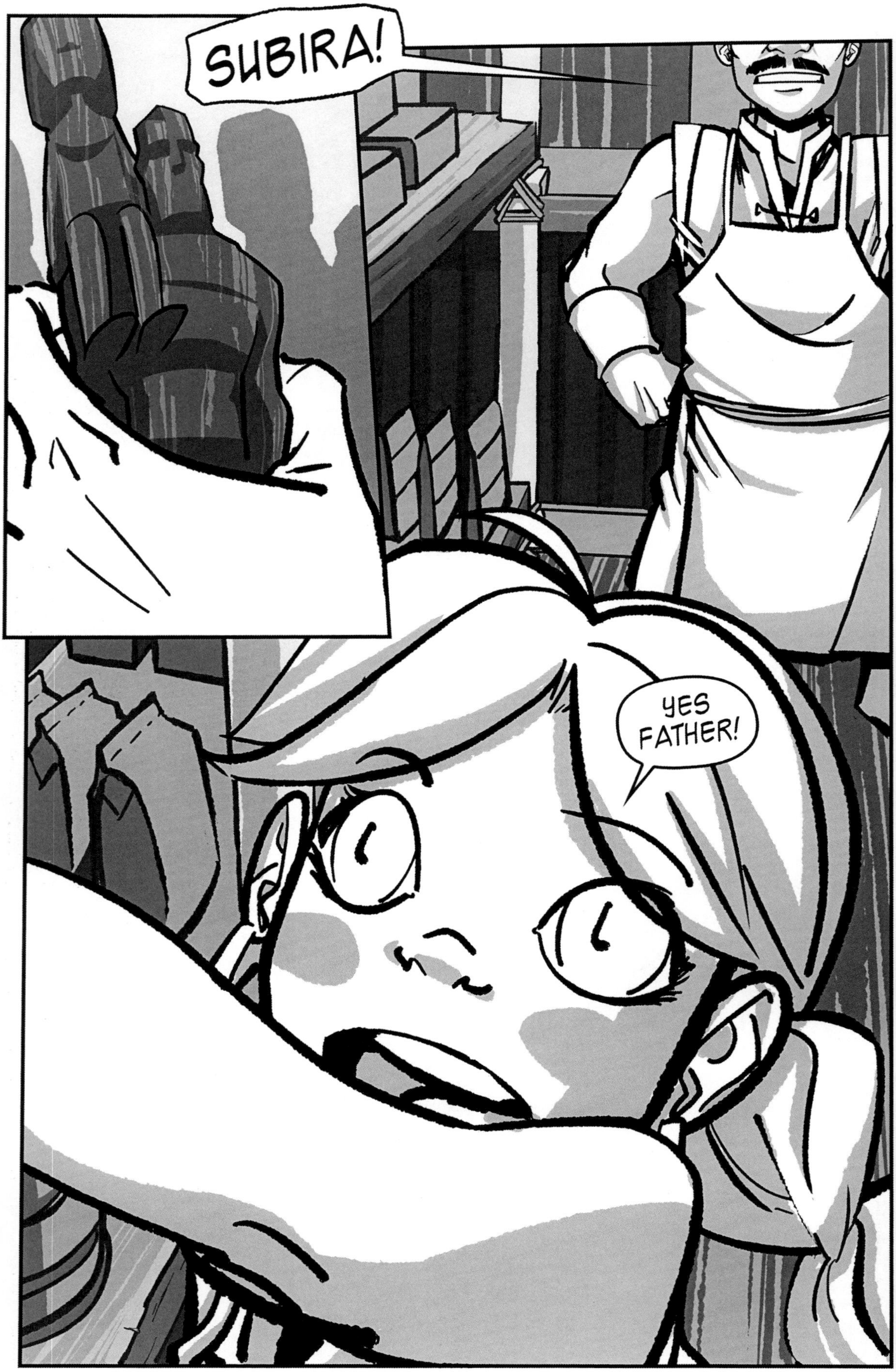
SUBIRA!
YES FATHER!

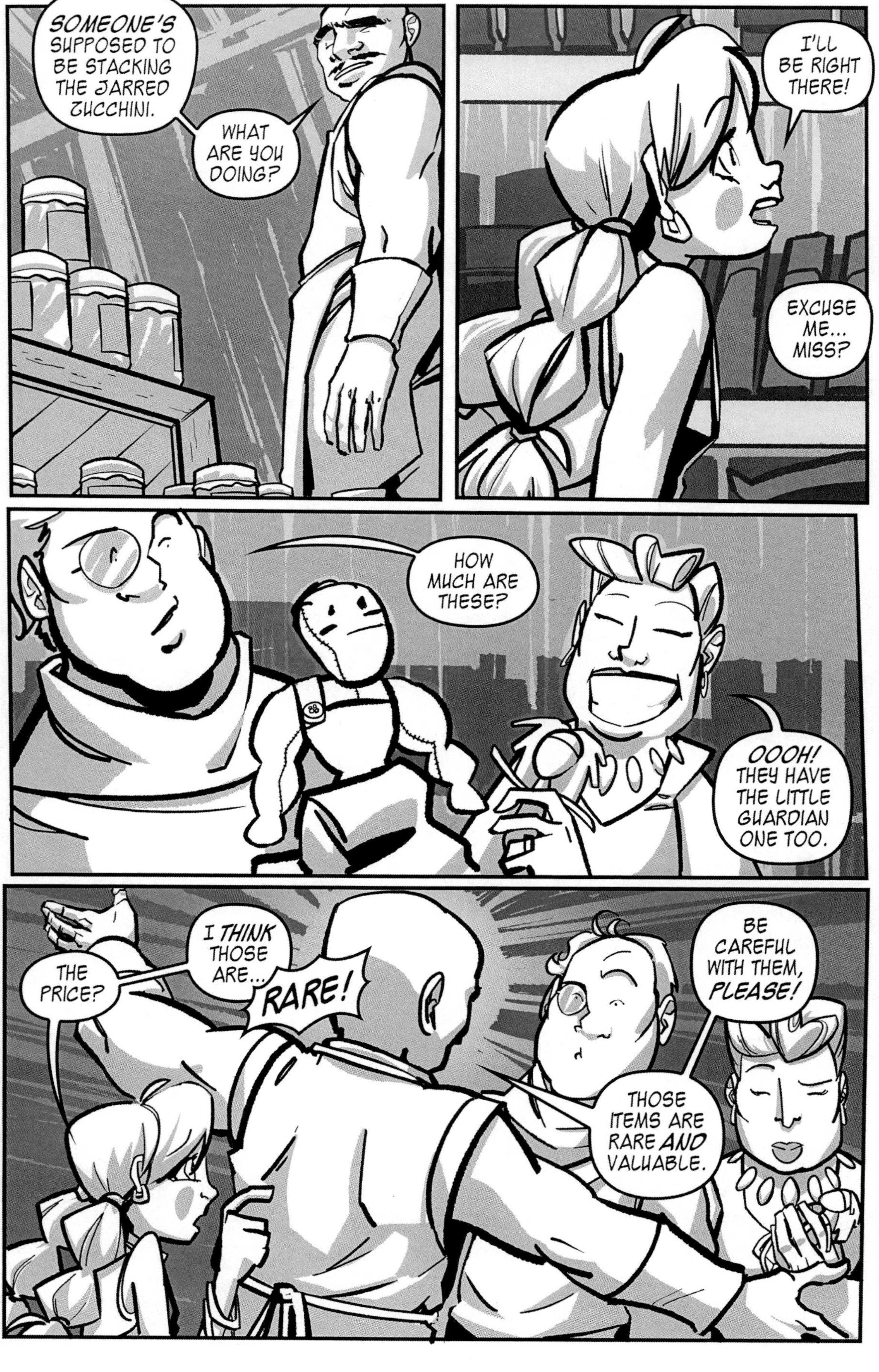
SOMEONE'S SUPPOSED TO BE STACKING THE JARRED ZUCCHINI.
WHAT ARE YOU DOING?
I'LL BE RIGHT THERE!
EXCUSE ME... MISS?
HOW MUCH ARE THESE?
OOOH! THEY HAVE THE LITTLE GUARDIAN ONE TOO.
THE PRICE?
I THINK THOSE ARE...
RARE!
BE CAREFUL WITH THEM, PLEASE!
THOSE ITEMS ARE RARE AND VALUABLE.

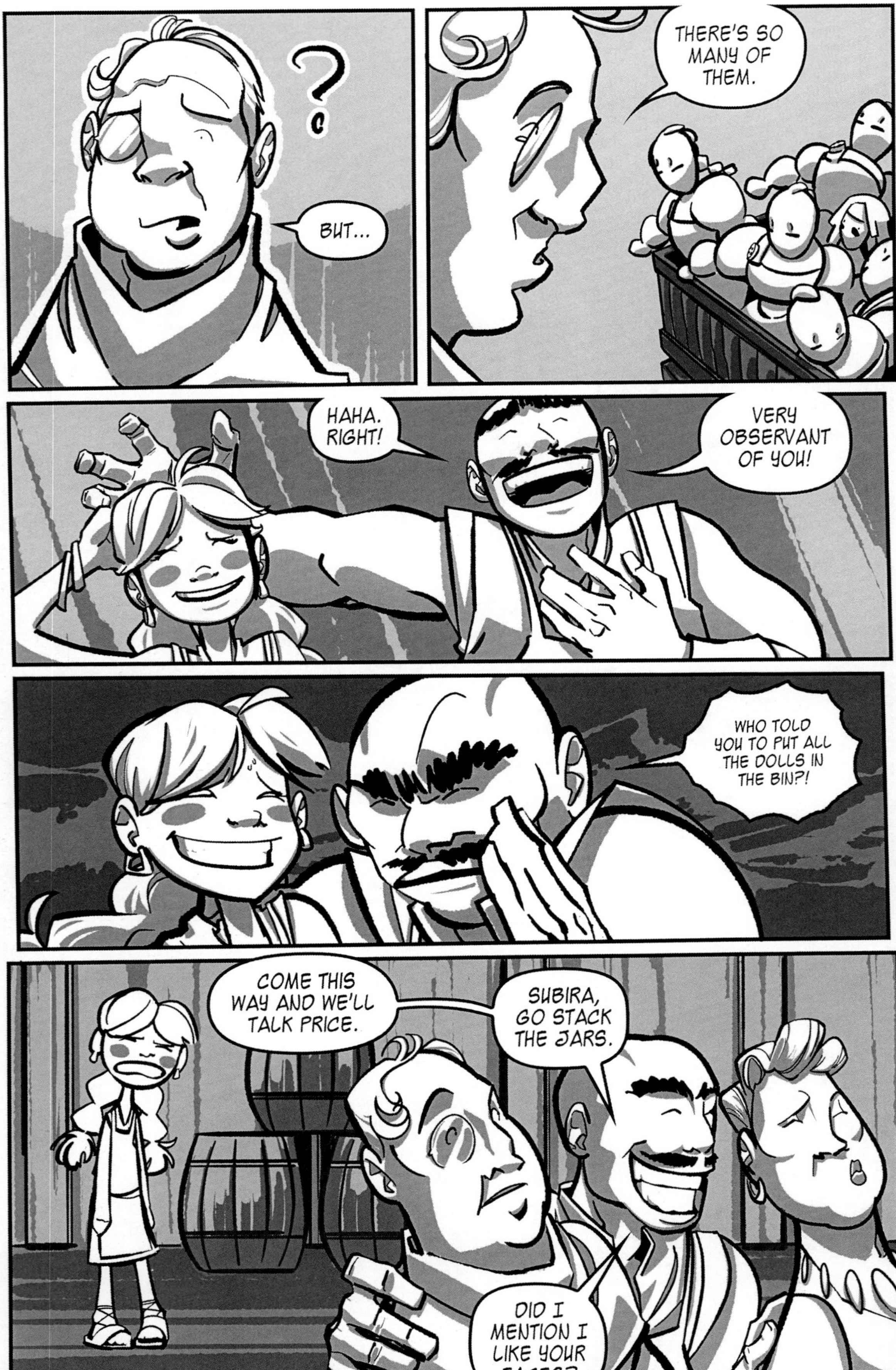
?
BUT...
THERE'S SO MANY OF THEM.
HAHA. RIGHT!
VERY OBSERVANT OF YOU!
WHO TOLD YOU TO PUT ALL THE DOLLS IN THE BIN?!
COME THIS WAY AND WE'LL TALK PRICE.
SUBIRA, GO STACK THE JARS.
DID I MENTION I LIKE YOUR FACES?

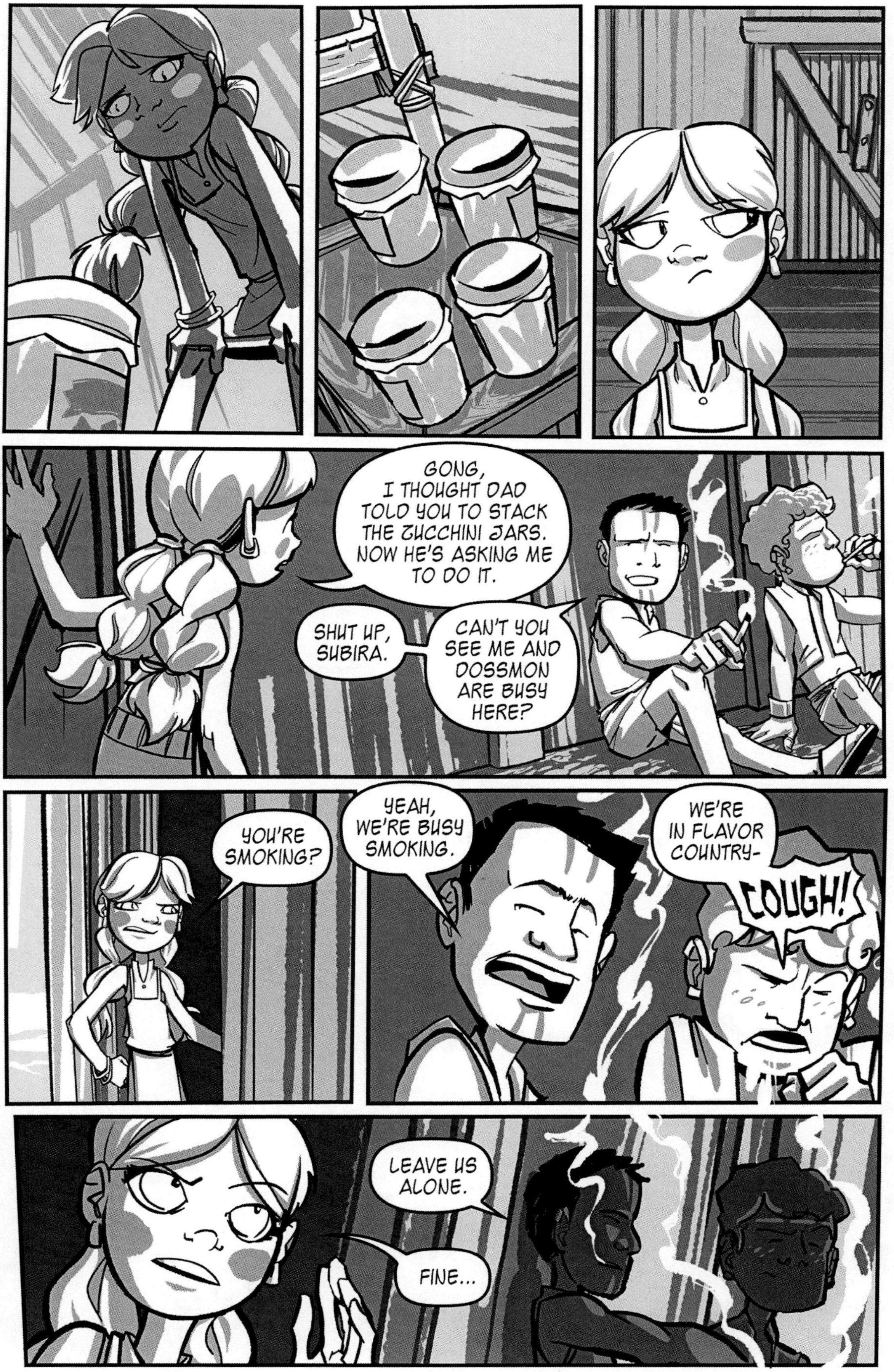
GONG, I THOUGHT DAD TOLD YOU TO STACK THE ZUCCHINI JARS. NOW HE'S ASKING ME TO DO IT.
SHUT UP, SUBIRA.
CAN'T YOU SEE ME AND DOSSMON ARE BUSY HERE?
YOU'RE SMOKING?
YEAH, WE'RE BUSY SMOKING.
WE'RE IN FLAVOR COUNTRY-
COUGH!
LEAVE US ALONE.
FINE...

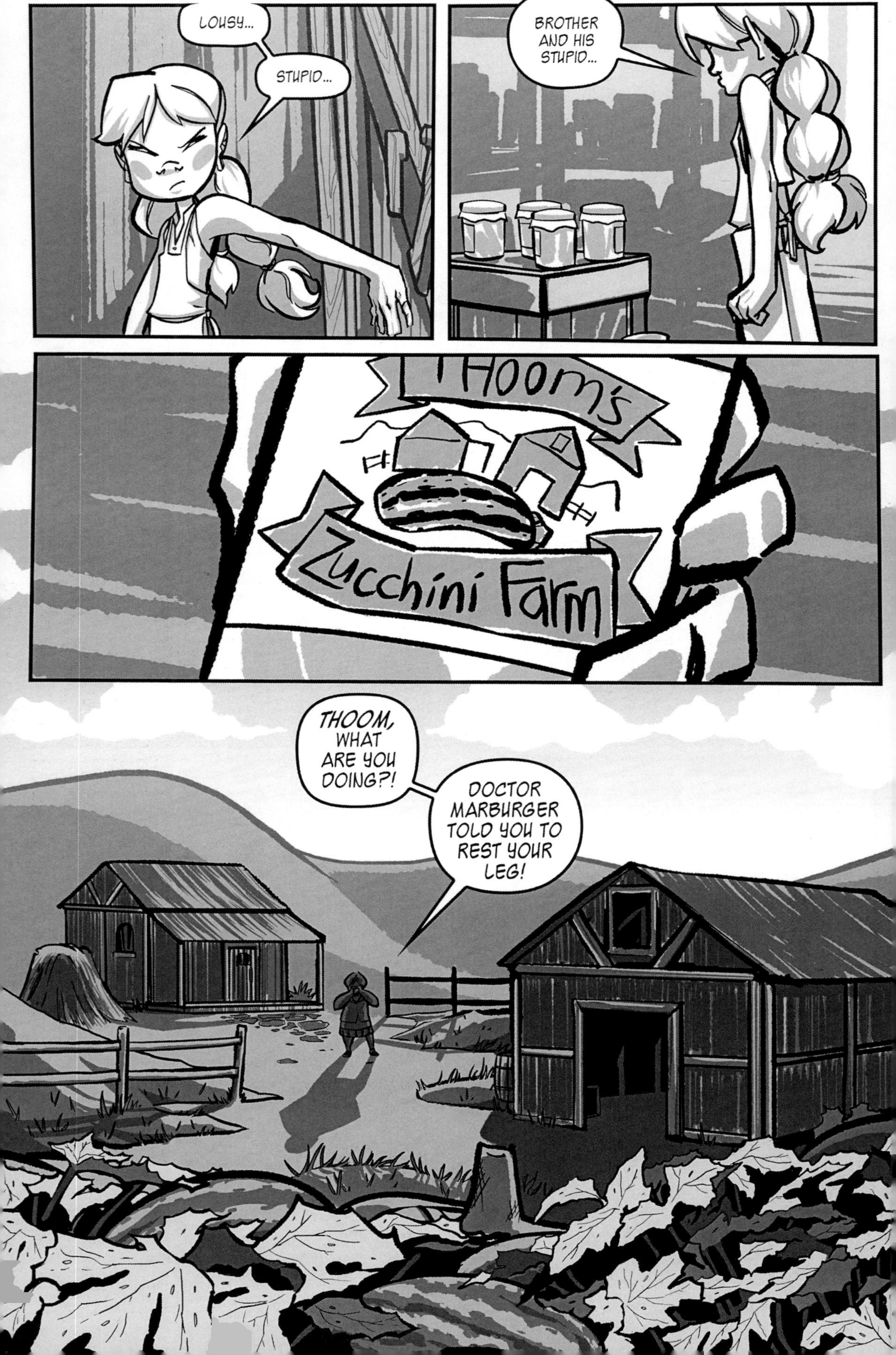
LOUSY...
STUPID...
BROTHER AND HIS STUPID...
Thoom's
Zucchini Farm
THOOM, WHAT ARE YOU DOING?!
DOCTOR MARBURGER TOLD YOU TO REST YOUR LEG!

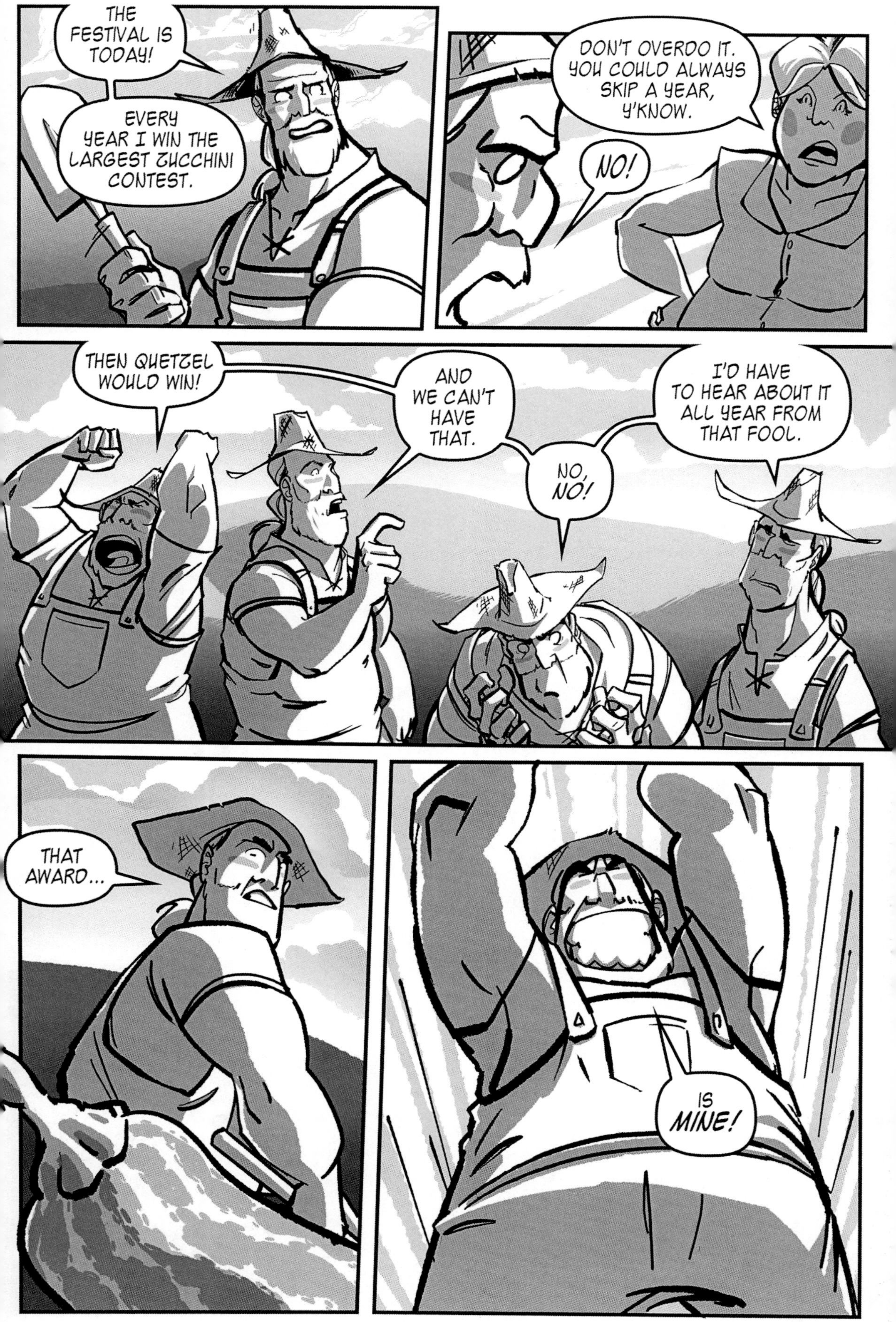
THE FESTIVAL IS TODAY!
EVERY YEAR I WIN THE LARGEST ZUCCHINI CONTEST.
DON'T OVERDO IT. YOU COULD ALWAYS SKIP A YEAR, Y'KNOW.
NO!
THEN QUETZEL WOULD WIN!
AND WE CAN'T HAVE THAT.
NO, NO!
I'D HAVE TO HEAR ABOUT IT ALL YEAR FROM THAT FOOL.
THAT AWARD...
IS MINE!

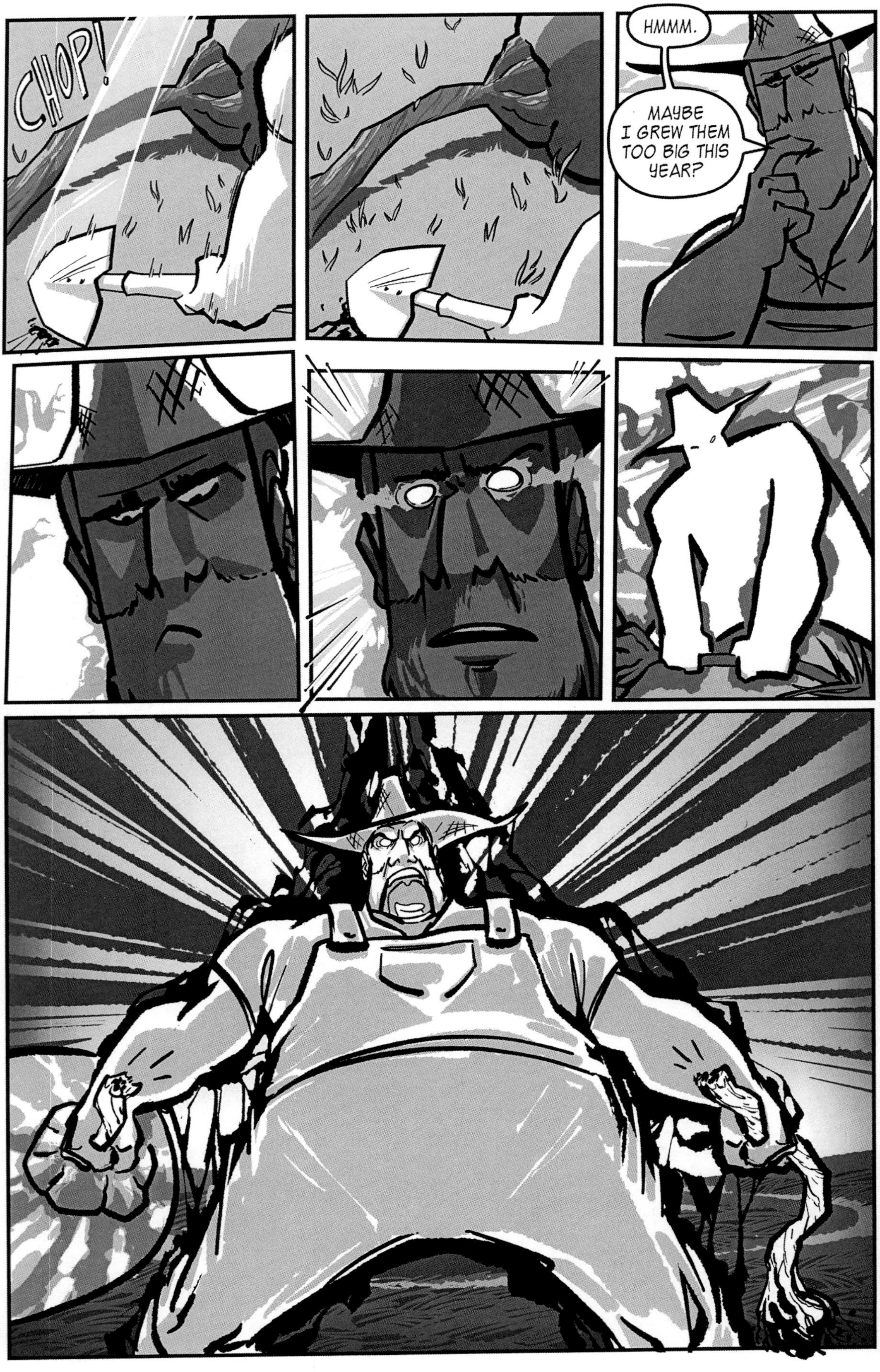
CHOP!
HMMM.
MAYBE I GREW THEM TOO BIG THIS YEAR?

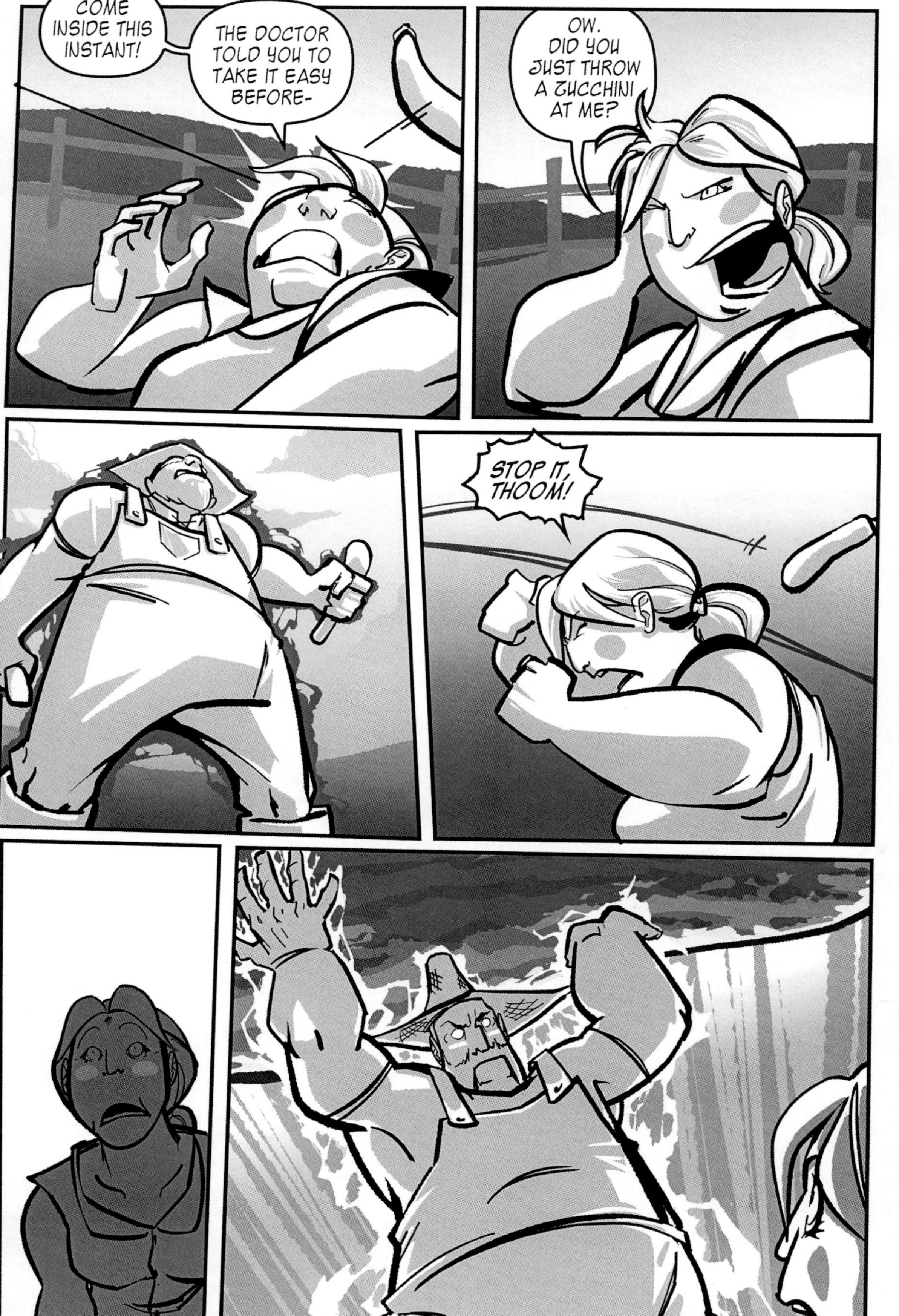
COME INSIDE THIS INSTANT!
THE DOCTOR TOLD YOU TO TAKE IT EASY BEFORE-
OW. DID YOU JUST THROW A ZUCCHINI AT ME?
STOP IT, THOOM!

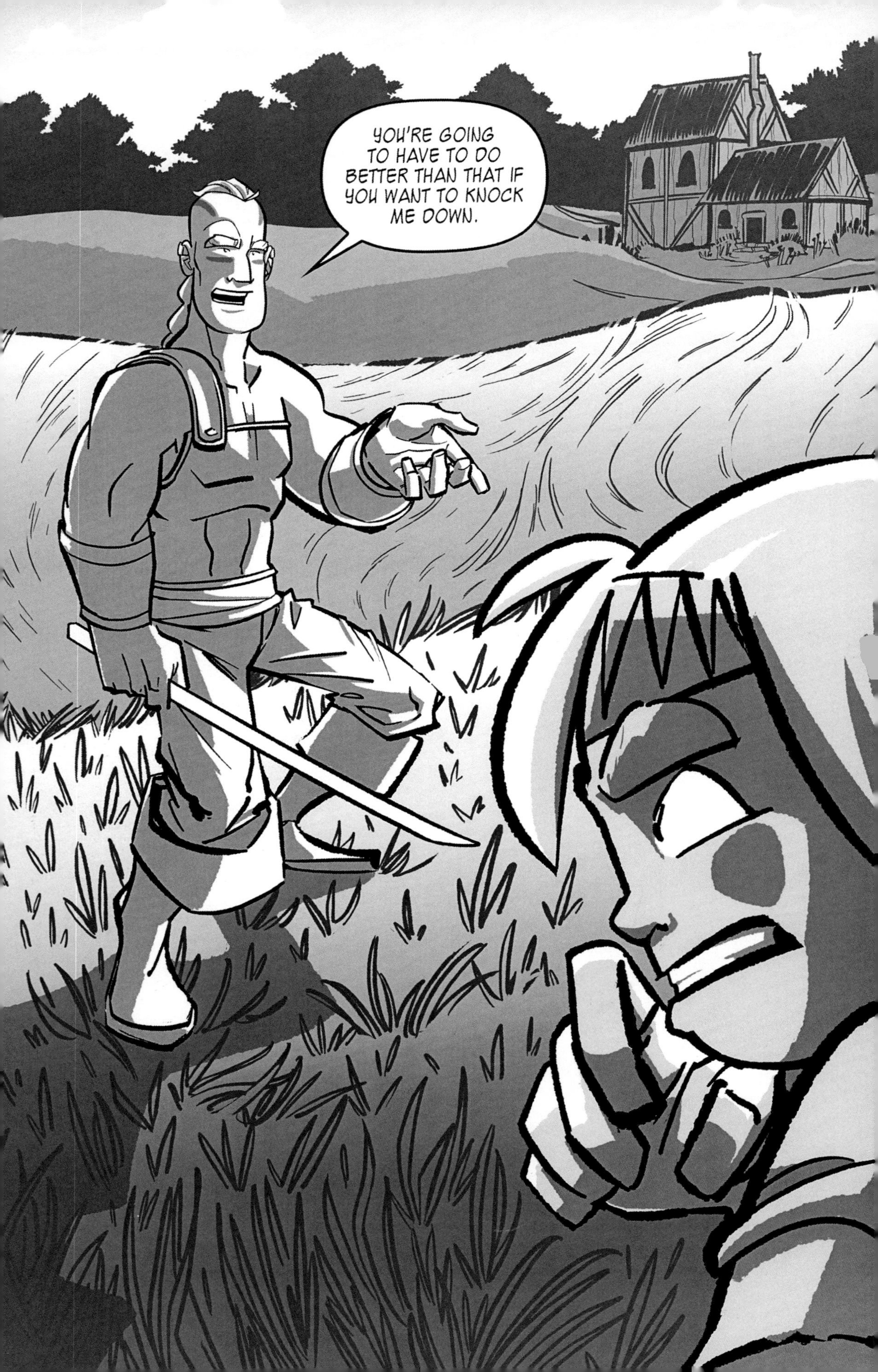
YOU'RE GOING TO HAVE TO DO BETTER THAN THAT IF YOU WANT TO KNOCK ME DOWN.

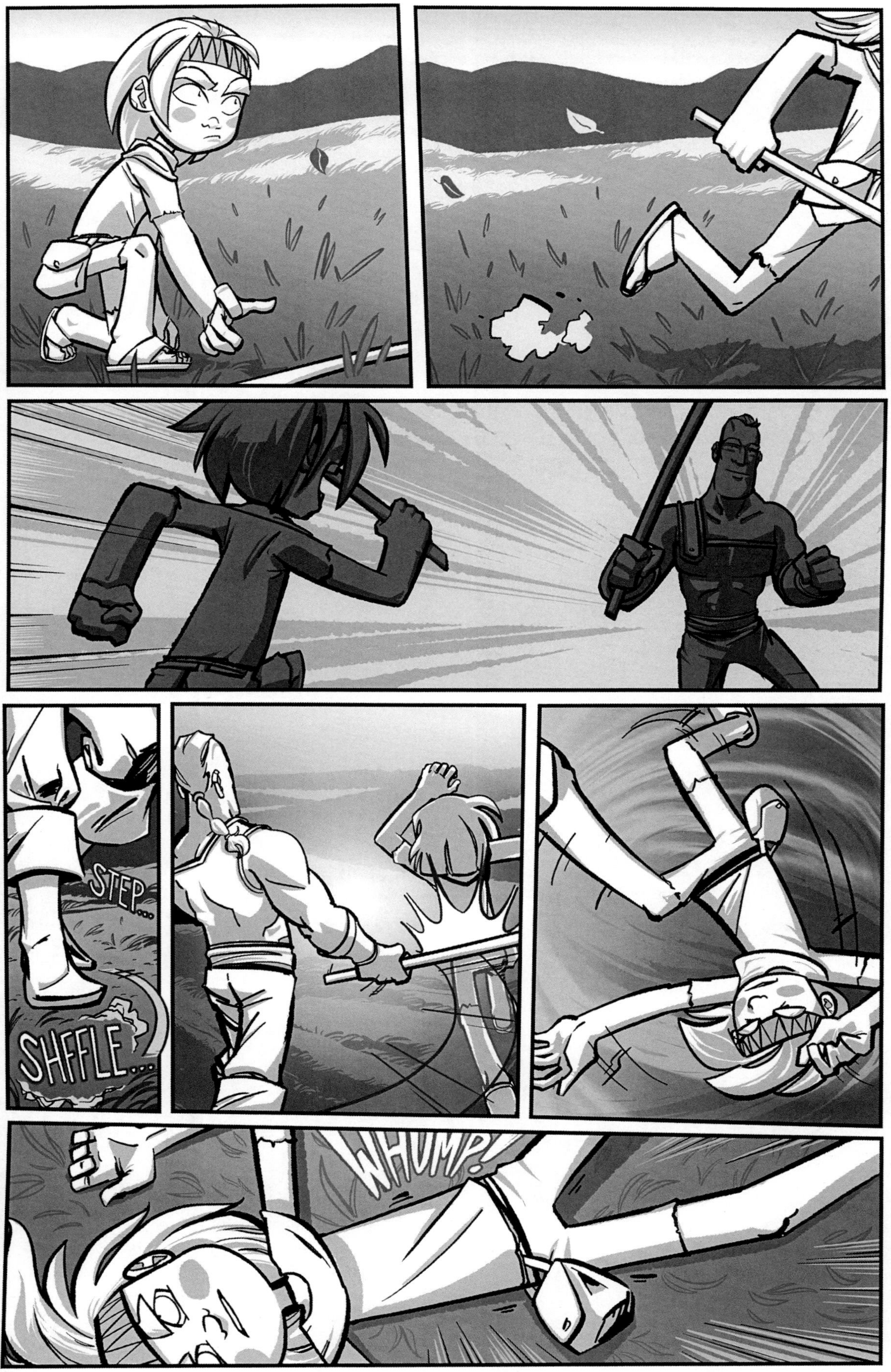

STEP...
SHFFLE...
WHUMP!

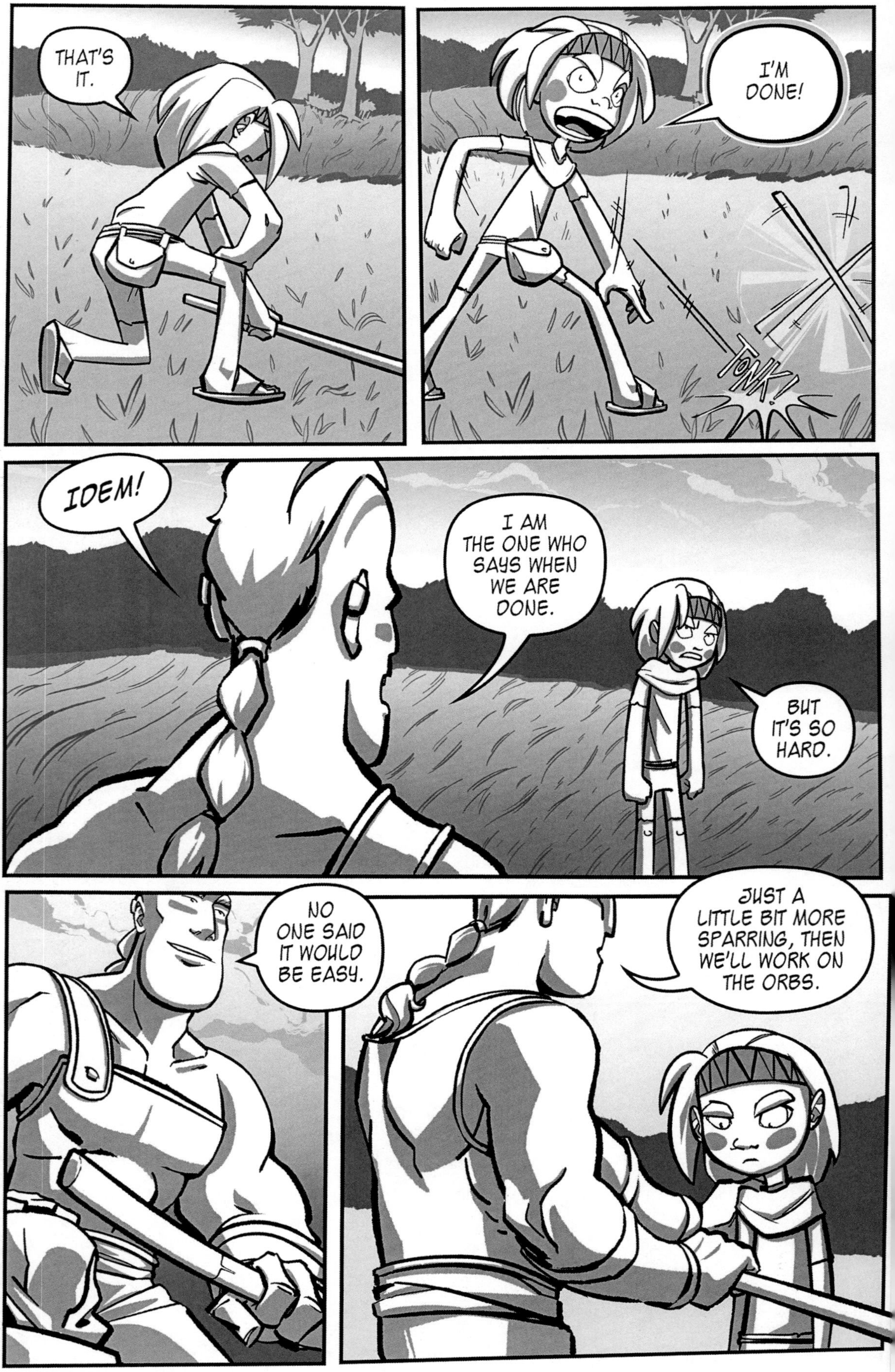
THAT'S IT.
I'M DONE!
TONK!
IDEM!
I AM THE ONE WHO SAYS WHEN WE ARE DONE.
BUT IT'S SO HARD.
NO ONE SAID IT WOULD BE EASY.
JUST A LITTLE BIT MORE SPARRING, THEN WE'LL WORK ON THE ORBS.

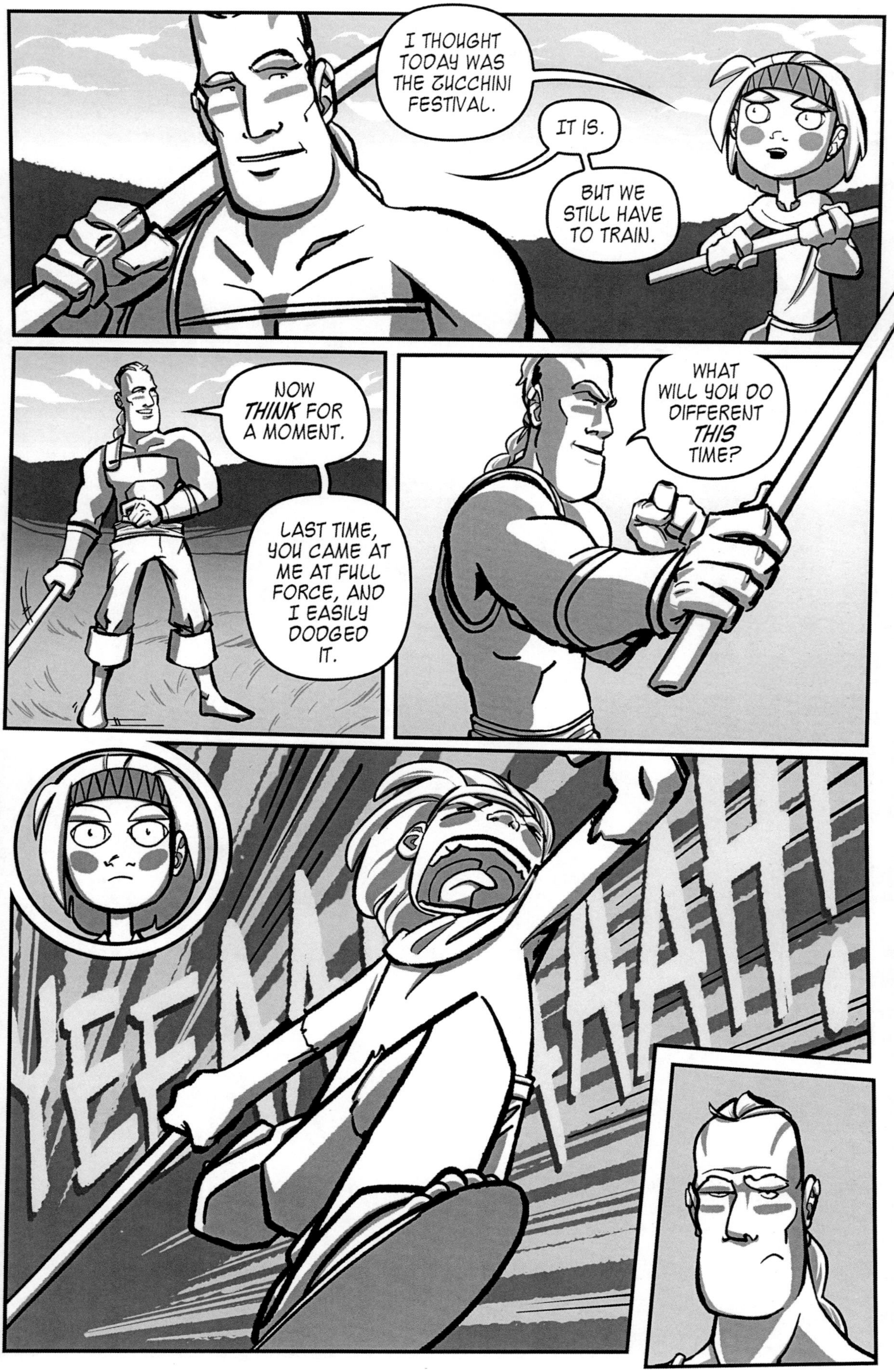
I THOUGHT TODAY WAS THE ZUCCHINI FESTIVAL.
IT IS.
BUT WE STILL HAVE TO TRAIN.
NOW THINK FOR A MOMENT.
LAST TIME, YOU CAME AT ME AT FULL FORCE, AND I EASILY DODGED IT.
WHAT WILL YOU DO DIFFERENT THIS TIME?

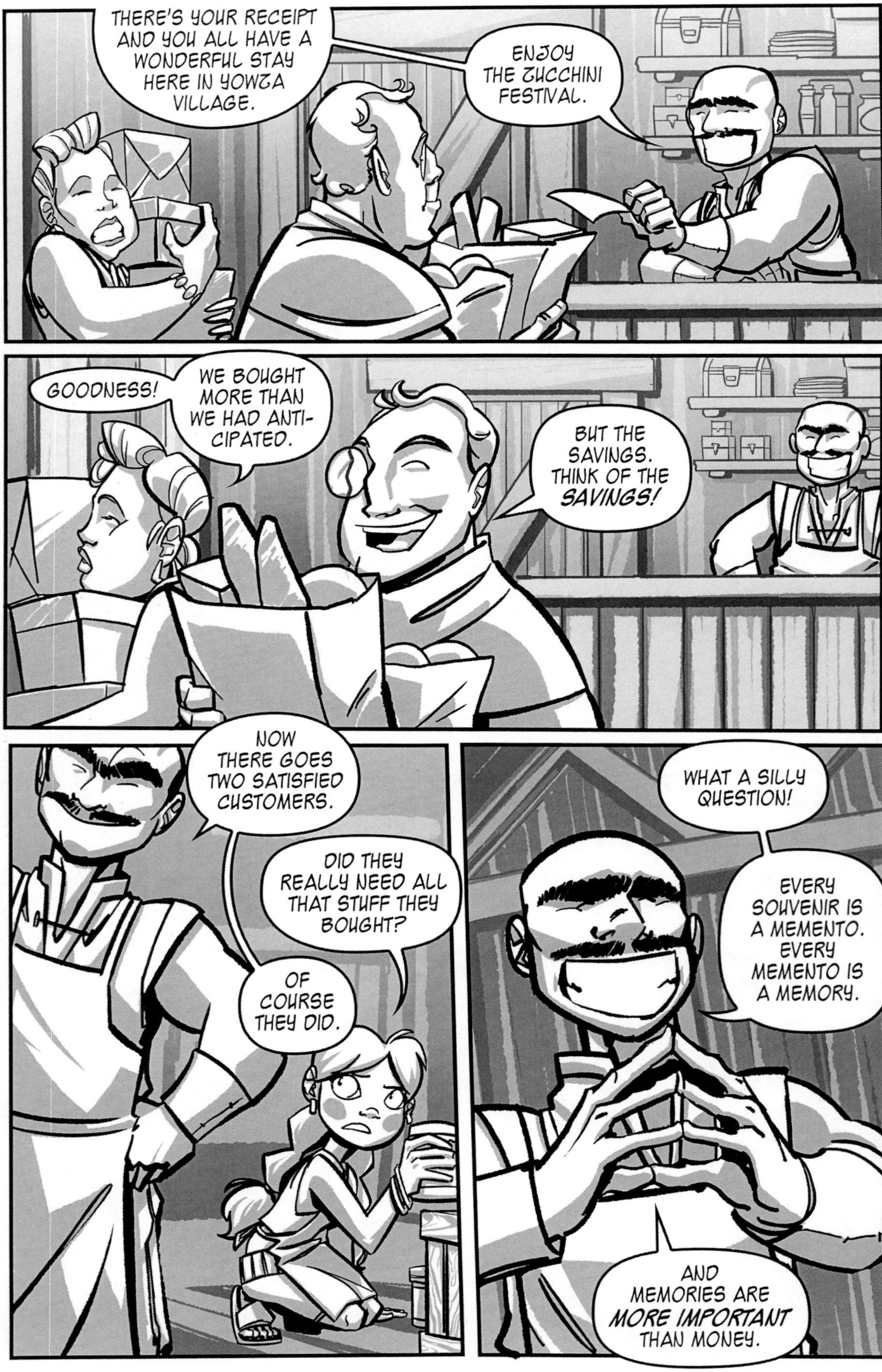
THERE'S YOUR RECEIPT AND YOU ALL HAVE A WONDERFUL STAY HERE IN YOWZA VILLAGE.
ENJOY THE ZUCCHINI FESTIVAL.
GOODNESS!
WE BOUGHT MORE THAN WE HAD ANTI-CIPATED.
BUT THE SAVINGS. THINK OF THE *SAVINGS!*
NOW THERE GOES TWO SATISFIED CUSTOMERS.
DID THEY REALLY NEED ALL THAT STUFF THEY BOUGHT?
OF COURSE THEY DID.
WHAT A SILLY QUESTION!
EVERY SOUVENIR IS A MEMENTO. EVERY MEMENTO IS A MEMORY.
AND MEMORIES ARE *MORE IMPORTANT* THAN MONEY.

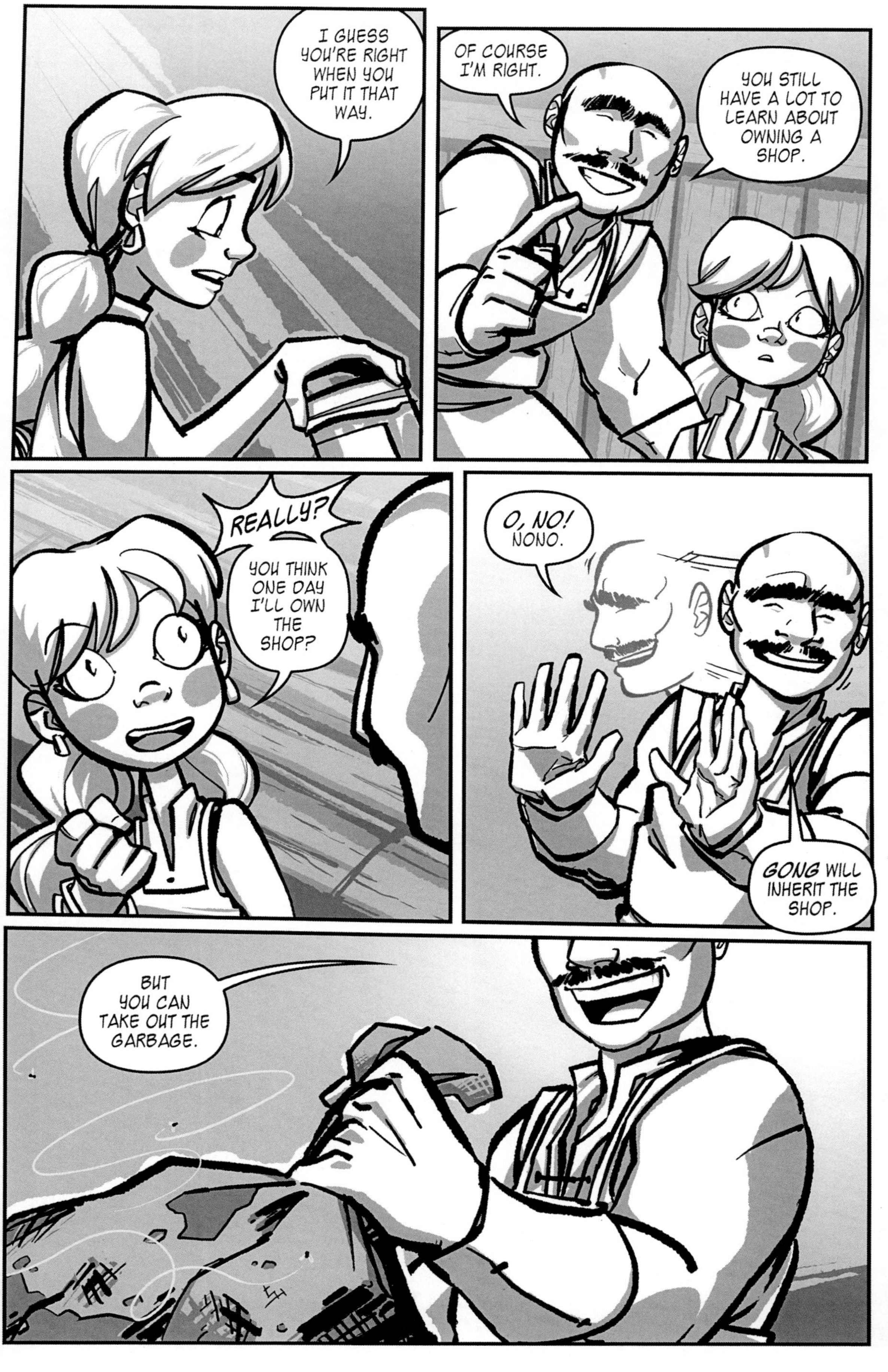
I GUESS YOU'RE RIGHT WHEN YOU PUT IT THAT WAY.
OF COURSE I'M RIGHT.
YOU STILL HAVE A LOT TO LEARN ABOUT OWNING A SHOP.
REALLY?
YOU THINK ONE DAY I'LL OWN THE SHOP?
O, NO! NONO.
GONG WILL INHERIT THE SHOP.
BUT YOU CAN TAKE OUT THE GARBAGE.

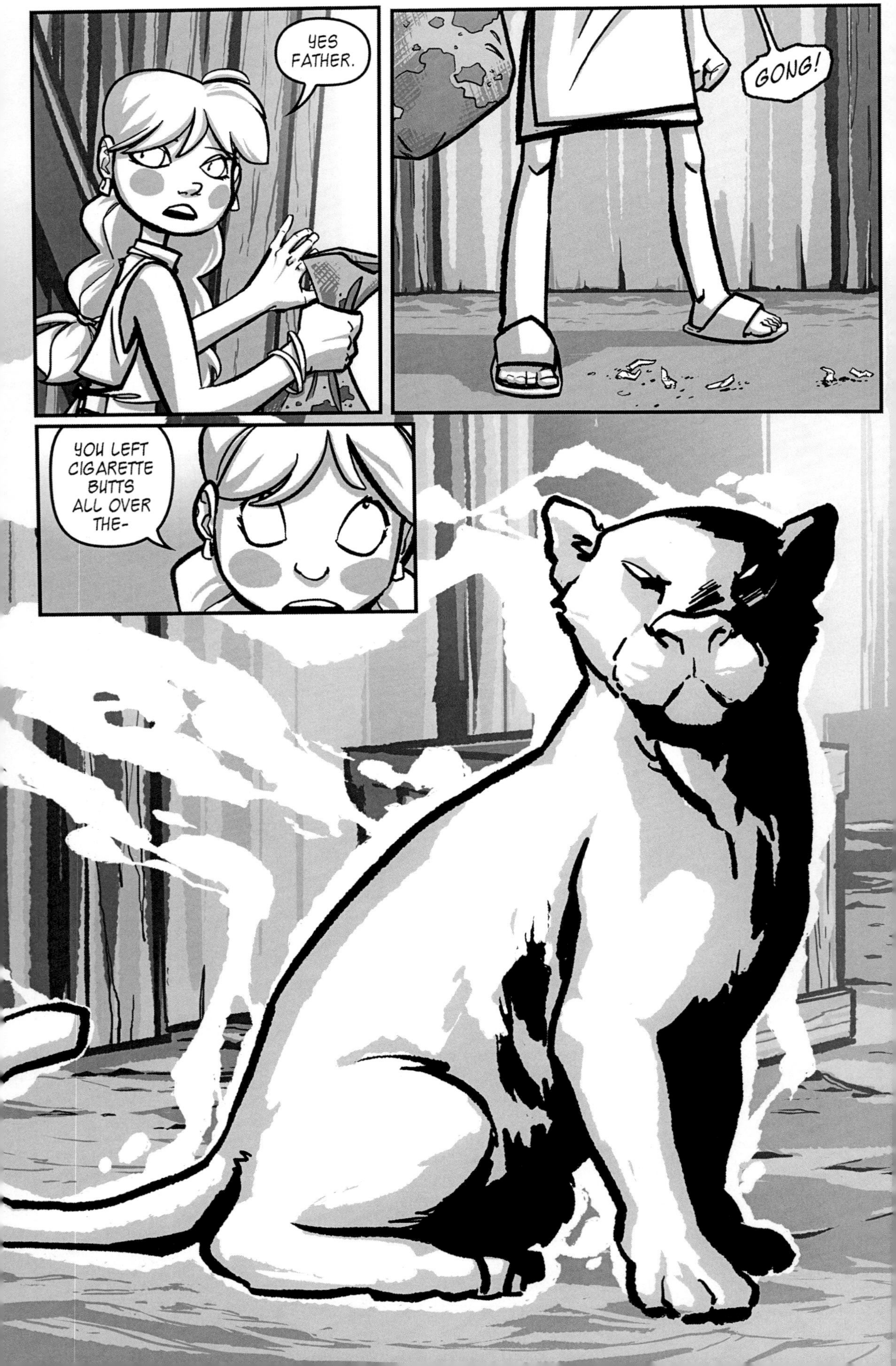
YES FATHER.
GONG!
YOU LEFT CIGARETTE BUTTS ALL OVER THE-

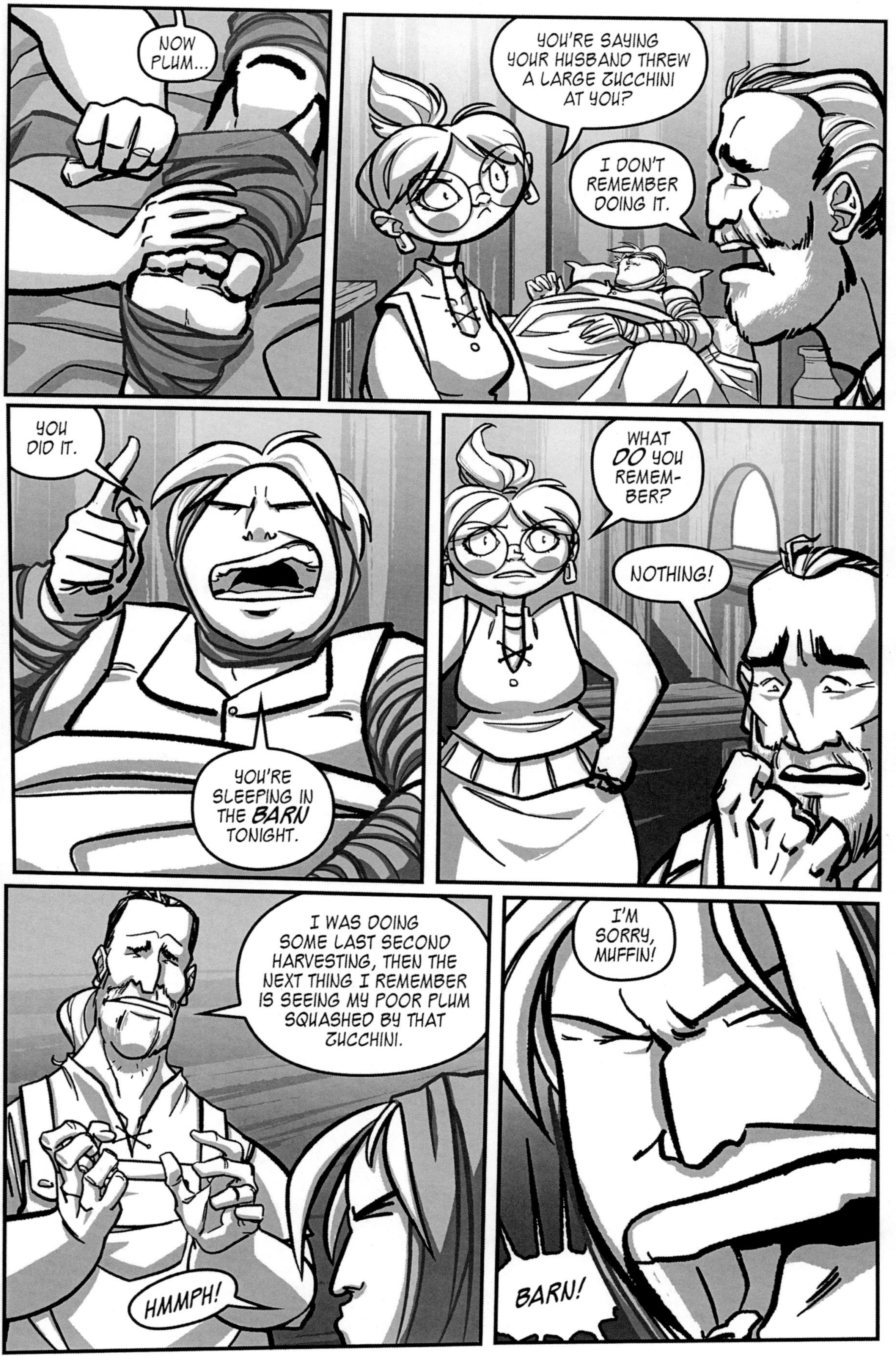
NOW PLUM...
YOU'RE SAYING YOUR HUSBAND THREW A LARGE ZUCCHINI AT YOU?
I DON'T REMEMBER DOING IT.
YOU DID IT.
YOU'RE SLEEPING IN THE BARN TONIGHT.
WHAT DO YOU REMEMBER?
NOTHING!
I WAS DOING SOME LAST SECOND HARVESTING, THEN THE NEXT THING I REMEMBER IS SEEING MY POOR PLUM SQUASHED BY THAT ZUCCHINI.
HMMPH!
I'M SORRY, MUFFIN!
BARN!

HARVESTING?

WITH YOUR BAD LEG?

YOU SHOULD BE RESTING IT.

THAT'S WHAT I SAID!

BAH!

IT'S FINE.

IF YOU ASK ME IT'S PROBABLY AN ALLERGIC REACTION TO SOME BAD MEDICINE I WAS GIVEN THE LAST TIME I WAS HERE.

EXCUSE ME? From what I recall you told me you were out feeding your chickens when something *bit* you.

YOW!

WHAT IN THE...

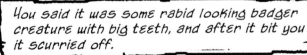

You said it was some rabid looking badger creature with big teeth, and after it bit you it scurried off.

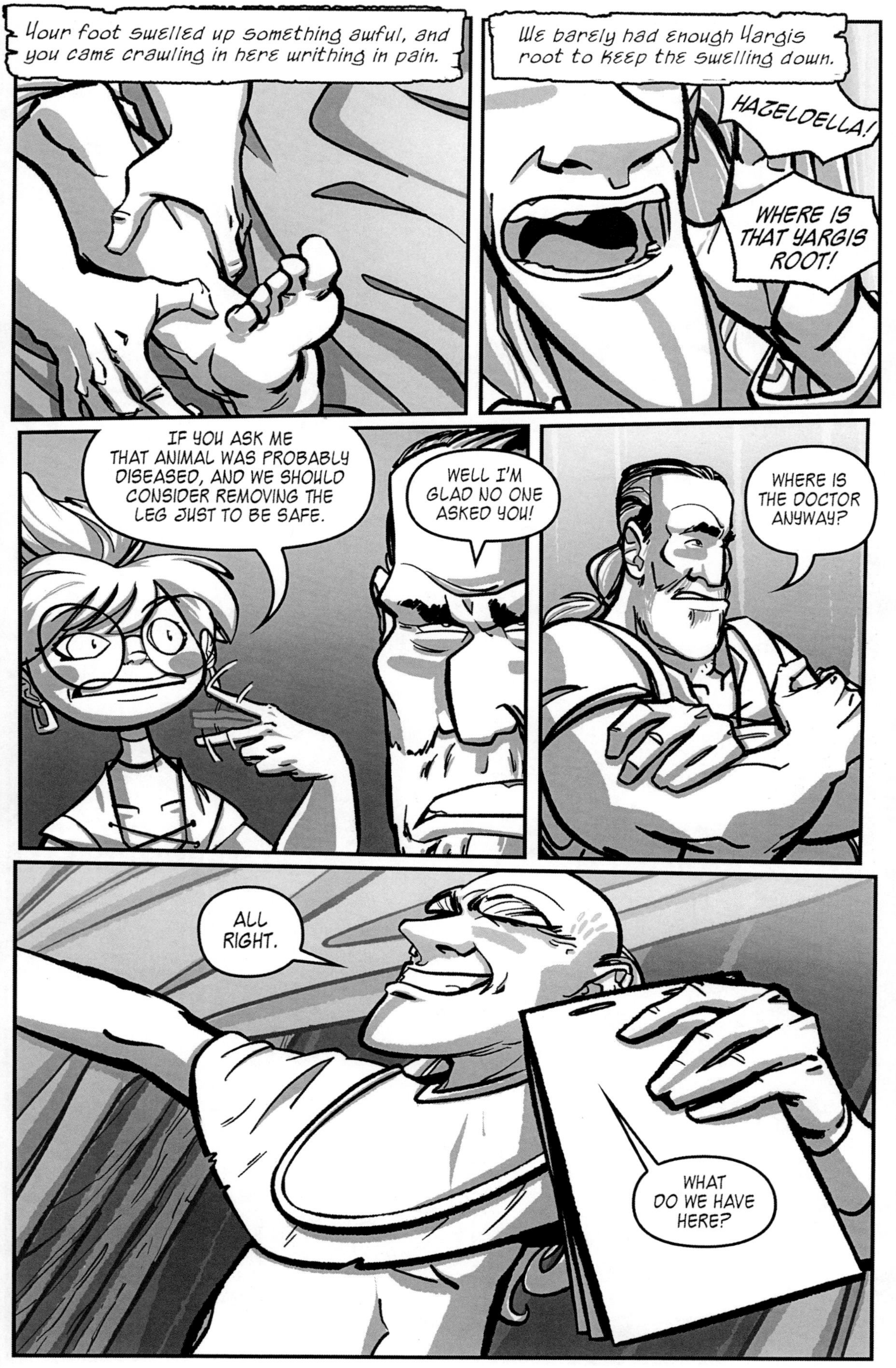
Your foot swelled up something awful, and you came crawling in here writhing in pain.
We barely had enough Yargis root to keep the swelling down.
HAZELDELLA!
WHERE IS THAT YARGIS ROOT!
IF YOU ASK ME THAT ANIMAL WAS PROBABLY DISEASED, AND WE SHOULD CONSIDER REMOVING THE LEG JUST TO BE SAFE.
WELL I'M GLAD NO ONE ASKED YOU!
WHERE IS THE DOCTOR ANYWAY?
ALL RIGHT.
WHAT DO WE HAVE HERE?

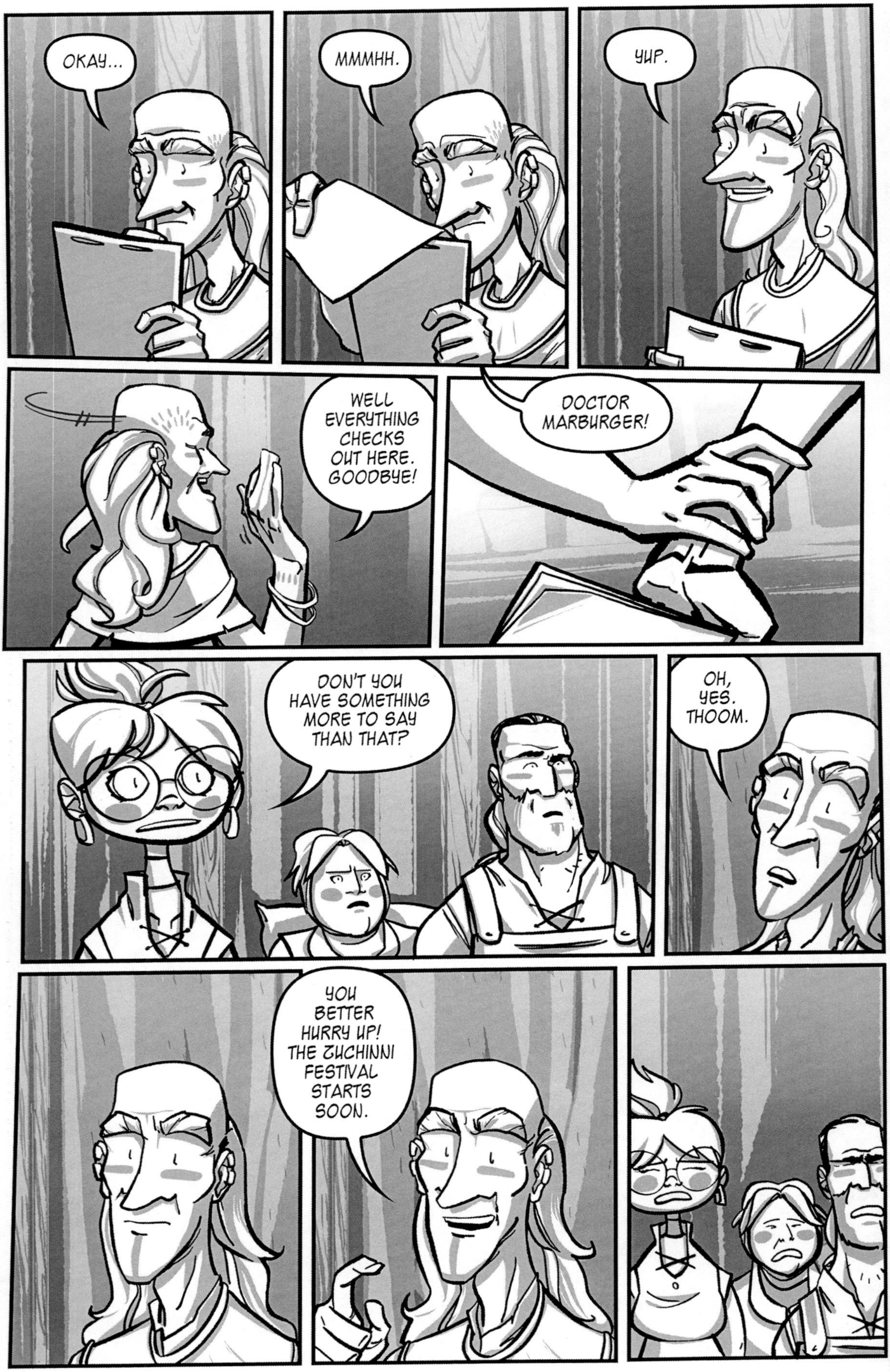
OKAY...
MMMHH.
YUP.
WELL EVERYTHING CHECKS OUT HERE. GOODBYE!
DOCTOR MARBURGER!
DON'T YOU HAVE SOMETHING MORE TO SAY THAN THAT?
OH, YES. THOOM.
YOU BETTER HURRY UP! THE ZUCHINNI FESTIVAL STARTS SOON.

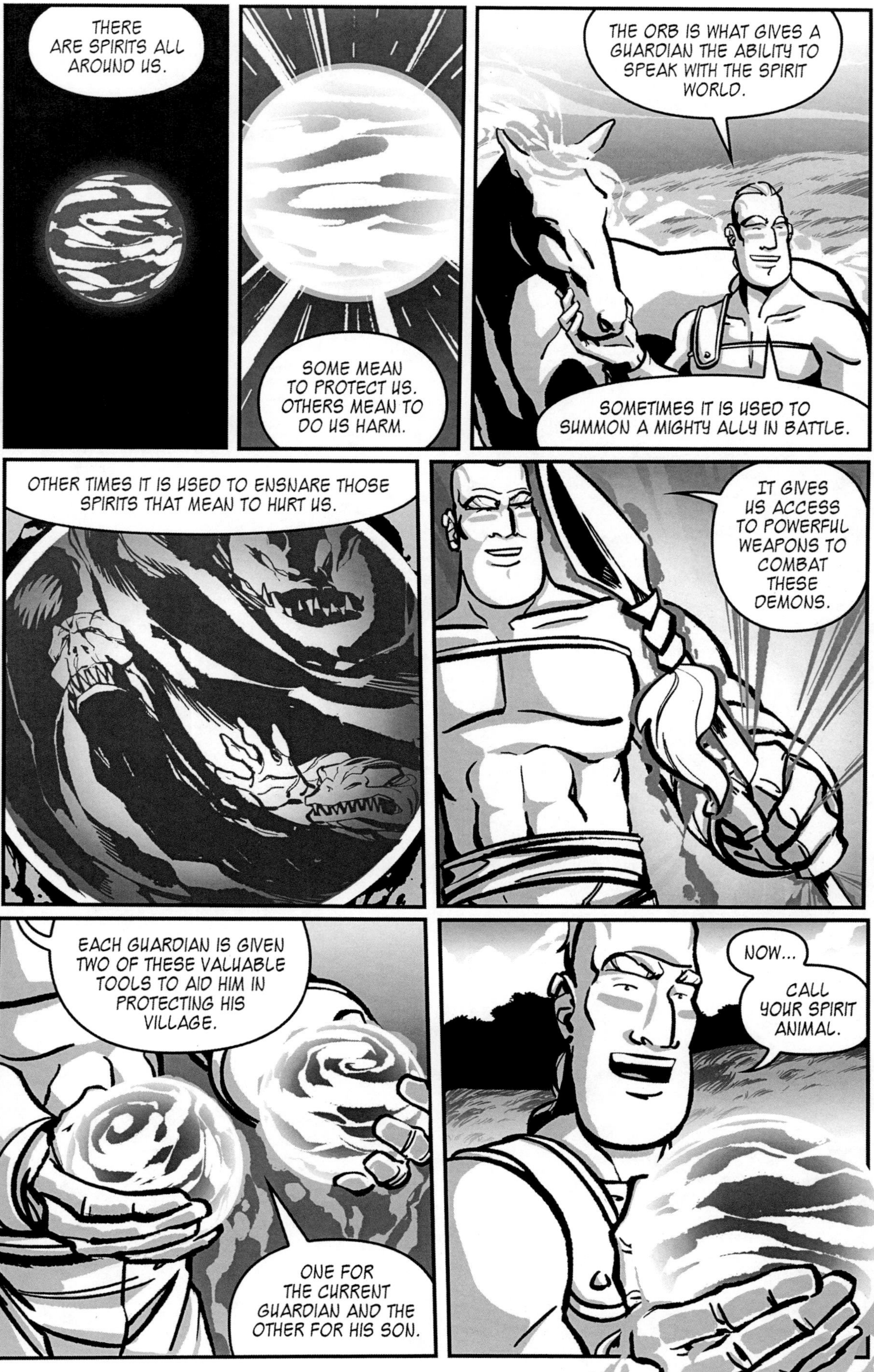
THERE ARE SPIRITS ALL AROUND US.
SOME MEAN TO PROTECT US. OTHERS MEAN TO DO US HARM.
THE ORB IS WHAT GIVES A GUARDIAN THE ABILITY TO SPEAK WITH THE SPIRIT WORLD.
SOMETIMES IT IS USED TO SUMMON A MIGHTY ALLY IN BATTLE.
OTHER TIMES IT IS USED TO ENSNARE THOSE SPIRITS THAT MEAN TO HURT US.
IT GIVES US ACCESS TO POWERFUL WEAPONS TO COMBAT THESE DEMONS.
EACH GUARDIAN IS GIVEN TWO OF THESE VALUABLE TOOLS TO AID HIM IN PROTECTING HIS VILLAGE.
ONE FOR THE CURRENT GUARDIAN AND THE OTHER FOR HIS SON.
NOW...
CALL YOUR SPIRIT ANIMAL.

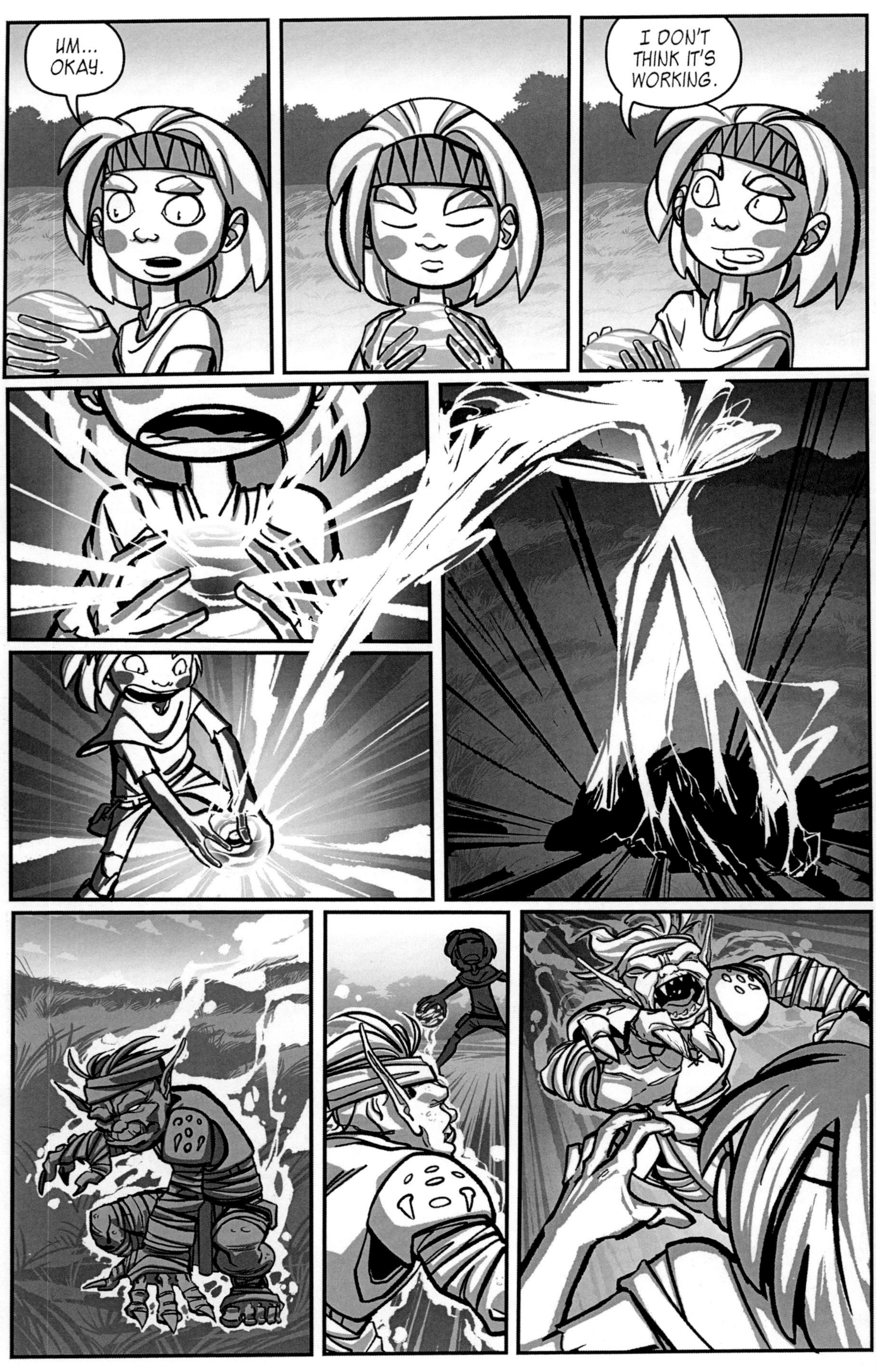
UM... OKAY.
I DON'T THINK IT'S WORKING.

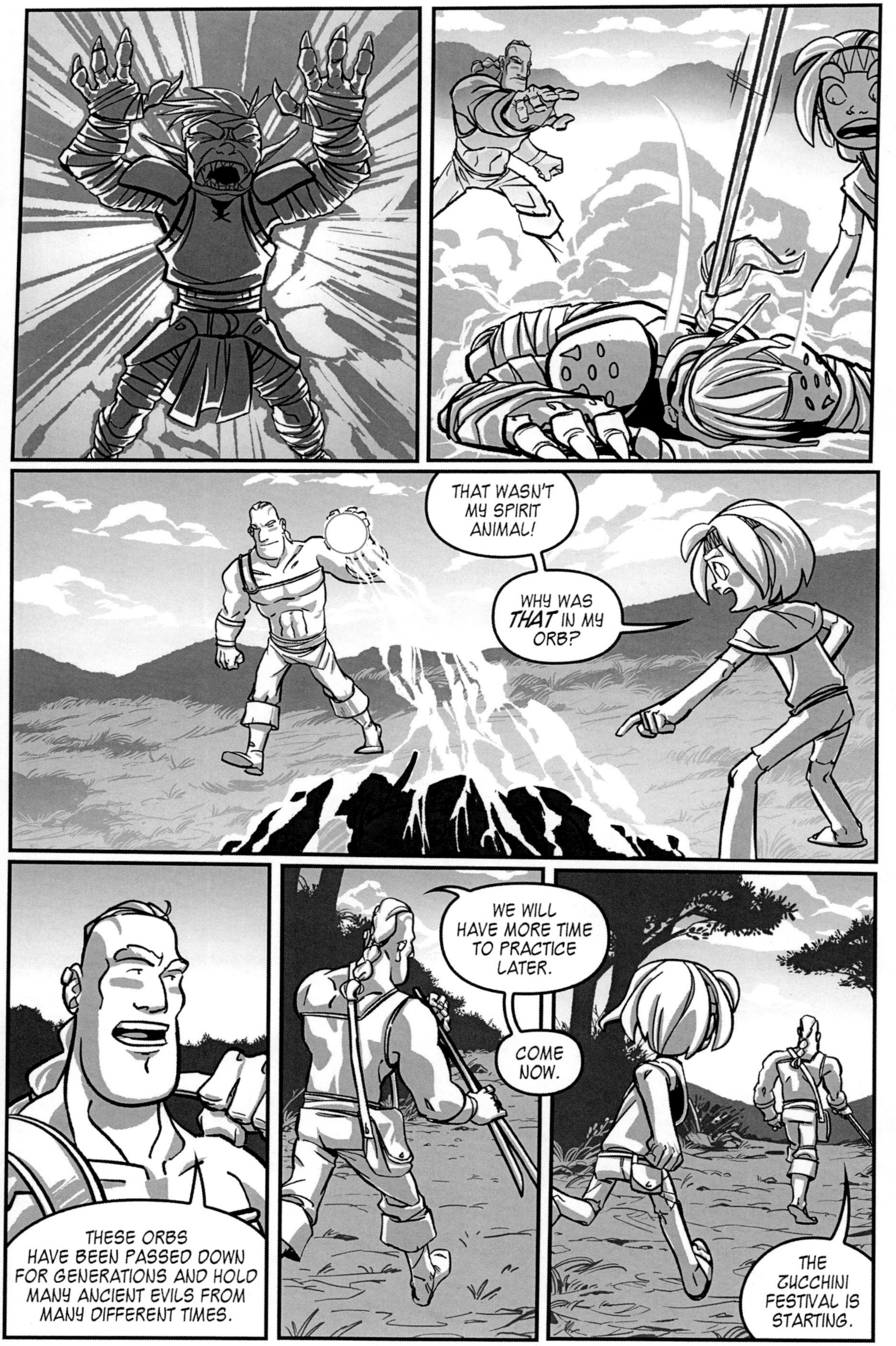
THAT WASN'T MY SPIRIT ANIMAL!
WHY WAS *THAT* IN MY ORB?
THESE ORBS HAVE BEEN PASSED DOWN FOR GENERATIONS AND HOLD MANY ANCIENT EVILS FROM MANY DIFFERENT TIMES.
WE WILL HAVE MORE TIME TO PRACTICE LATER.
COME NOW.
THE ZUCCHINI FESTIVAL IS STARTING.

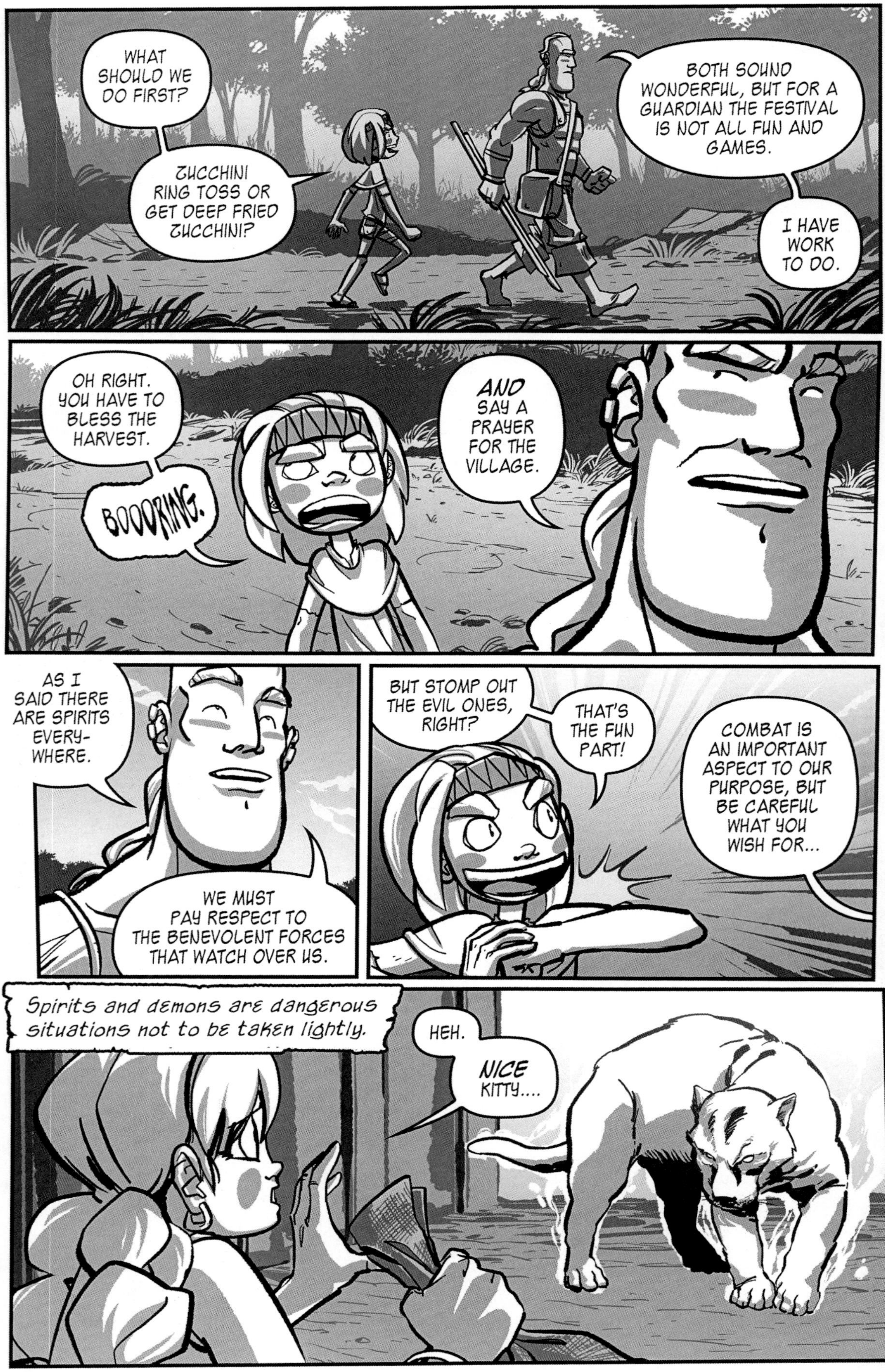
WHAT SHOULD WE DO FIRST?
ZUCCHINI RING TOSS OR GET DEEP FRIED ZUCCHINI?
BOTH SOUND WONDERFUL, BUT FOR A GUARDIAN THE FESTIVAL IS NOT ALL FUN AND GAMES.
I HAVE WORK TO DO.
OH RIGHT. YOU HAVE TO BLESS THE HARVEST.
BOOORING.
AND SAY A PRAYER FOR THE VILLAGE.
AS I SAID THERE ARE SPIRITS EVERY-WHERE.
WE MUST PAY RESPECT TO THE BENEVOLENT FORCES THAT WATCH OVER US.
BUT STOMP OUT THE EVIL ONES, RIGHT?
THAT'S THE FUN PART!
COMBAT IS AN IMPORTANT ASPECT TO OUR PURPOSE, BUT BE CAREFUL WHAT YOU WISH FOR...
Spirits and demons are dangerous situations not to be taken lightly.
HEH.
NICE KITTY....

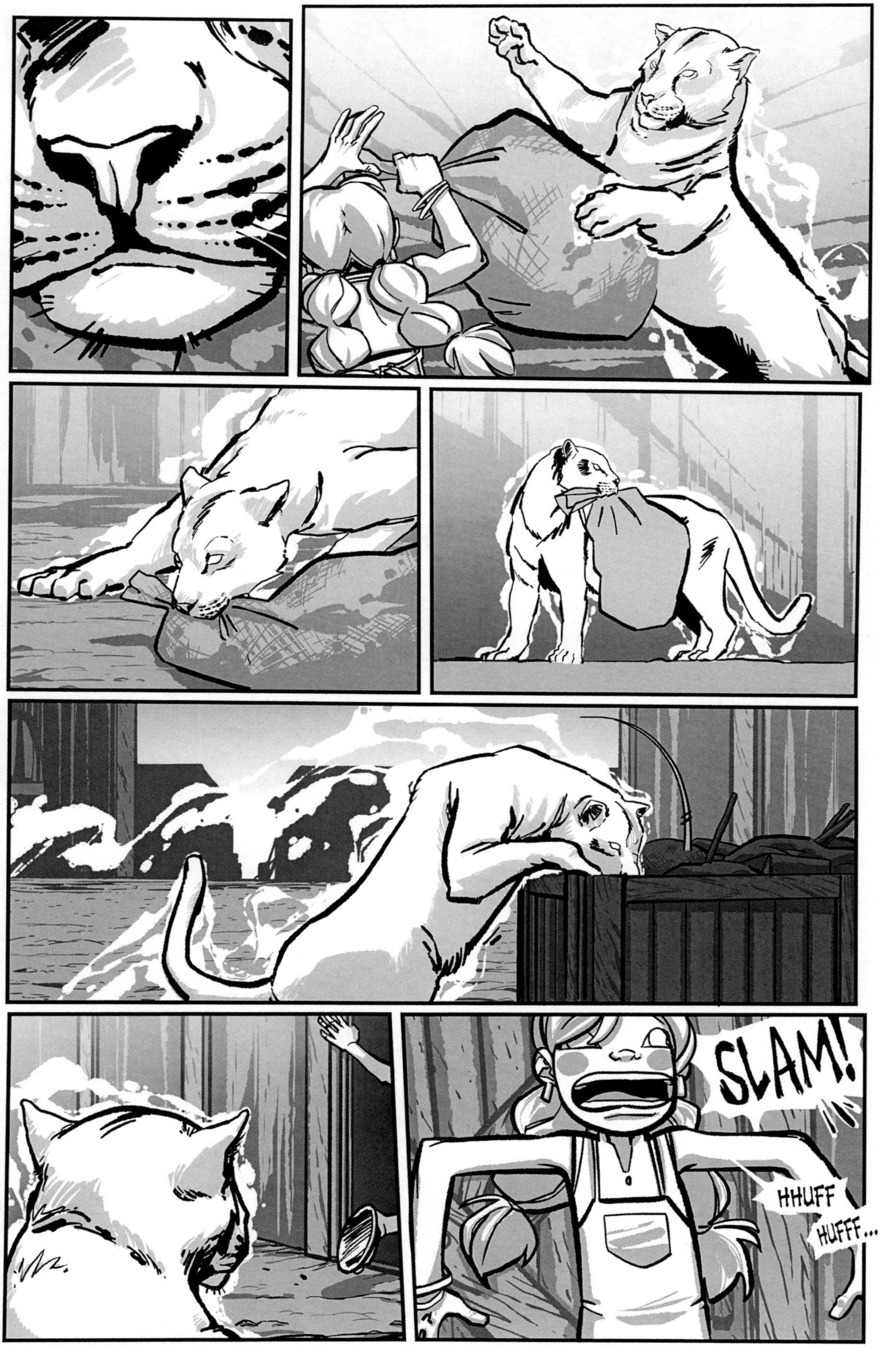
SLAM!
HHUFF
HUFFF...

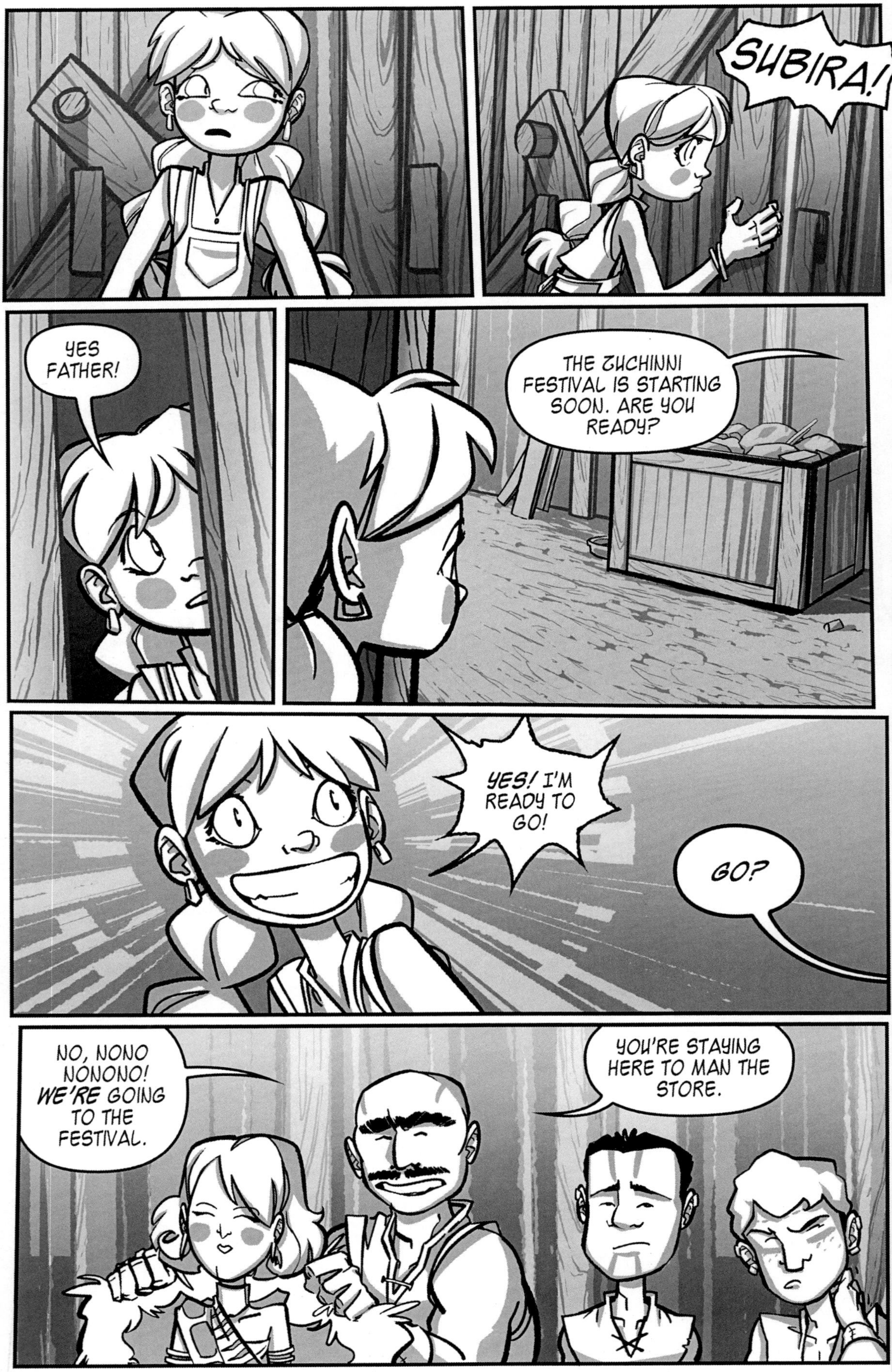
SUBIRA!
YES FATHER!
THE ZUCHINNI FESTIVAL IS STARTING SOON. ARE YOU READY?
YES! I'M READY TO GO!
GO?
NO, NONO NONONO! WE'RE GOING TO THE FESTIVAL.
YOU'RE STAYING HERE TO MAN THE STORE.

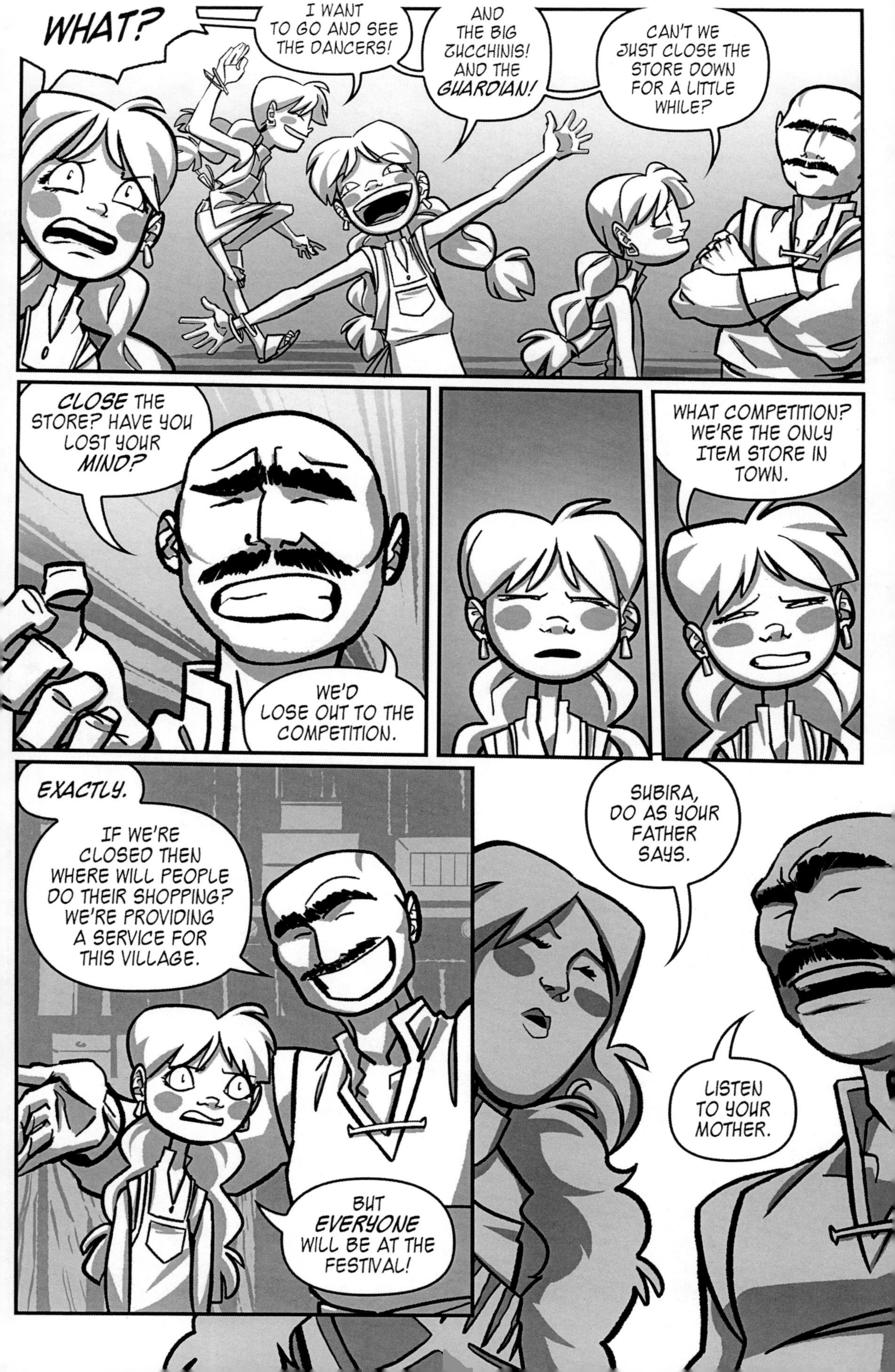
WHAT?
I WANT TO GO AND SEE THE DANCERS!
AND THE BIG ZUCCHINIS! AND THE GUARDIAN!
CAN'T WE JUST CLOSE THE STORE DOWN FOR A LITTLE WHILE?
CLOSE THE STORE? HAVE YOU LOST YOUR MIND?
WE'D LOSE OUT TO THE COMPETITION.
WHAT COMPETITION? WE'RE THE ONLY ITEM STORE IN TOWN.
EXACTLY.
IF WE'RE CLOSED THEN WHERE WILL PEOPLE DO THEIR SHOPPING? WE'RE PROVIDING A SERVICE FOR THIS VILLAGE.
BUT EVERYONE WILL BE AT THE FESTIVAL!
SUBIRA, DO AS YOUR FATHER SAYS.
LISTEN TO YOUR MOTHER.

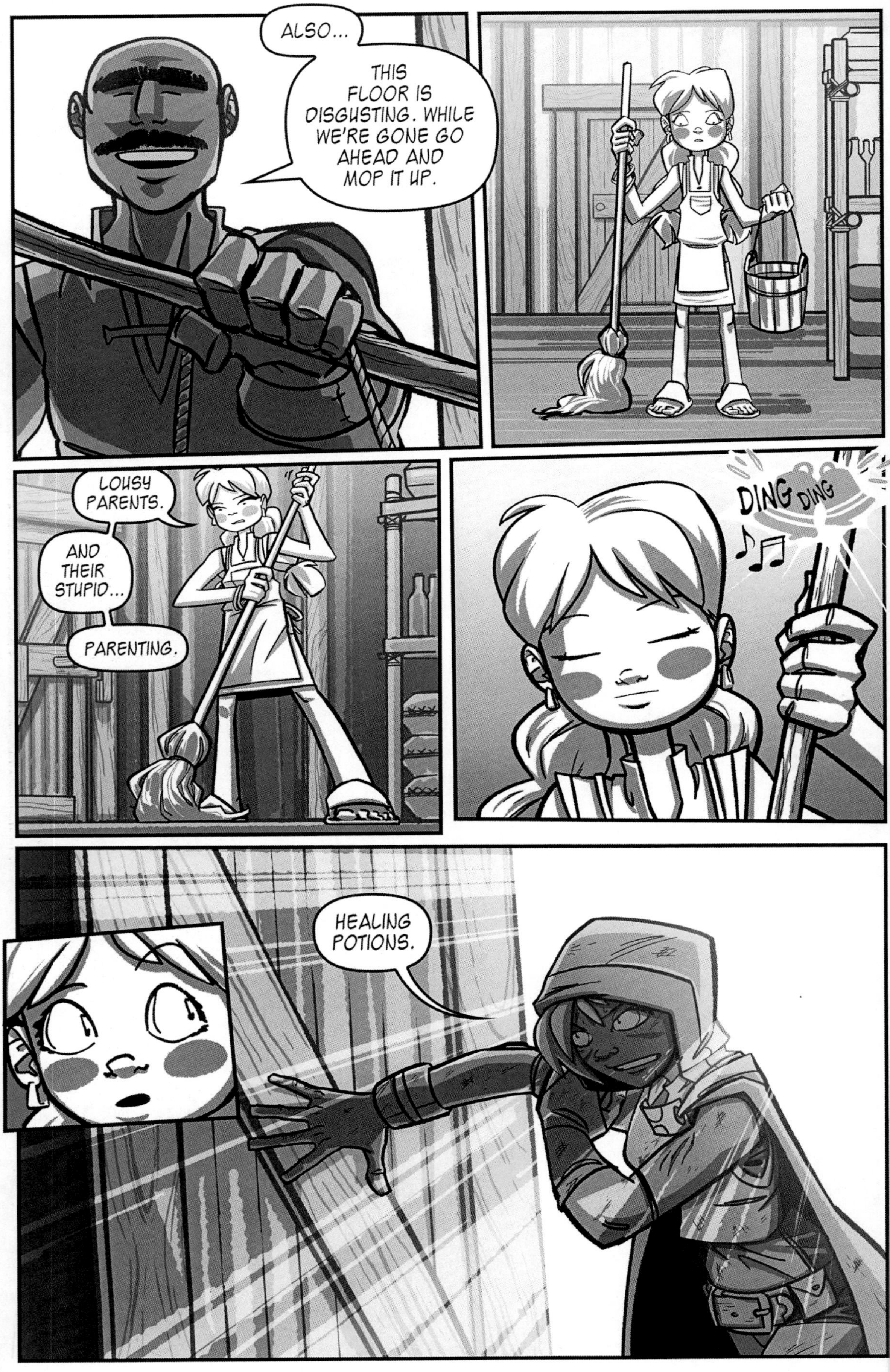
ALSO...
THIS FLOOR IS DISGUSTING. WHILE WE'RE GONE GO AHEAD AND MOP IT UP.
LOUSY PARENTS.
AND THEIR STUPID...
PARENTING.
DING DING
HEALING POTIONS.

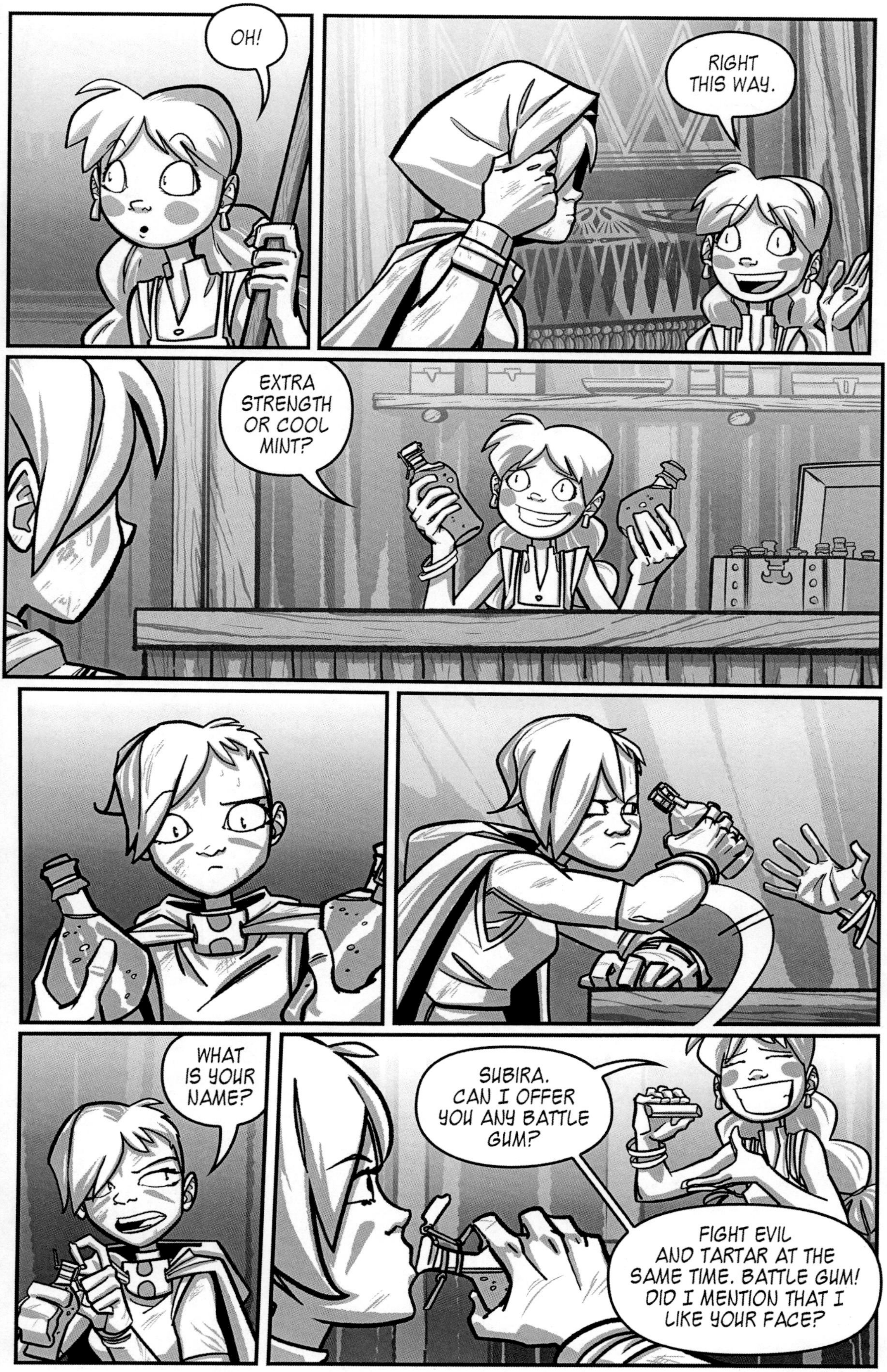
OH!
RIGHT THIS WAY.
EXTRA STRENGTH OR COOL MINT?
WHAT IS YOUR NAME?
SUBIRA. CAN I OFFER YOU ANY BATTLE GUM?
FIGHT EVIL AND TARTAR AT THE SAME TIME. BATTLE GUM! DID I MENTION THAT I LIKE YOUR FACE?

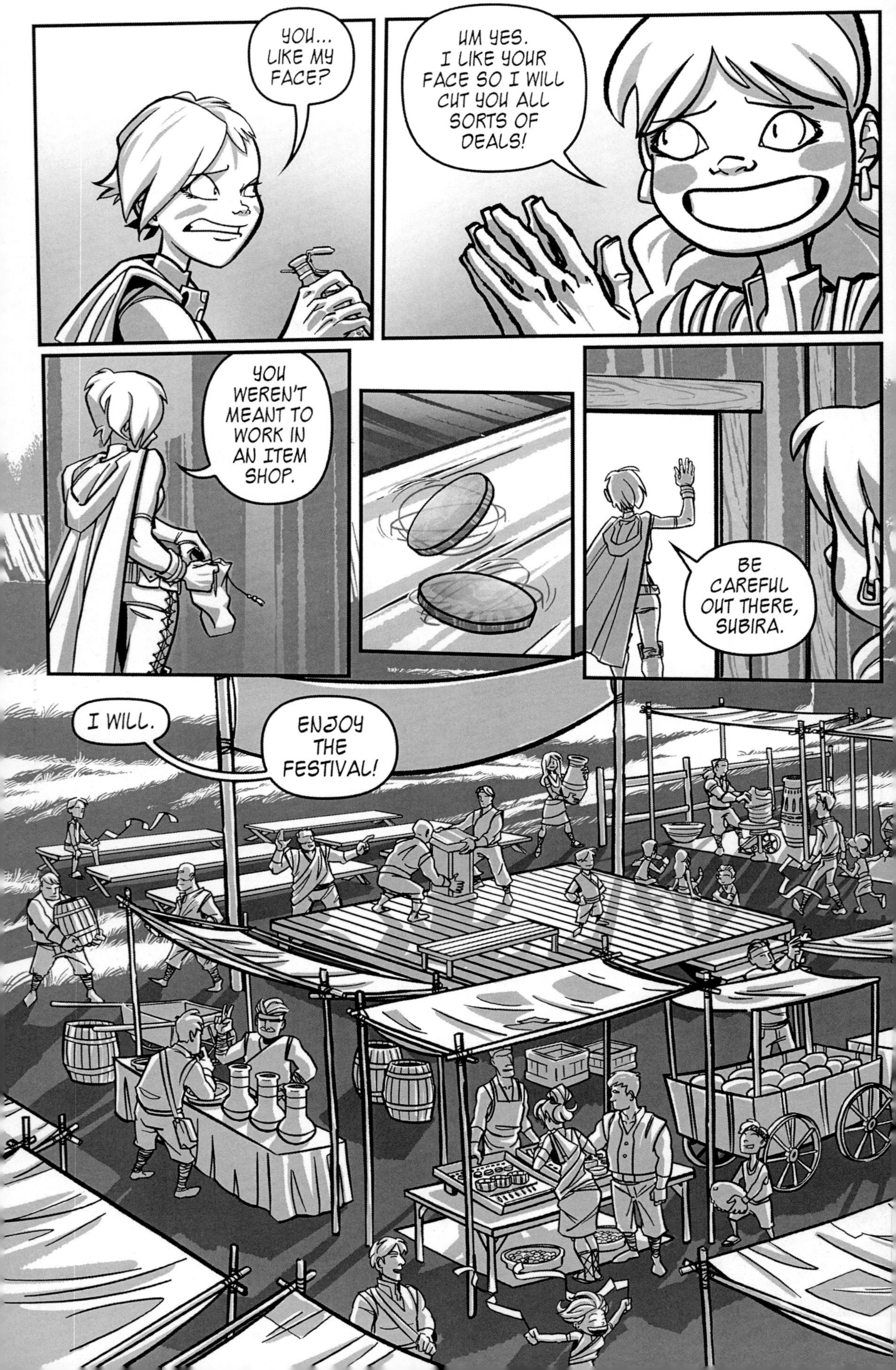
YOU... LIKE MY FACE?
UM YES. I LIKE YOUR FACE SO I WILL CUT YOU ALL SORTS OF DEALS!
YOU WEREN'T MEANT TO WORK IN AN ITEM SHOP.
BE CAREFUL OUT THERE, SUBIRA.
I WILL.
ENJOY THE FESTIVAL!

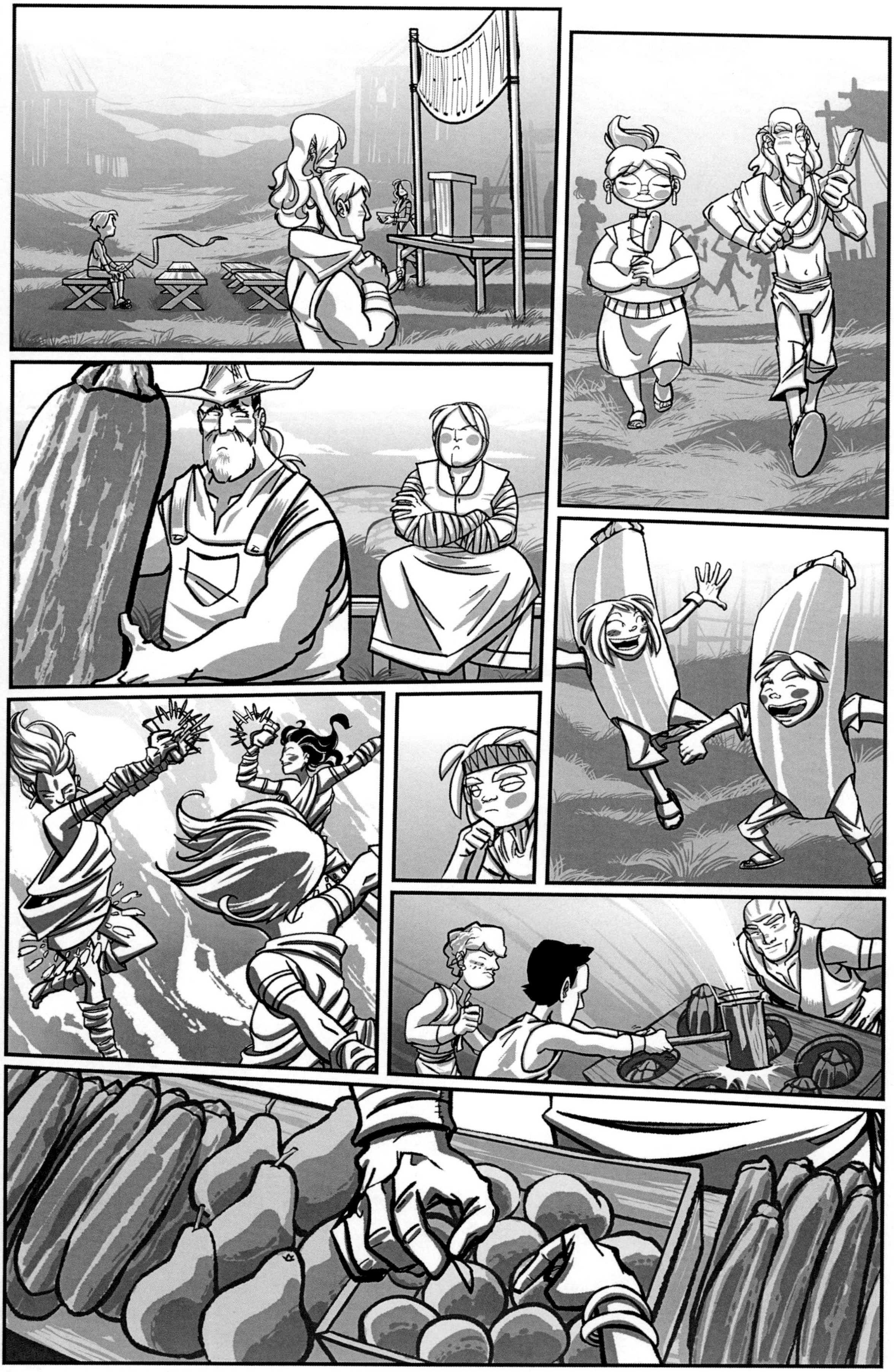
UCCHINI FESTIVAL

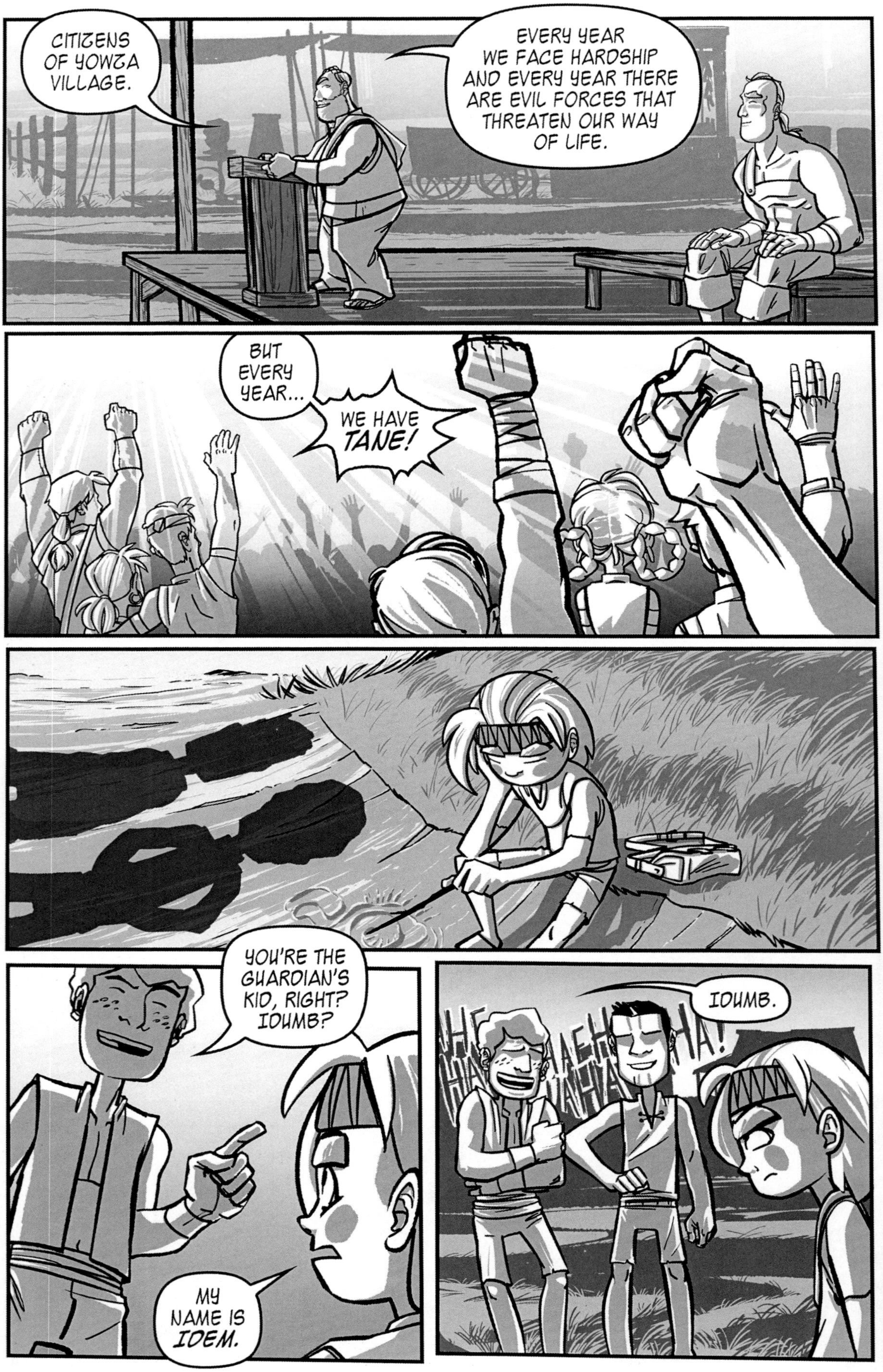
CITIZENS OF YOWZA VILLAGE.
EVERY YEAR WE FACE HARDSHIP AND EVERY YEAR THERE ARE EVIL FORCES THAT THREATEN OUR WAY OF LIFE.
BUT EVERY YEAR...
WE HAVE TANE!
YOU'RE THE GUARDIAN'S KID, RIGHT? IDUMB?
MY NAME IS IDEM.
IDUMB.
HAHAHAHA!

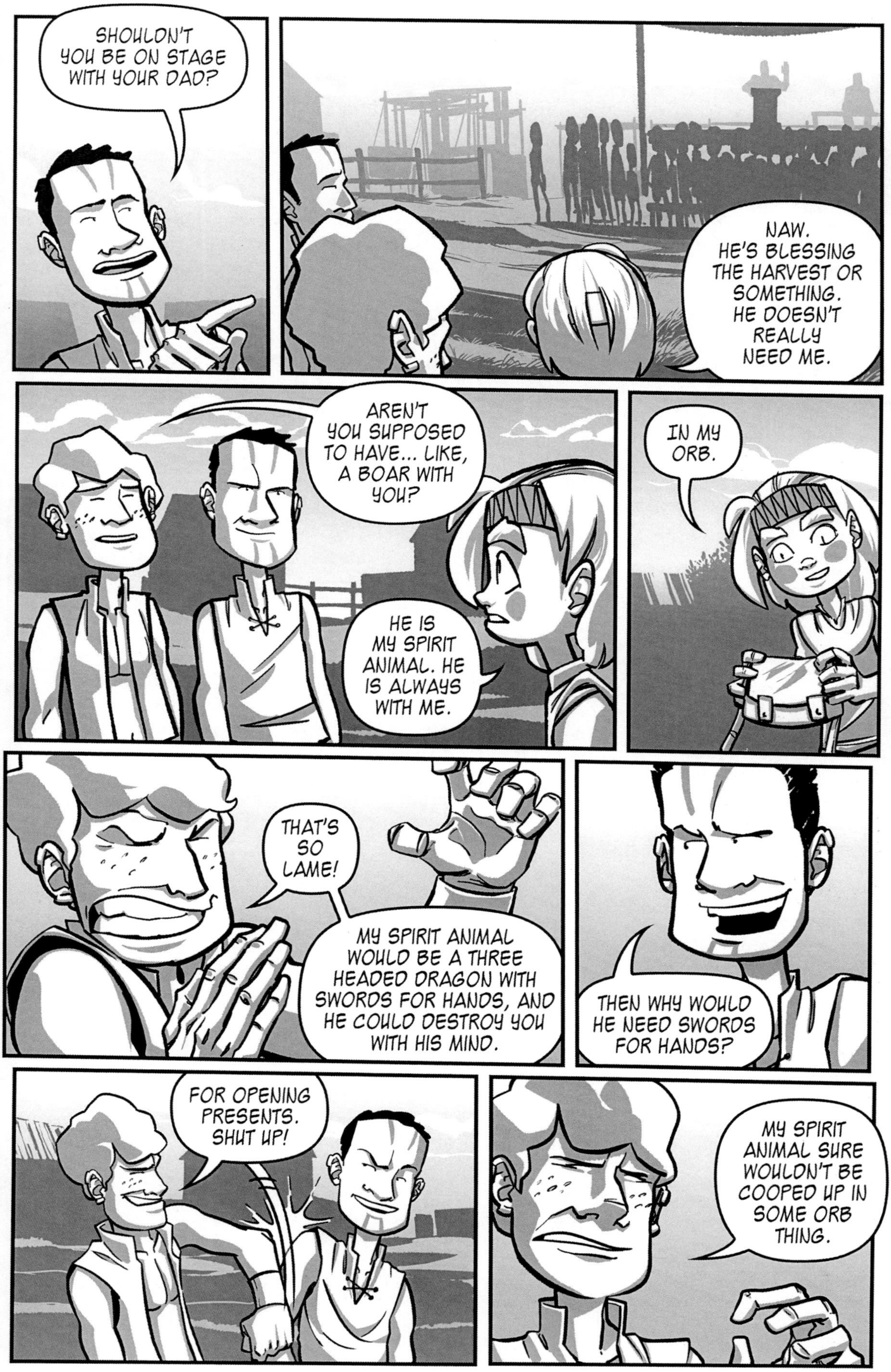
SHOULDN'T YOU BE ON STAGE WITH YOUR DAD?
NAW. HE'S BLESSING THE HARVEST OR SOMETHING. HE DOESN'T REALLY NEED ME.
AREN'T YOU SUPPOSED TO HAVE... LIKE, A BOAR WITH YOU?
HE IS MY SPIRIT ANIMAL. HE IS ALWAYS WITH ME.
IN MY ORB.
THAT'S SO LAME!
MY SPIRIT ANIMAL WOULD BE A THREE HEADED DRAGON WITH SWORDS FOR HANDS, AND HE COULD DESTROY YOU WITH HIS MIND.
THEN WHY WOULD HE NEED SWORDS FOR HANDS?
FOR OPENING PRESENTS. SHUT UP!
MY SPIRIT ANIMAL SURE WOULDN'T BE COOPED UP IN SOME ORB THING.

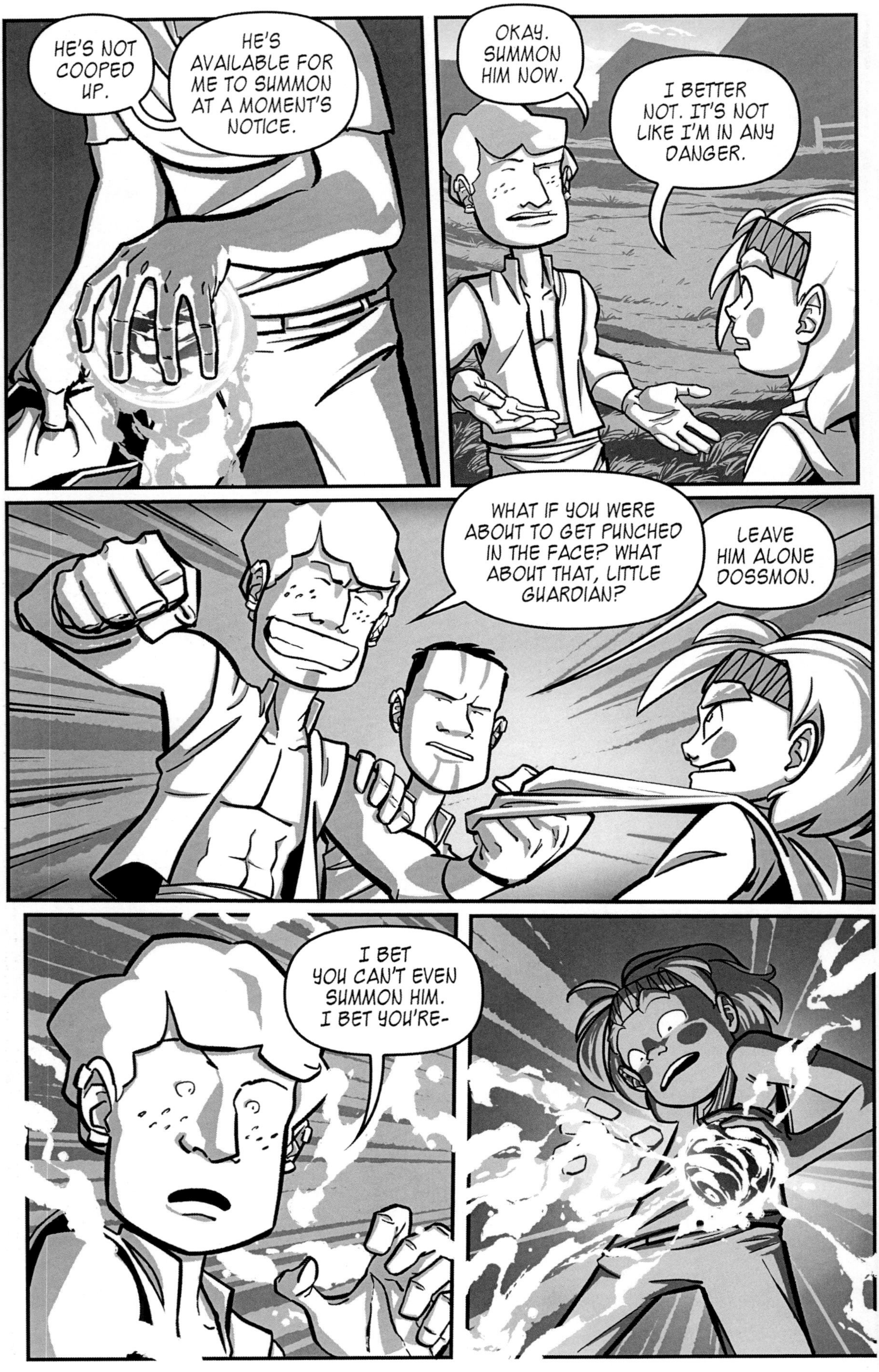
HE'S NOT COOPED UP.
HE'S AVAILABLE FOR ME TO SUMMON AT A MOMENT'S NOTICE.
OKAY. SUMMON HIM NOW.
I BETTER NOT. IT'S NOT LIKE I'M IN ANY DANGER.
WHAT IF YOU WERE ABOUT TO GET PUNCHED IN THE FACE? WHAT ABOUT THAT, LITTLE GUARDIAN?
LEAVE HIM ALONE DOSSMON.
I BET YOU CAN'T EVEN SUMMON HIM. I BET YOU'RE-

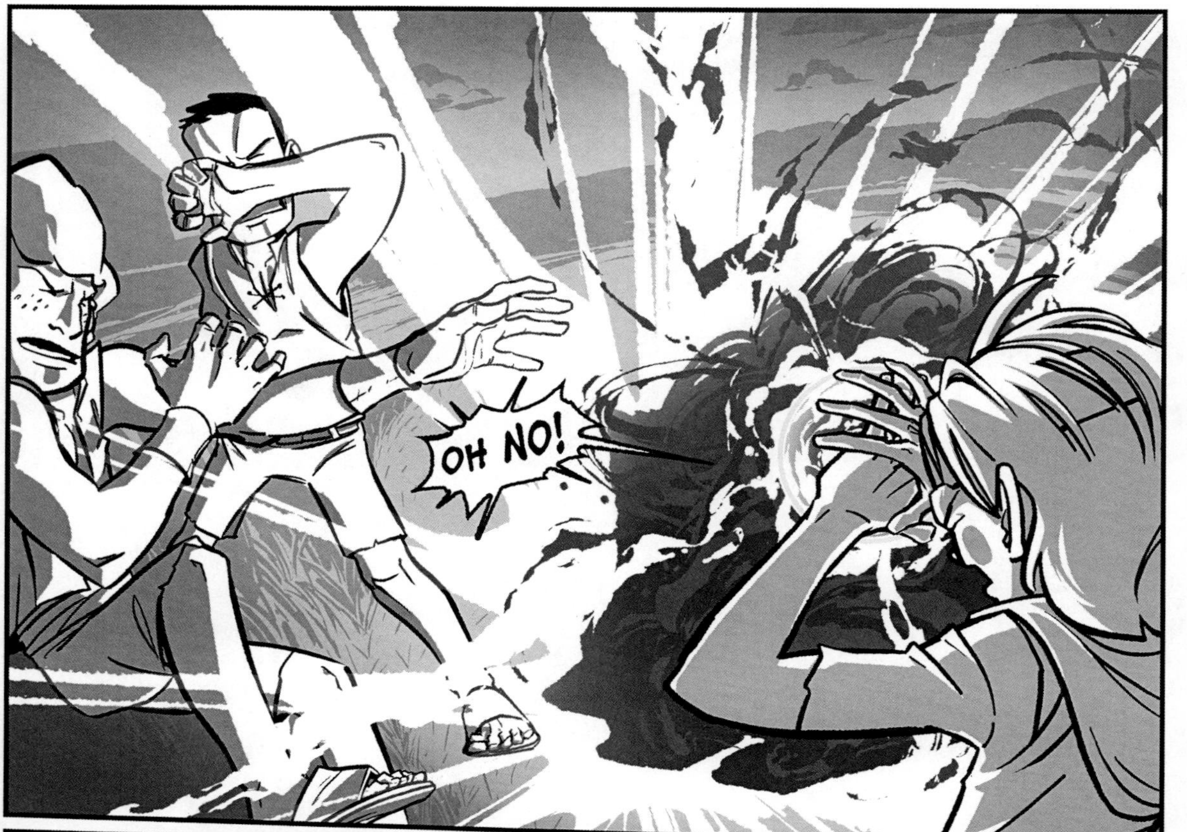
OH NO!

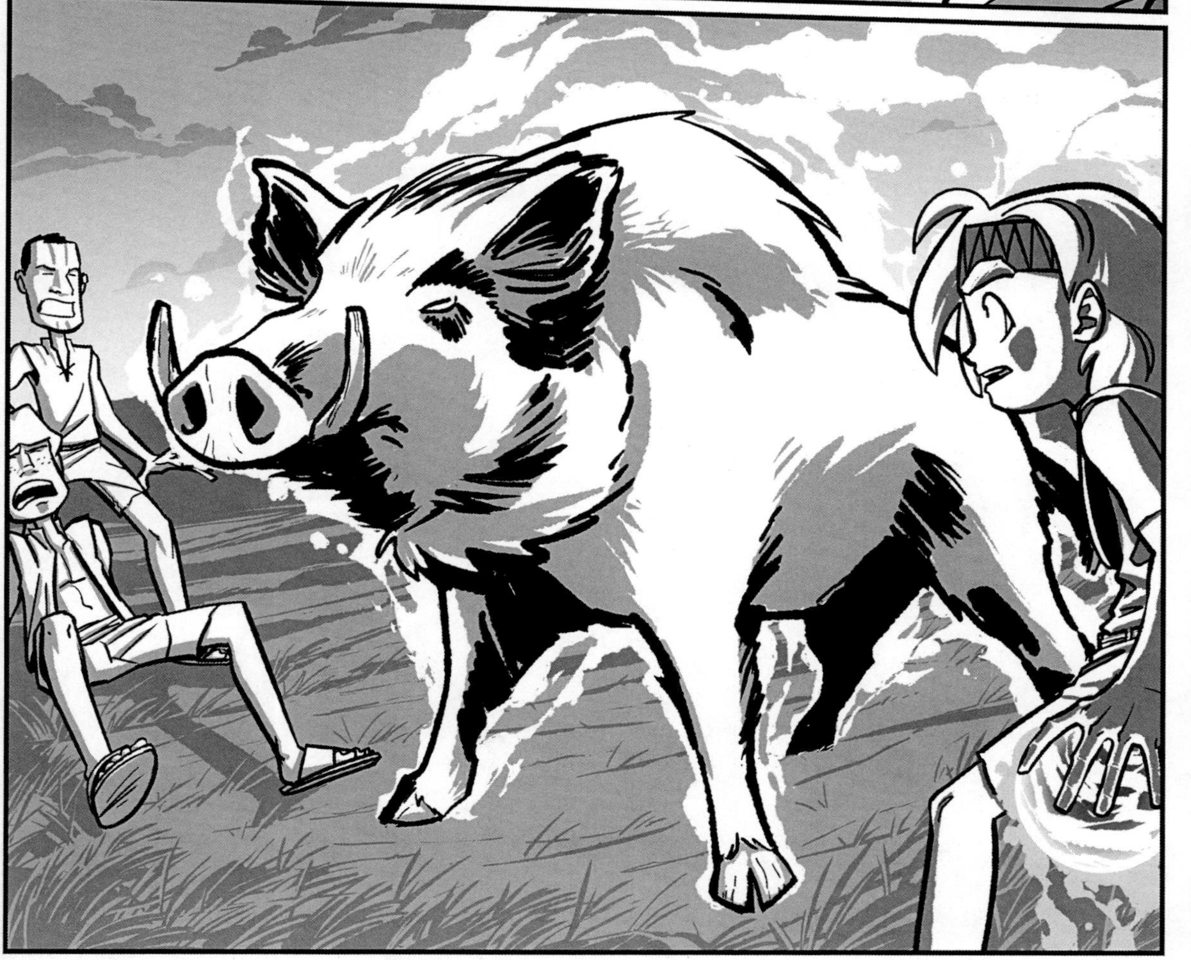

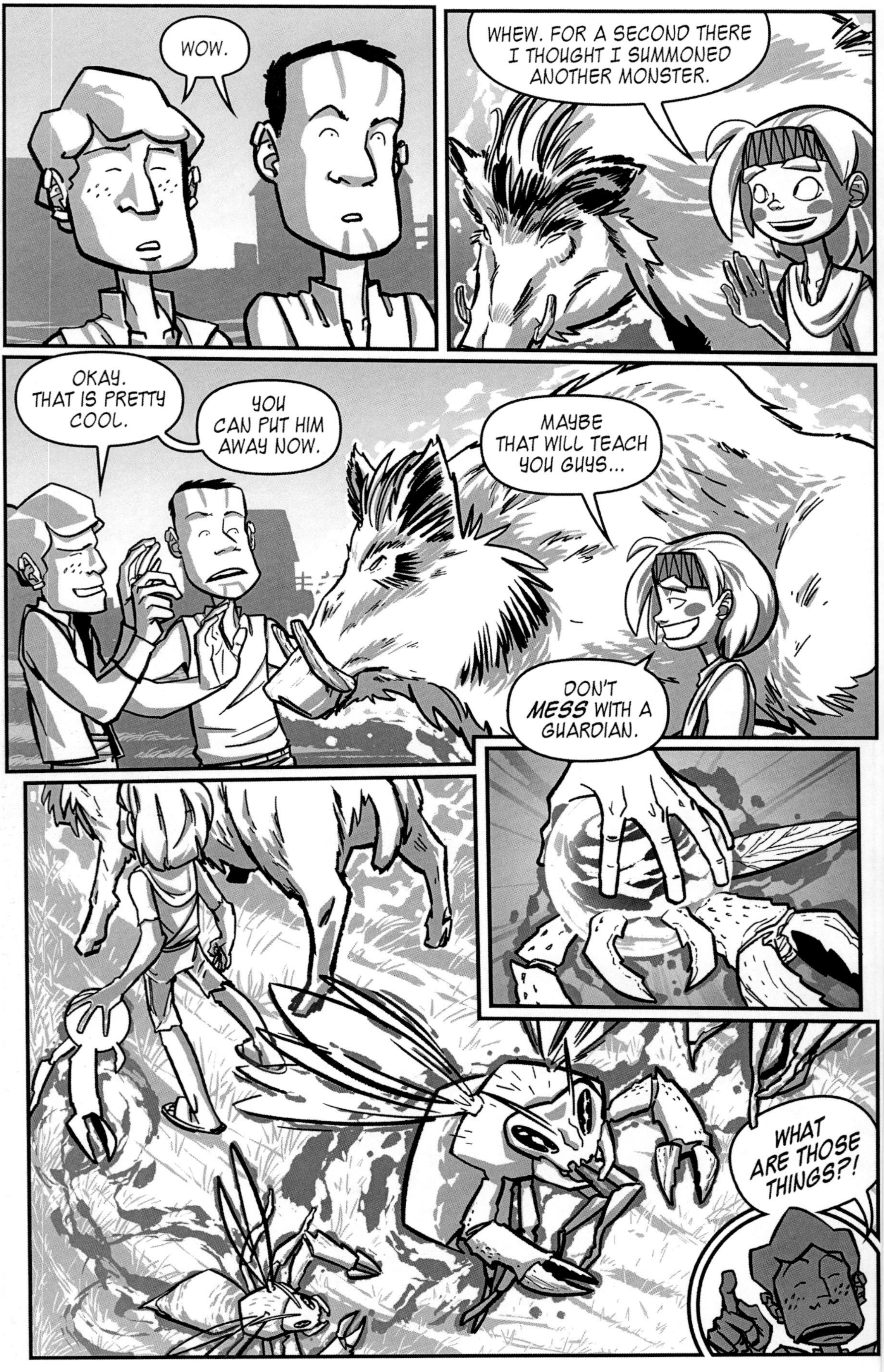
WOW.
WHEW. FOR A SECOND THERE I THOUGHT I SUMMONED ANOTHER MONSTER.
OKAY. THAT IS PRETTY COOL.
YOU CAN PUT HIM AWAY NOW.
MAYBE THAT WILL TEACH YOU GUYS...
DON'T MESS WITH A GUARDIAN.
WHAT ARE THOSE THINGS?!

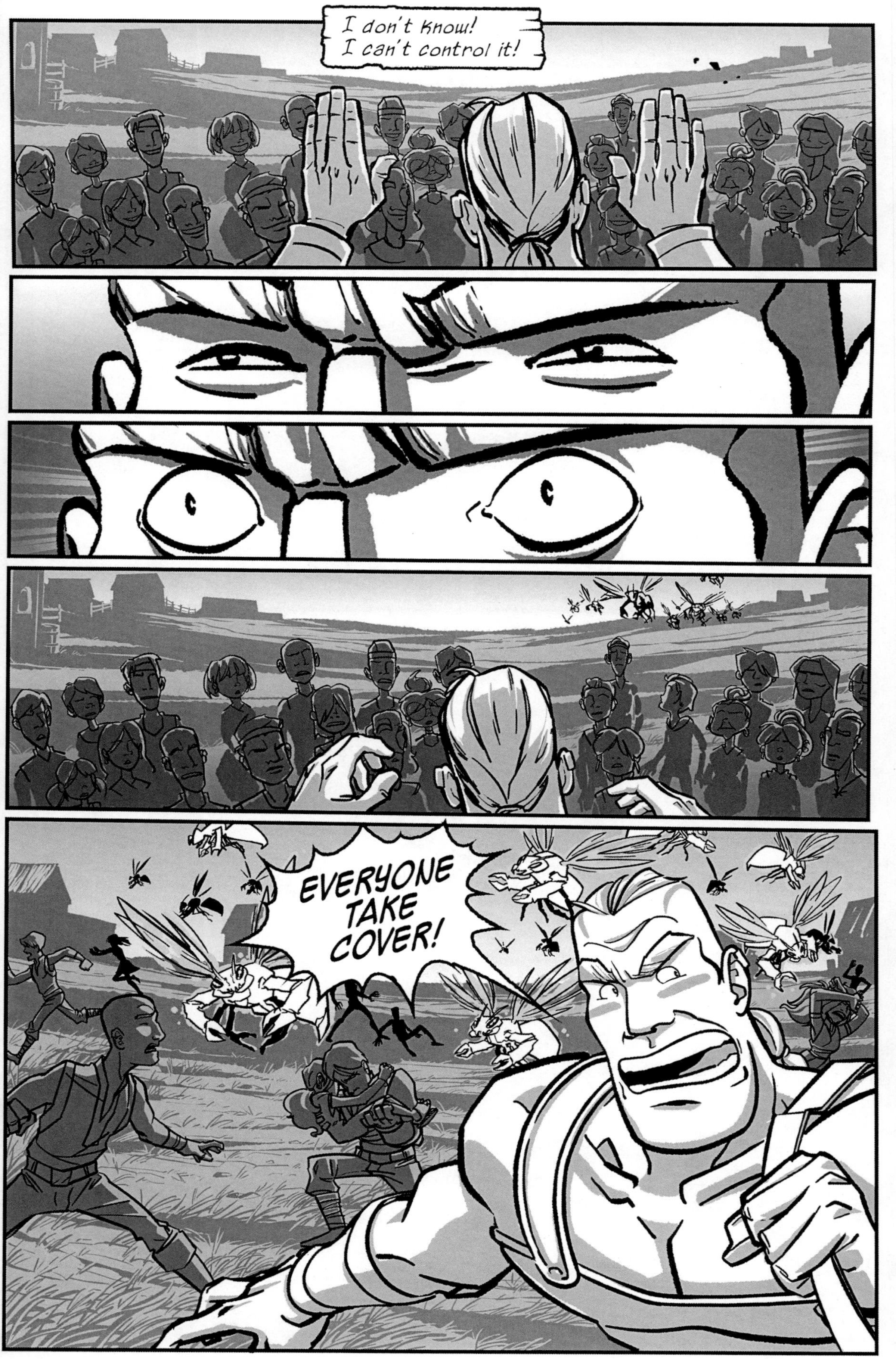
I don't know!
I can't control it!
EVERYONE TAKE COVER!

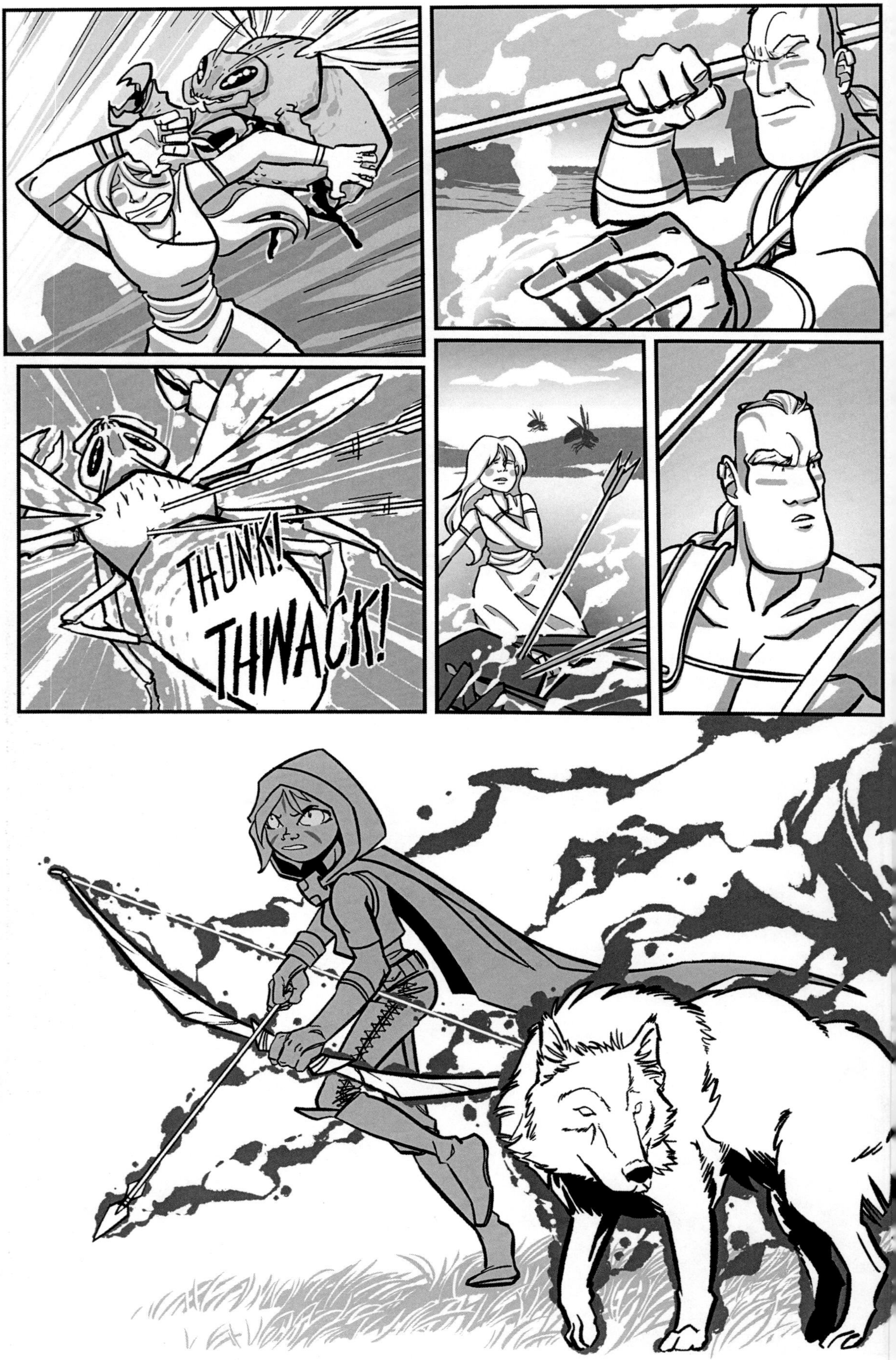
THUNK!
THWACK!

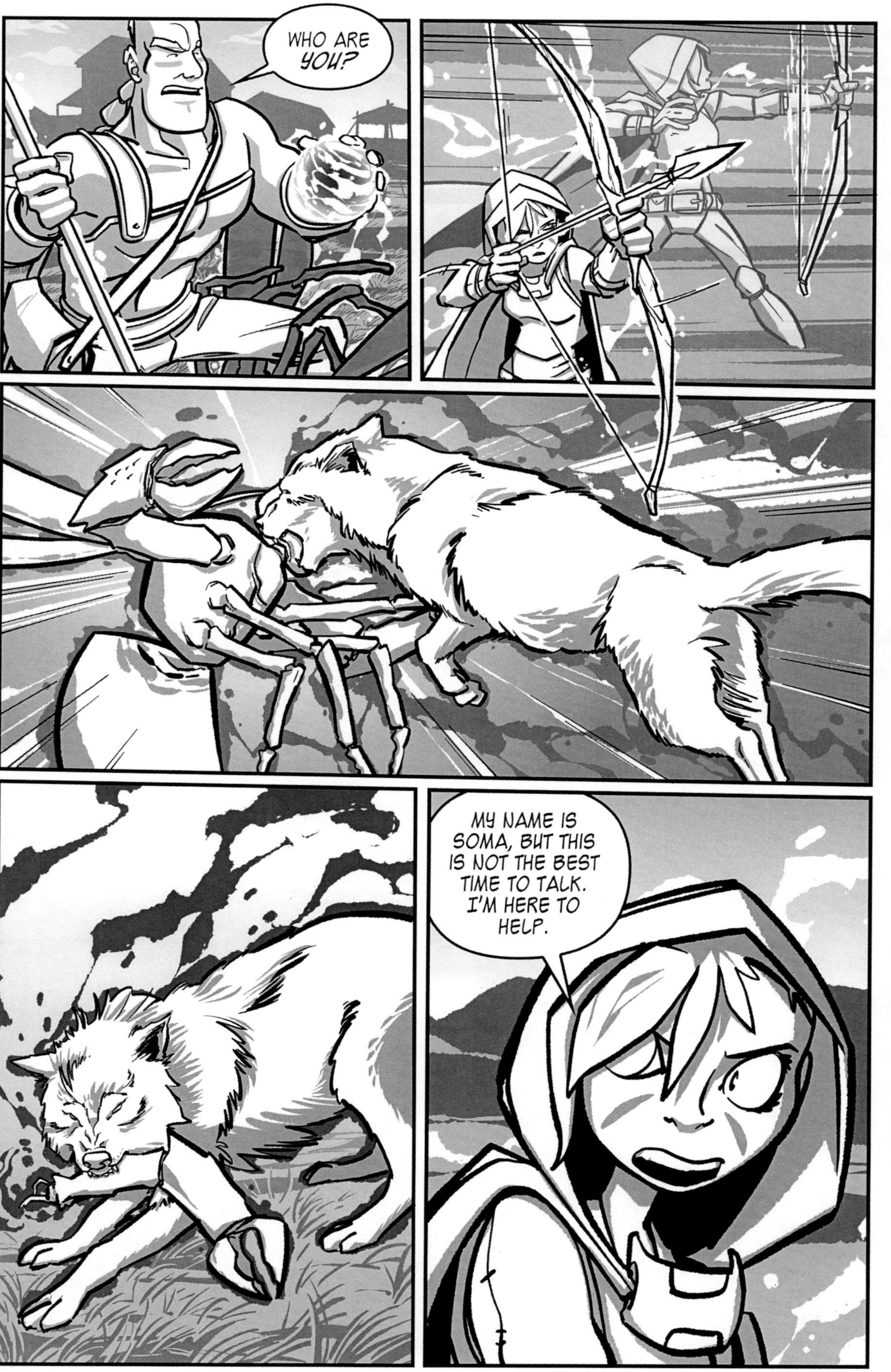
WHO ARE YOU?
MY NAME IS SOMA, BUT THIS IS NOT THE BEST TIME TO TALK. I'M HERE TO HELP.

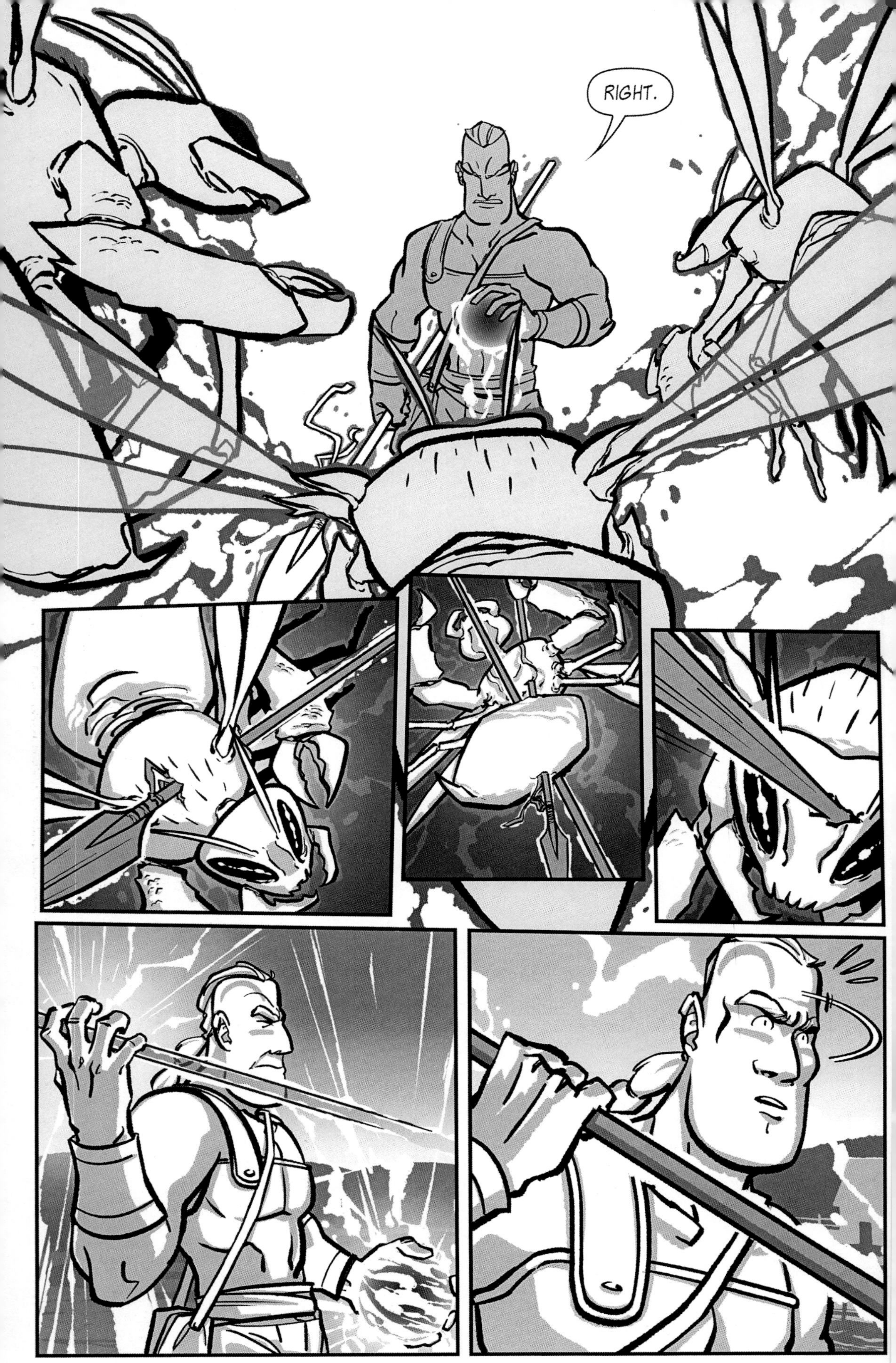
RIGHT.

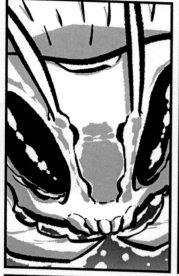

TAKE THE WOMAN!

BUT SPARE ME! I'M A DOCTOR!

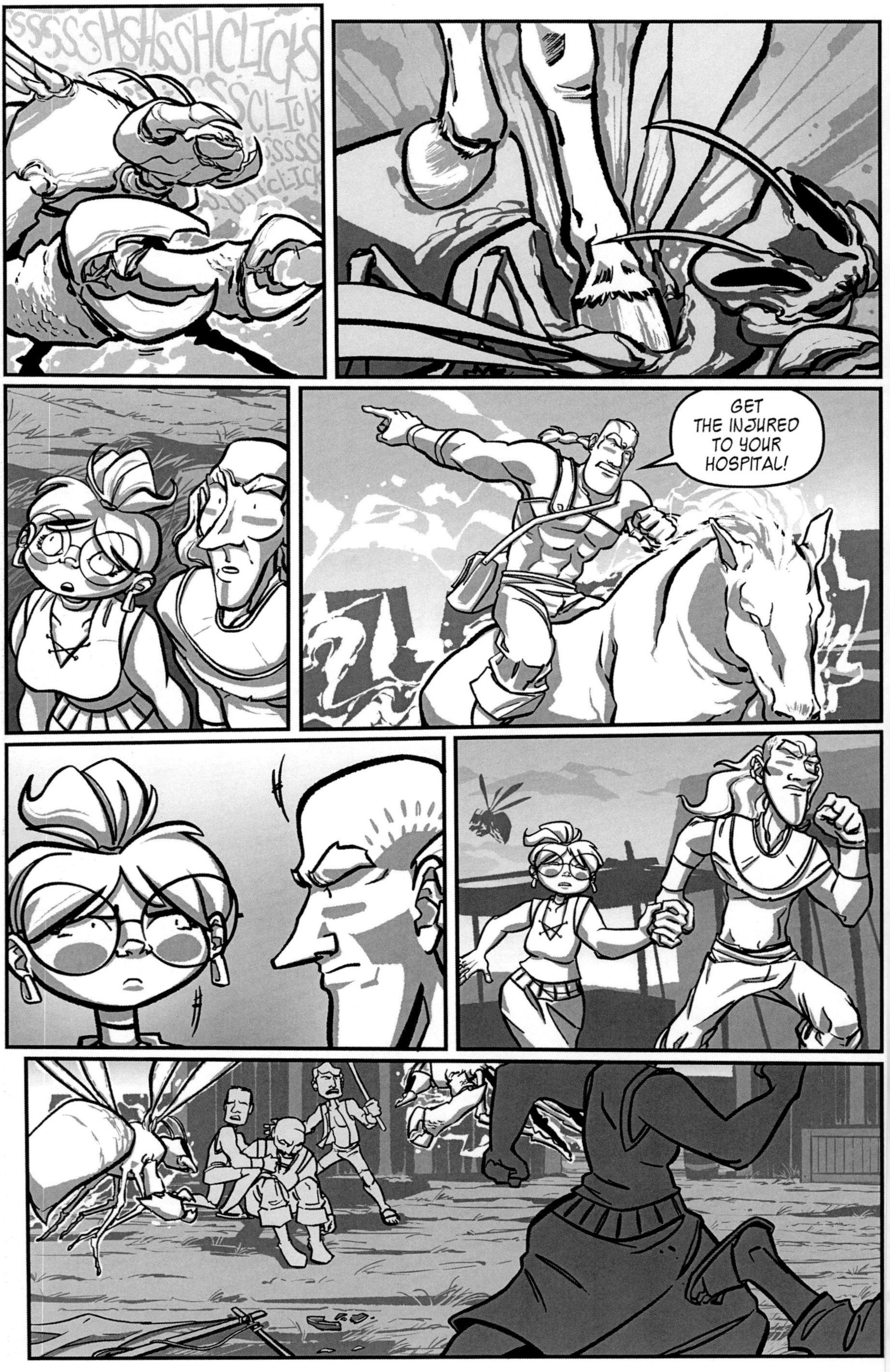
SSSSSHSHSSSHCLICKS
SSSSCLICK
SSSSSS
CLICK
GET THE INJURED TO YOUR HOSPITAL!

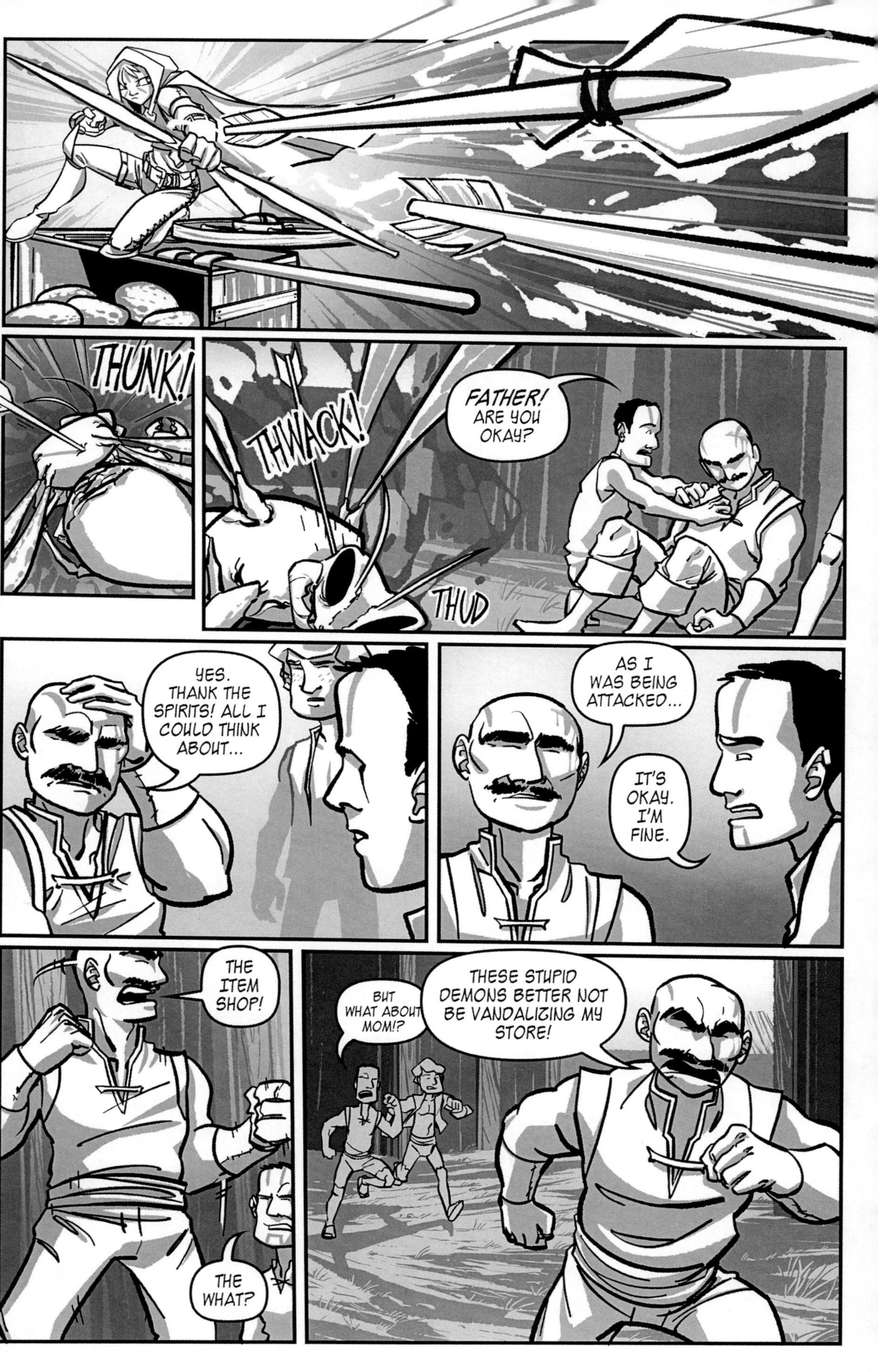
THUNK!
THWACK!
THUD
FATHER! ARE YOU OKAY?
YES. THANK THE SPIRITS! ALL I COULD THINK ABOUT...
AS I WAS BEING ATTACKED...
IT'S OKAY. I'M FINE.
THE ITEM SHOP!
THE WHAT?
THESE STUPID DEMONS BETTER NOT BE VANDALIZING MY STORE!
BUT WHAT ABOUT MOM!?

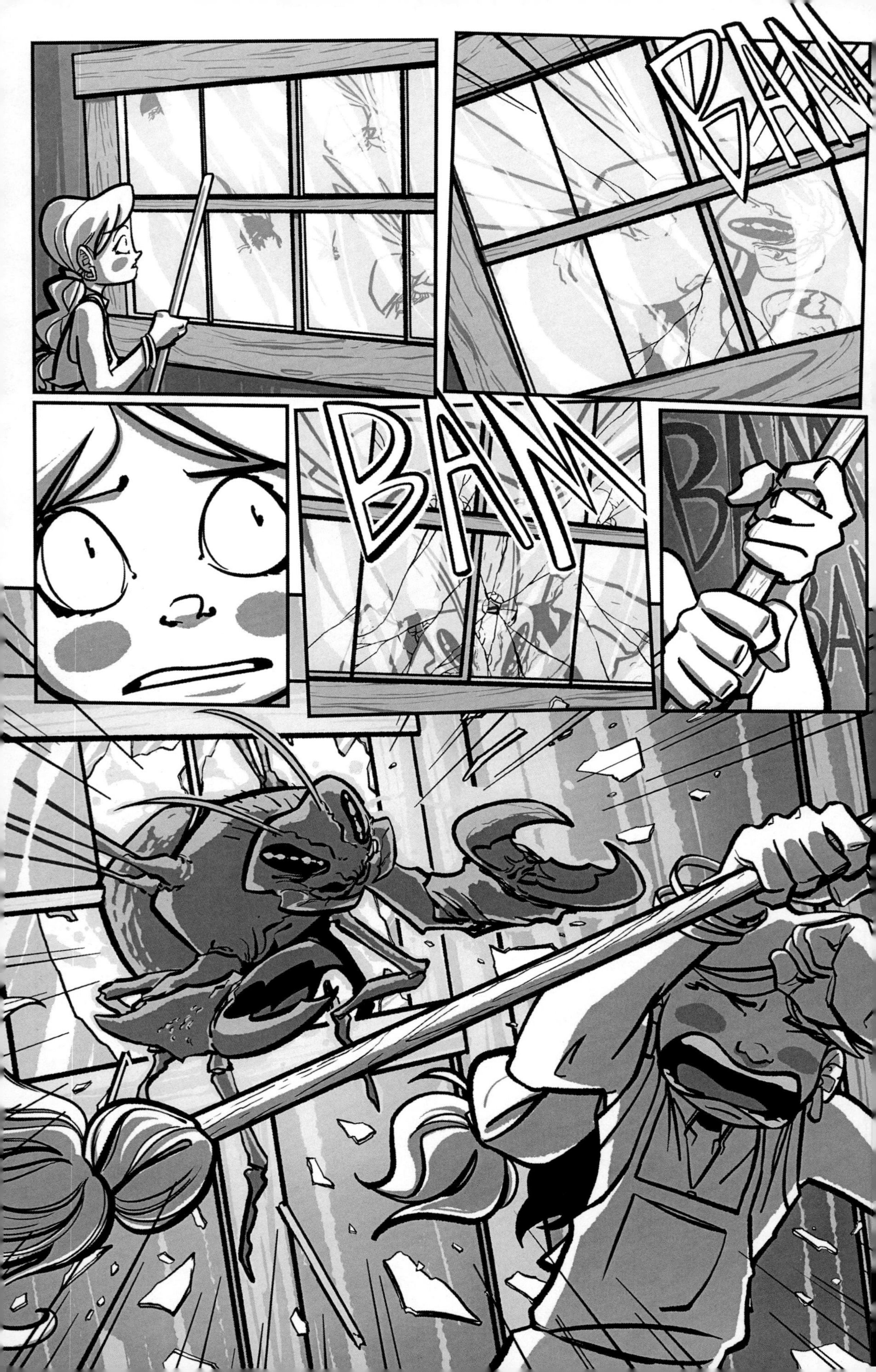

BAM
BAM
BAM
BAM

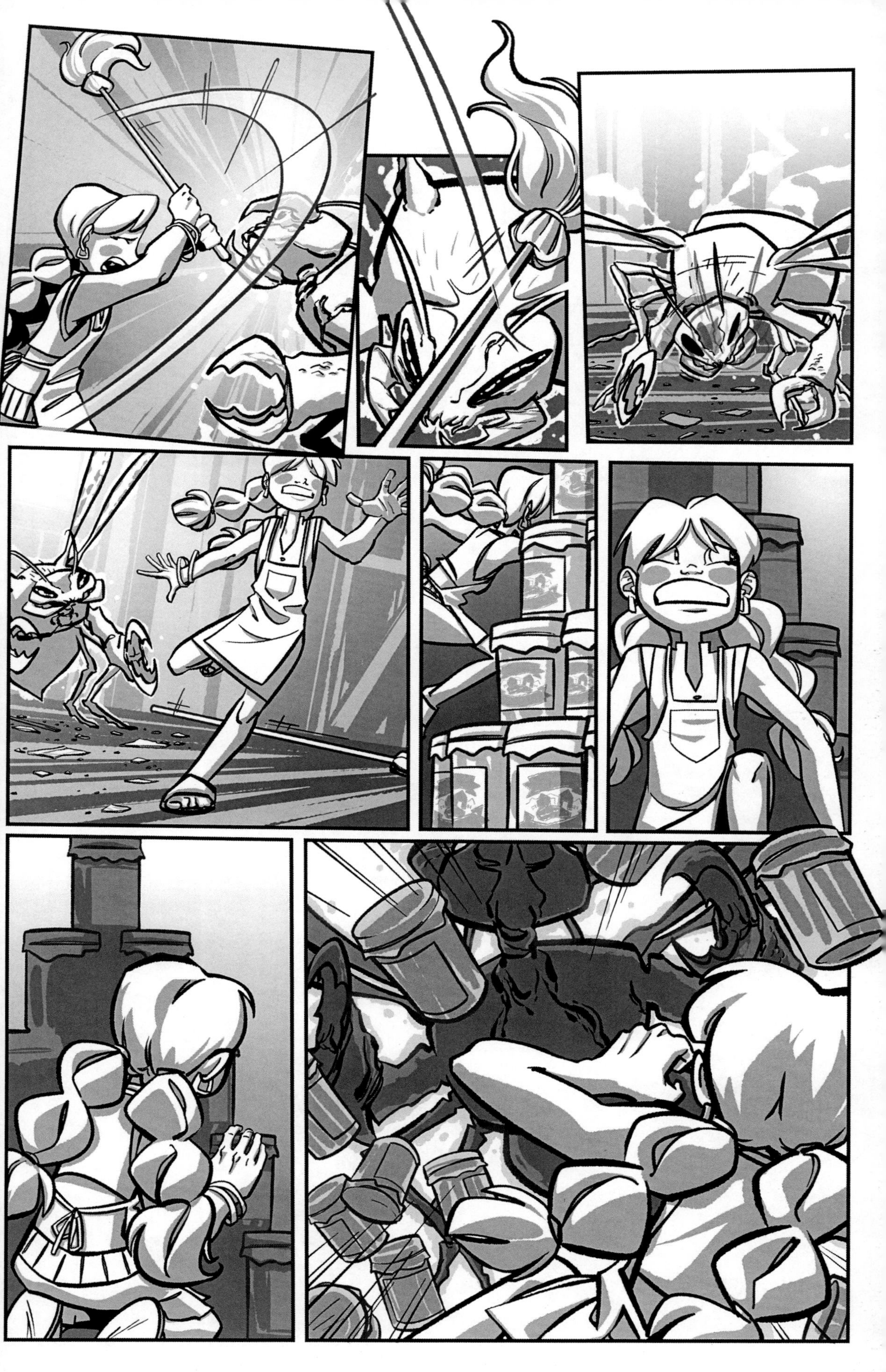

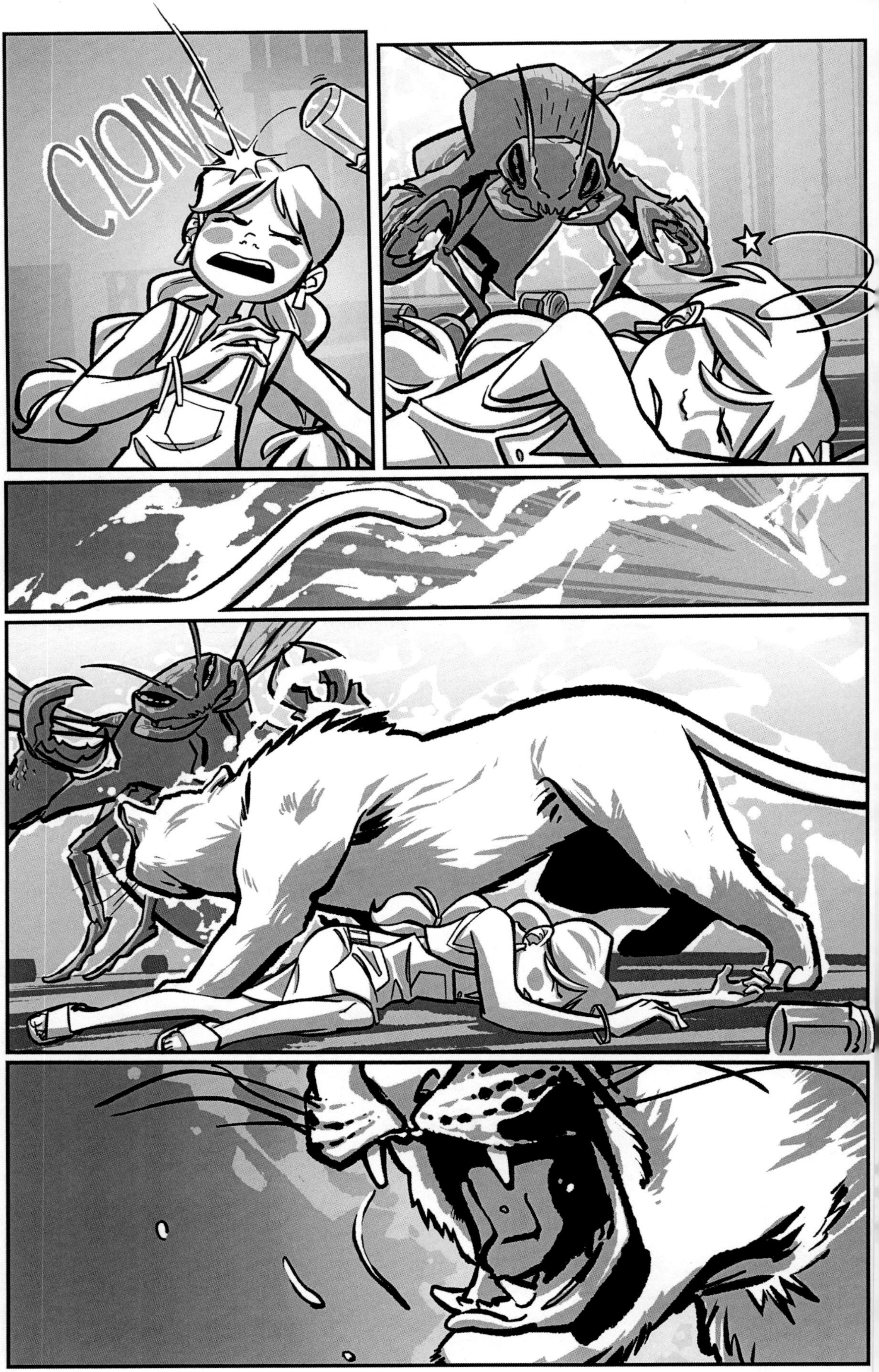
CLONK

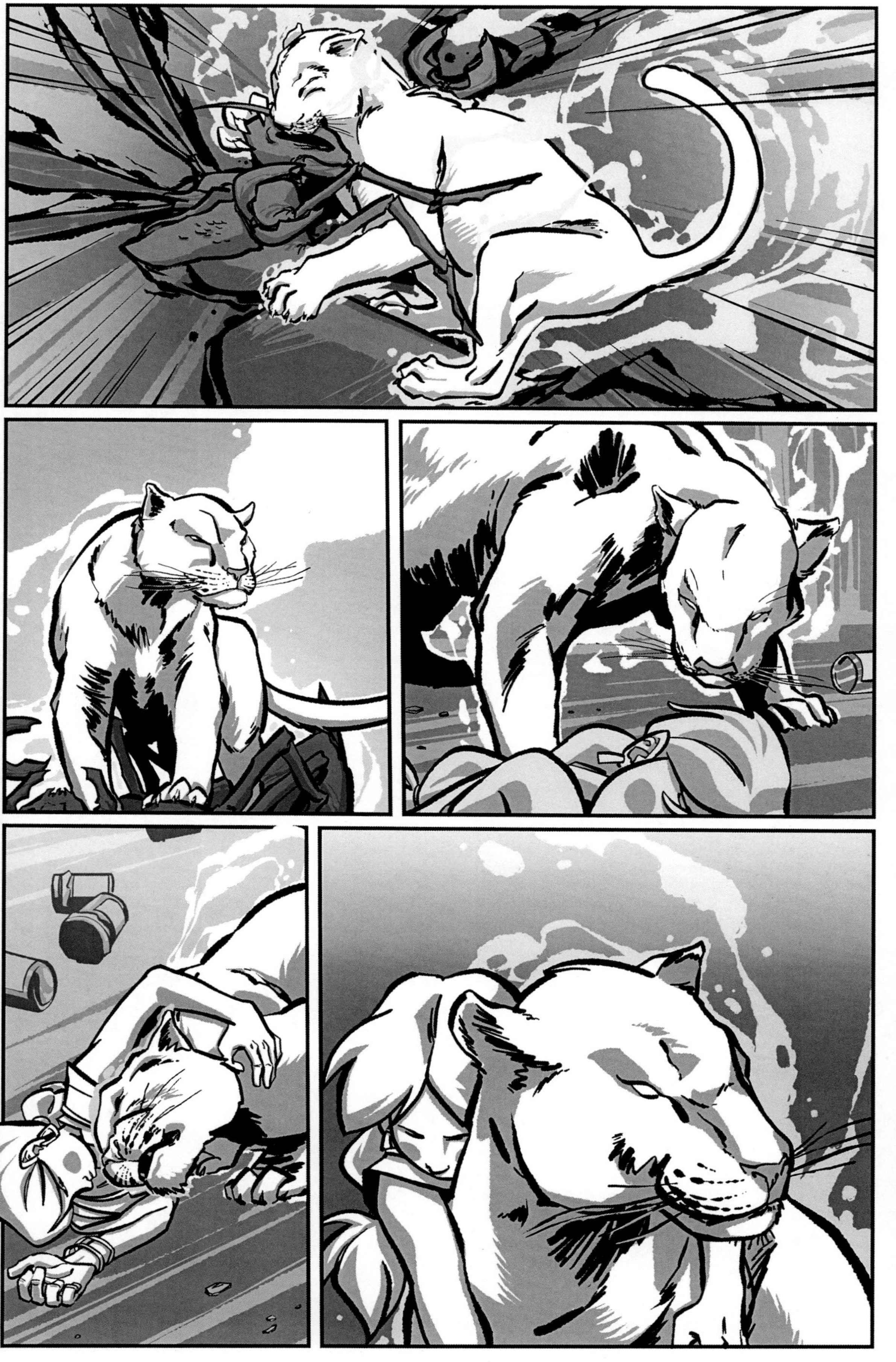

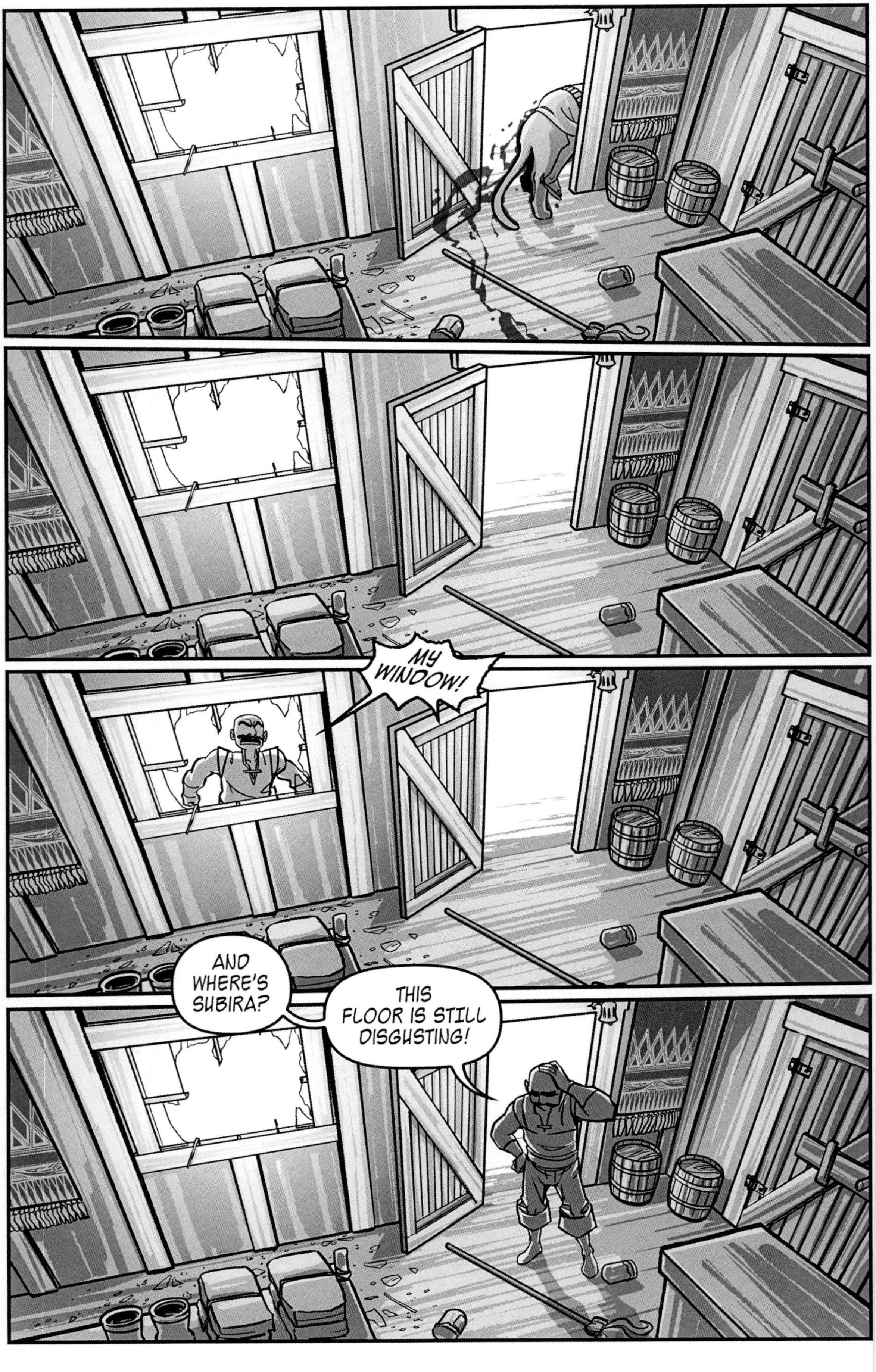
MY WINDOW!
AND WHERE'S SUBIRA?
THIS FLOOR IS STILL DISGUSTING!

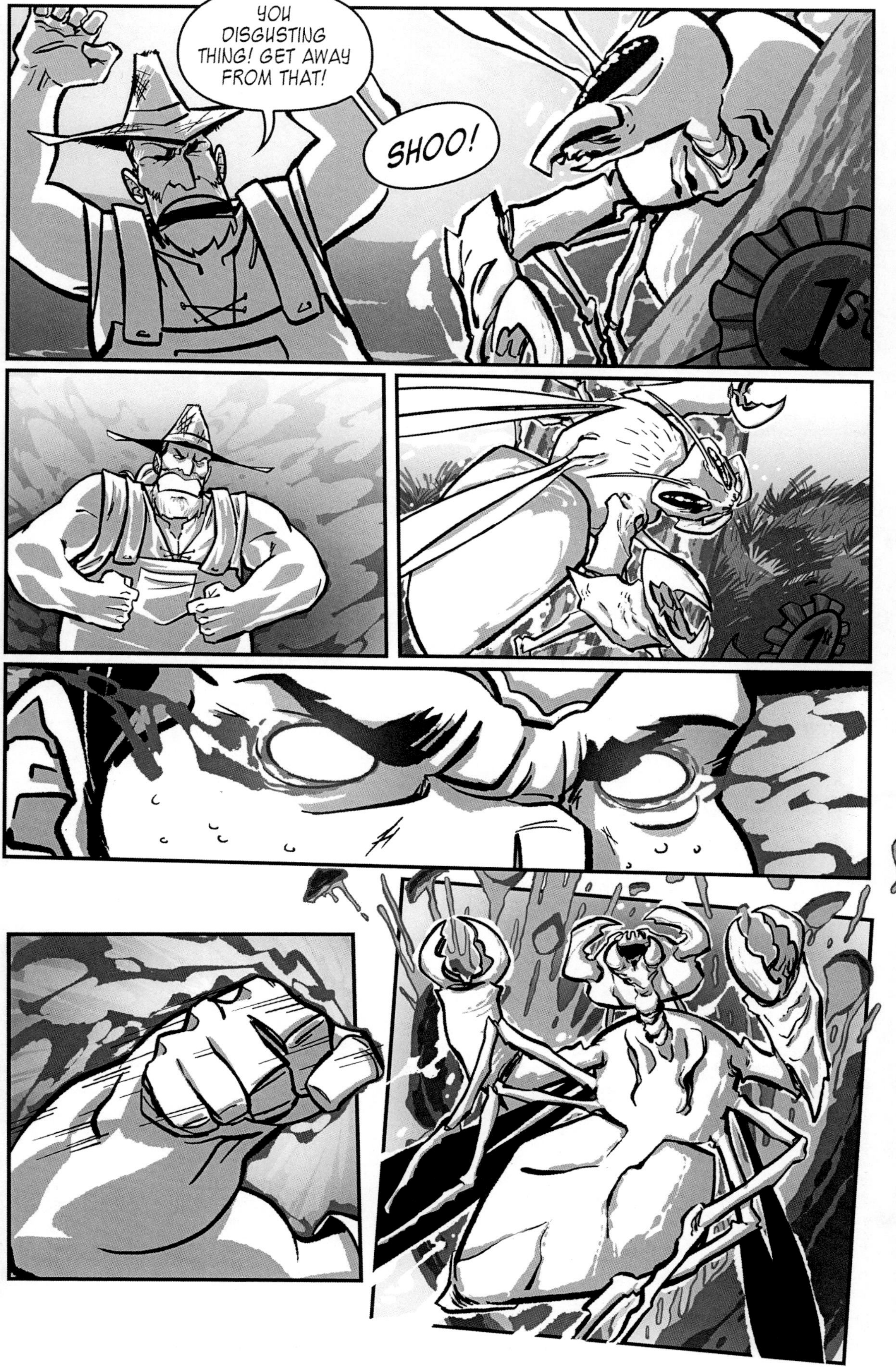
YOU DISGUSTING THING! GET AWAY FROM THAT!
SHOO!
1st

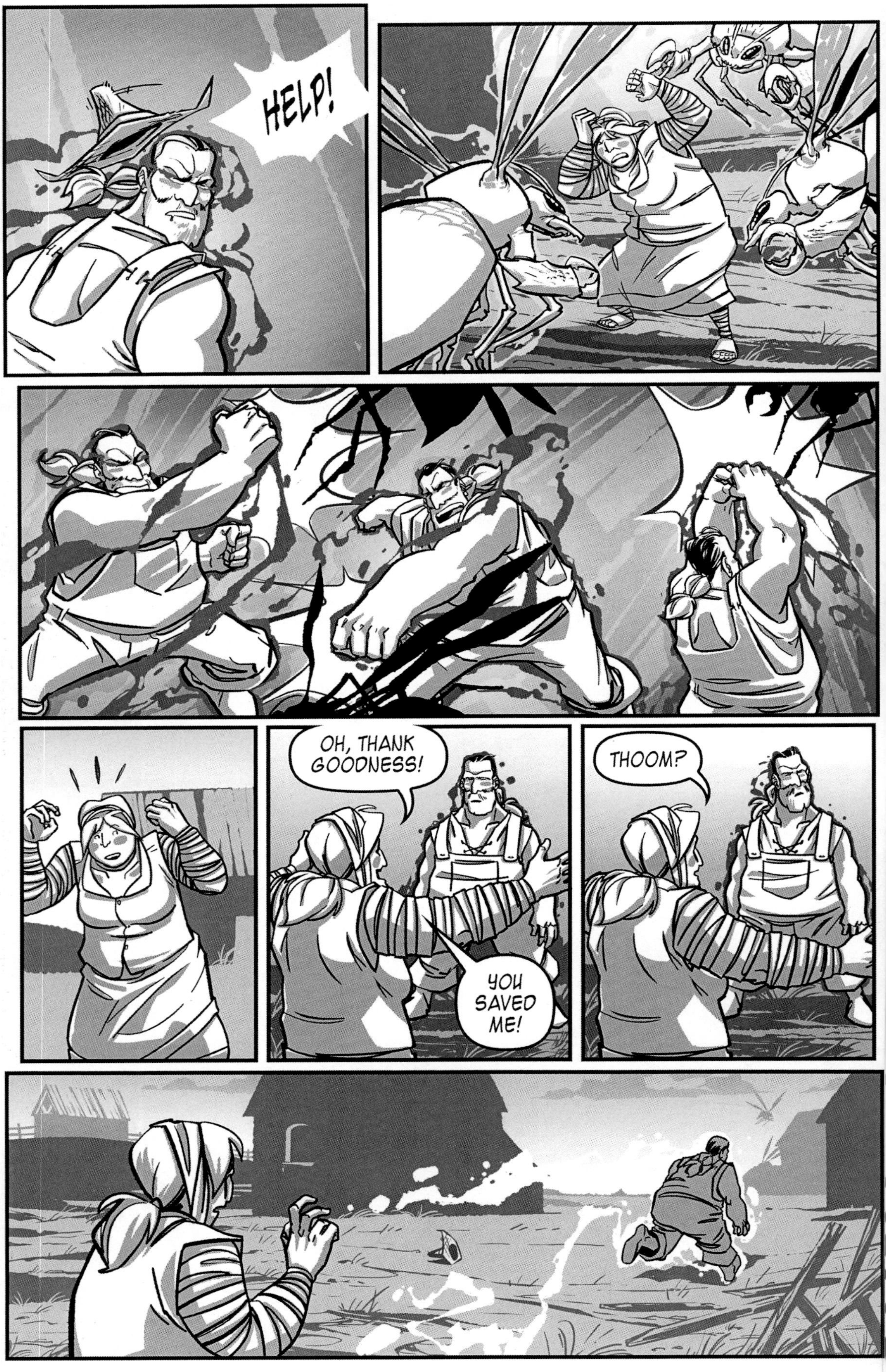
HELP!
OH, THANK GOODNESS!
YOU SAVED ME!
THOOM?

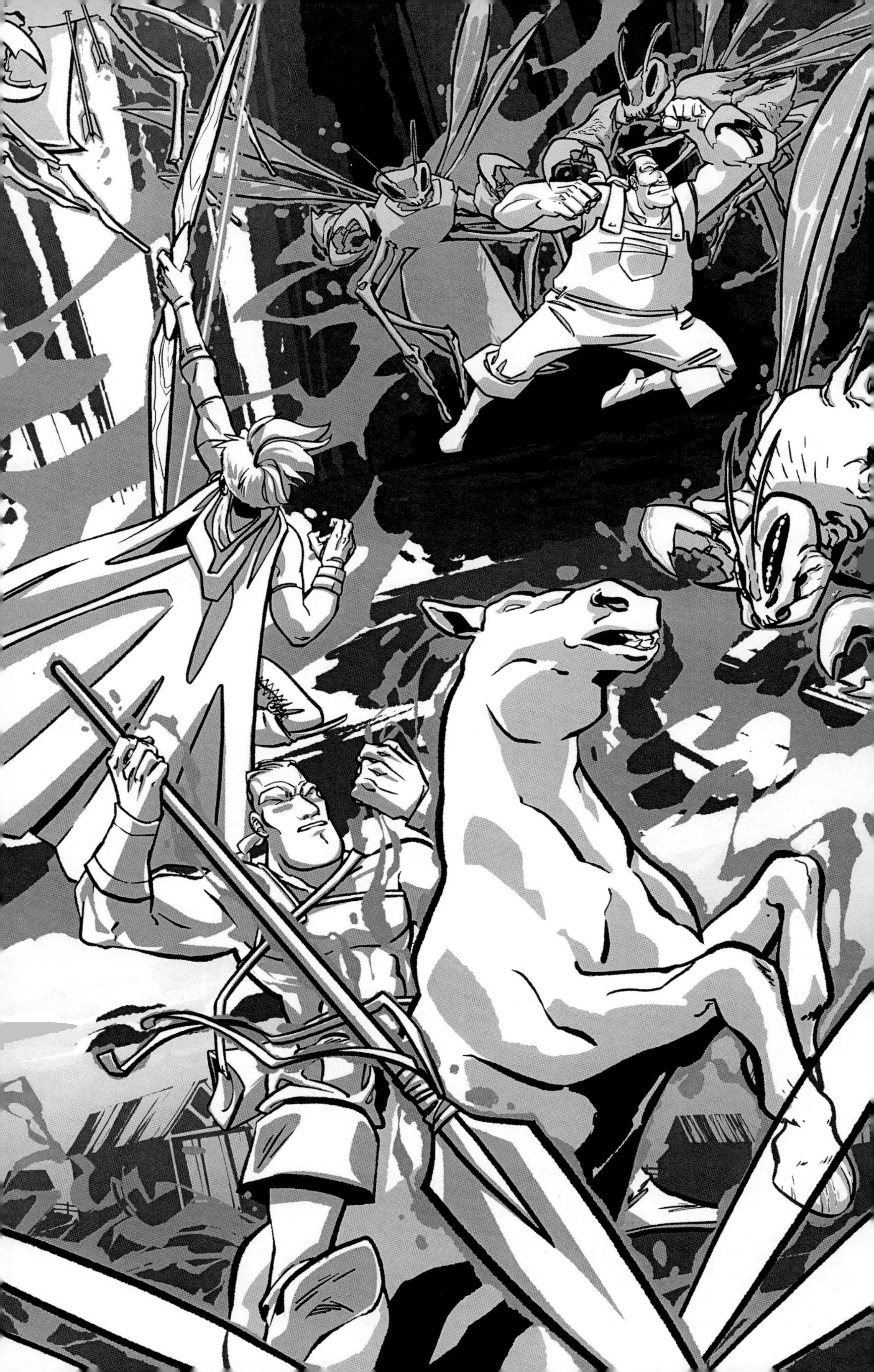

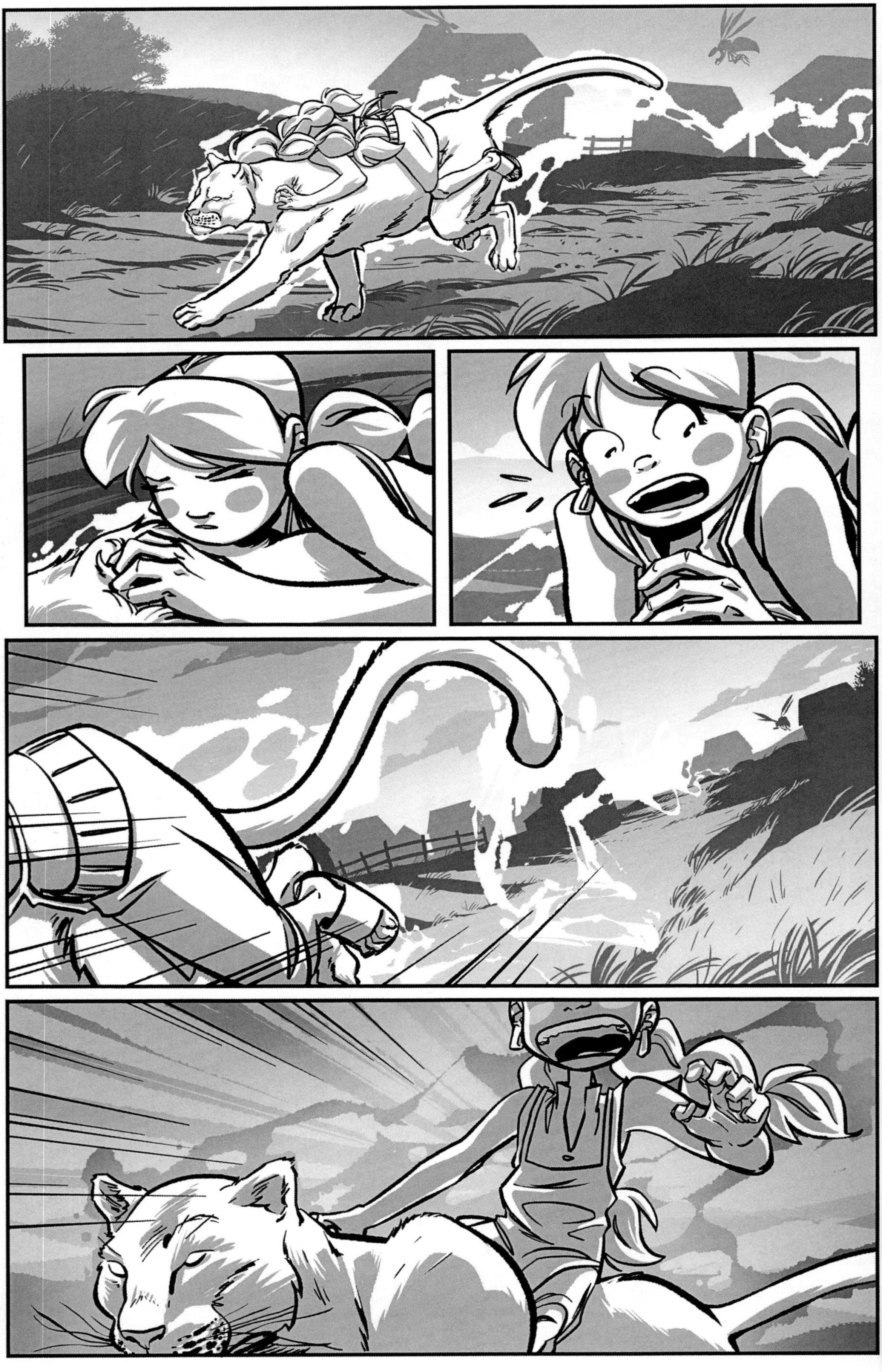

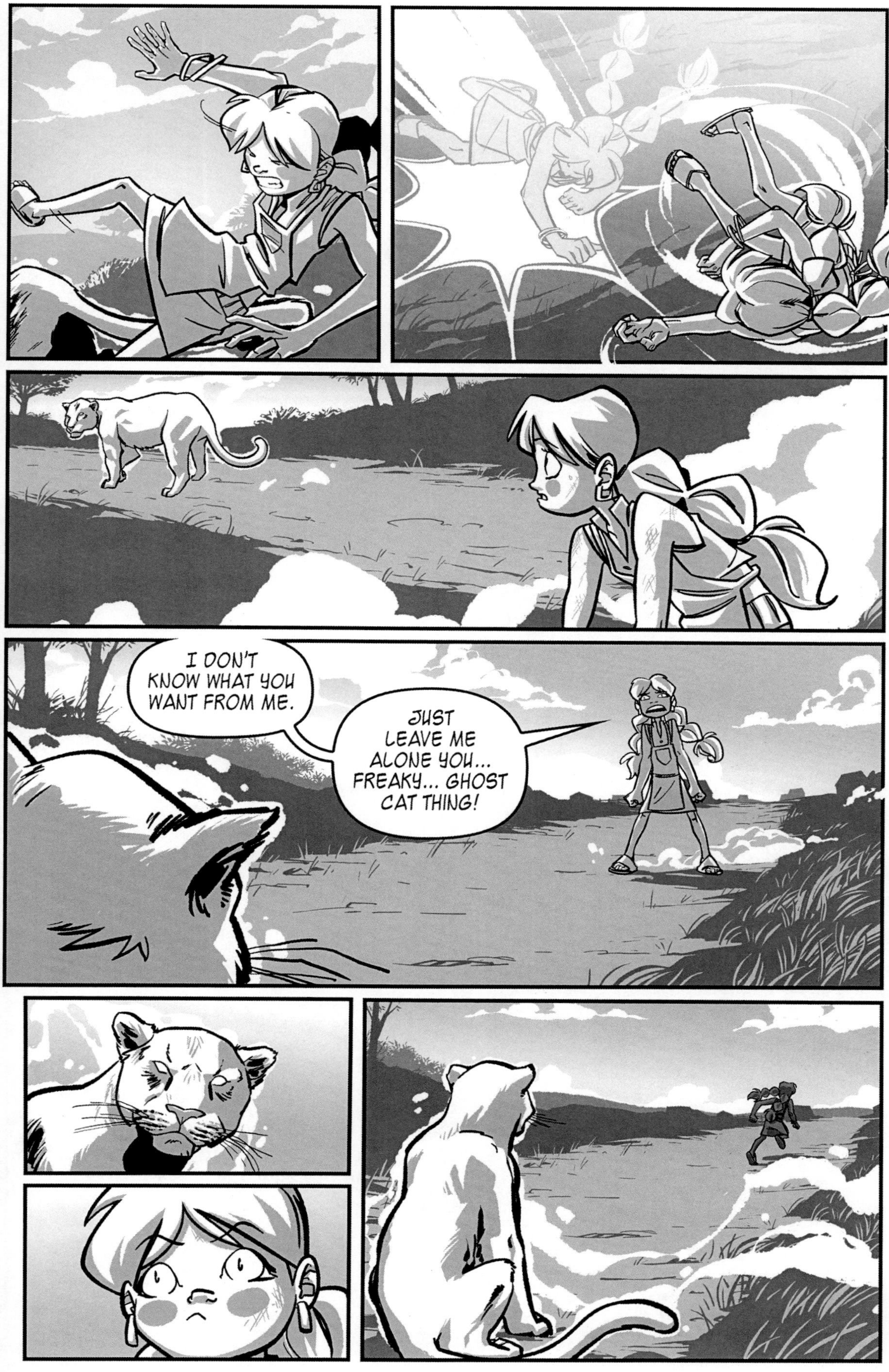
I DON'T KNOW WHAT YOU WANT FROM ME.
JUST LEAVE ME ALONE YOU... FREAKY... GHOST CAT THING!

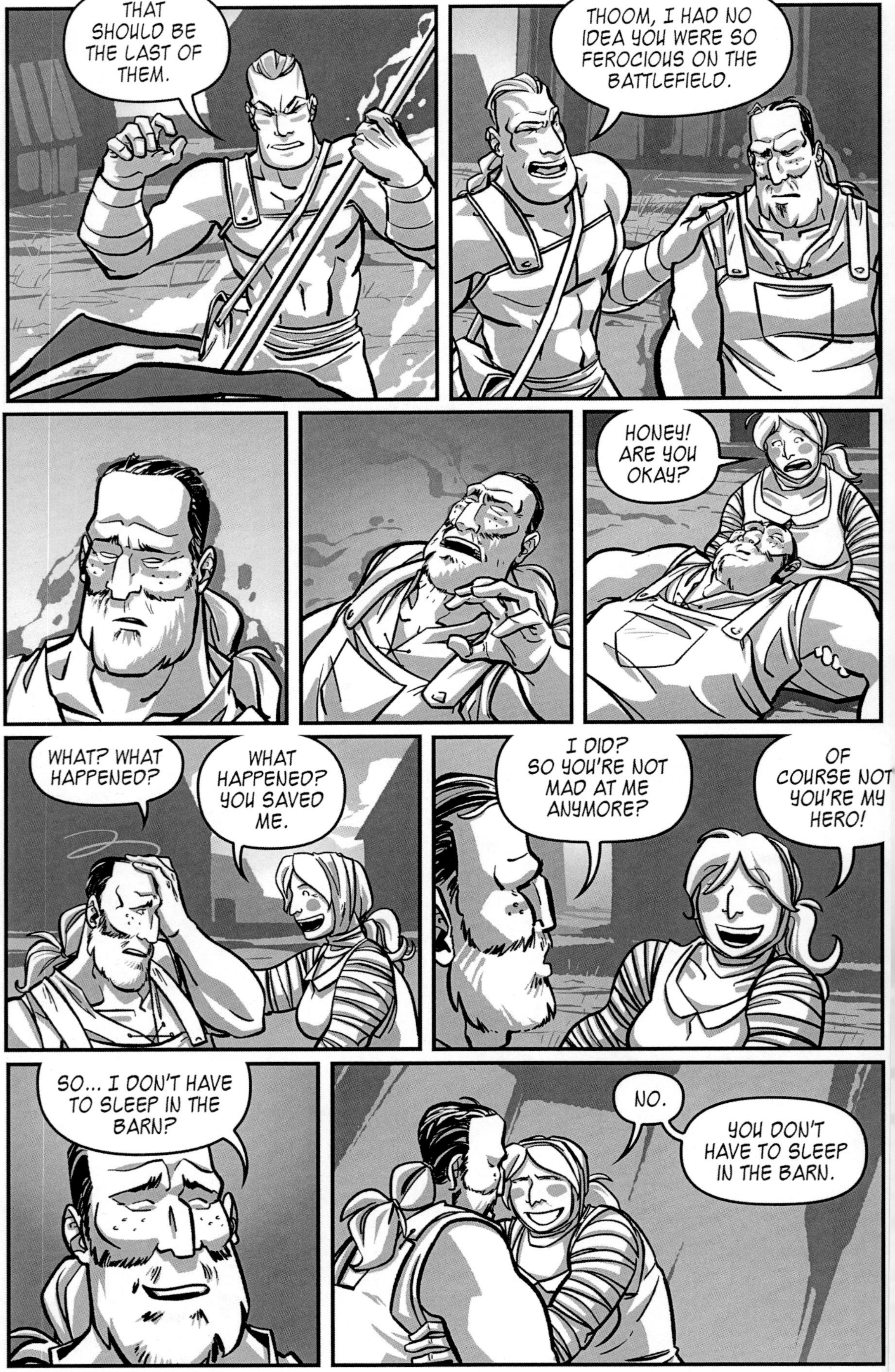
THAT SHOULD BE THE LAST OF THEM.
THOOM, I HAD NO IDEA YOU WERE SO FEROCIOUS ON THE BATTLEFIELD.
HONEY! ARE YOU OKAY?
WHAT? WHAT HAPPENED?
WHAT HAPPENED? YOU SAVED ME.
I DID? SO YOU'RE NOT MAD AT ME ANYMORE?
OF COURSE NOT YOU'RE MY HERO!
SO... I DON'T HAVE TO SLEEP IN THE BARN?
NO.
YOU DON'T HAVE TO SLEEP IN THE BARN.

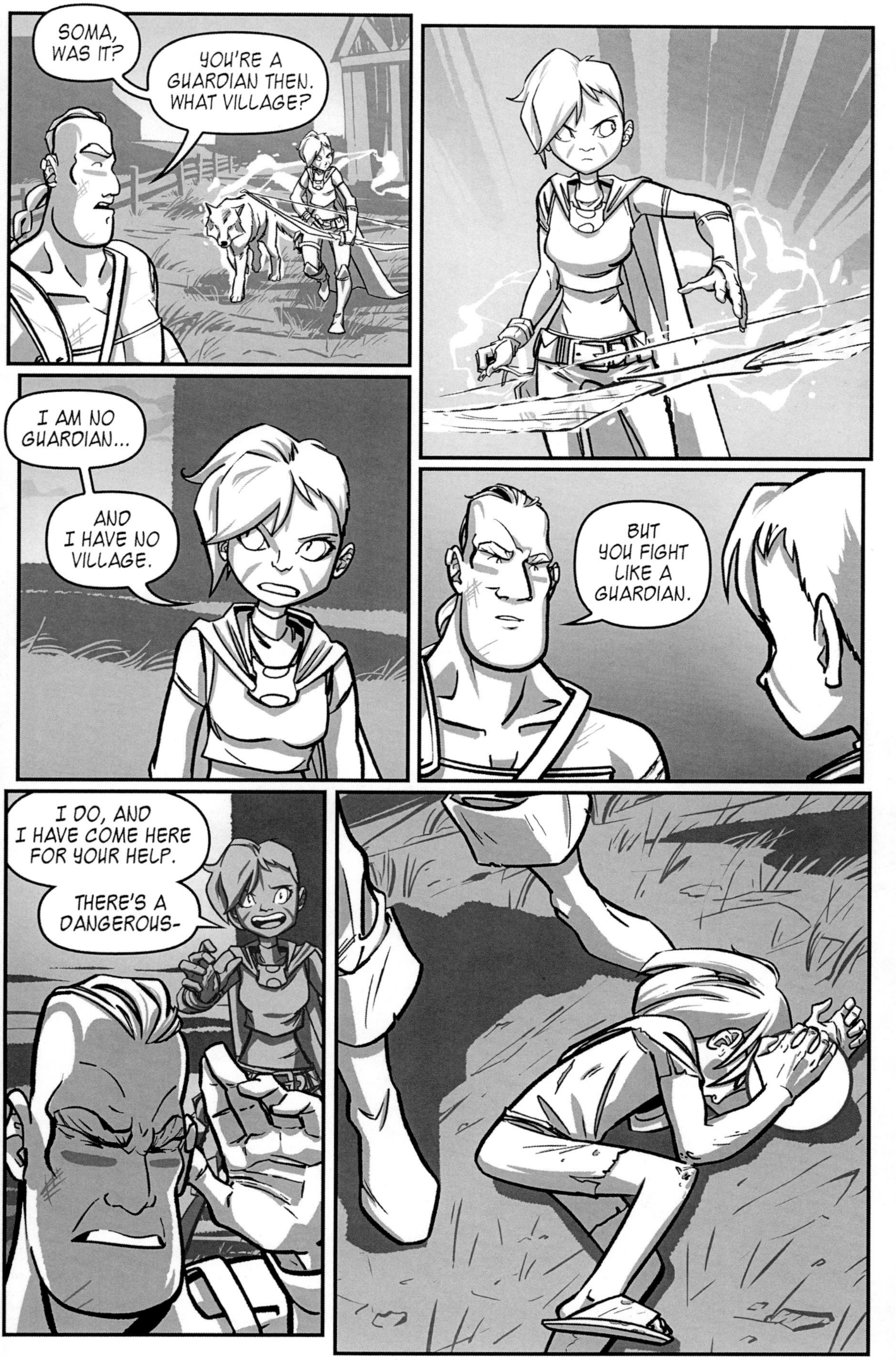
SOMA, WAS IT?
YOU'RE A GUARDIAN THEN. WHAT VILLAGE?
I AM NO GUARDIAN...
AND I HAVE NO VILLAGE.
BUT YOU FIGHT LIKE A GUARDIAN.
I DO, AND I HAVE COME HERE FOR YOUR HELP.
THERE'S A DANGEROUS-

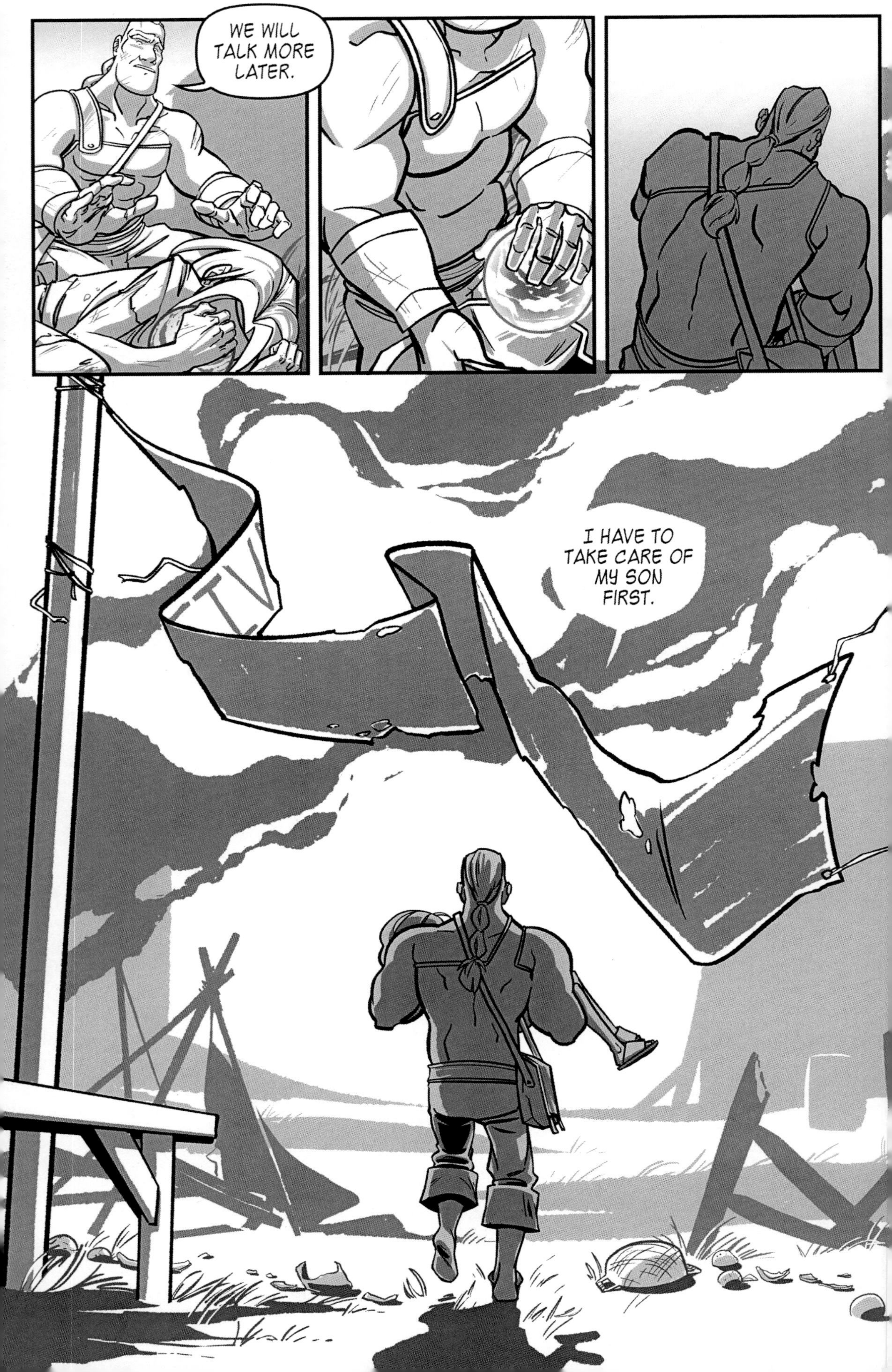
WE WILL TALK MORE LATER.
I HAVE TO TAKE CARE OF MY SON FIRST.

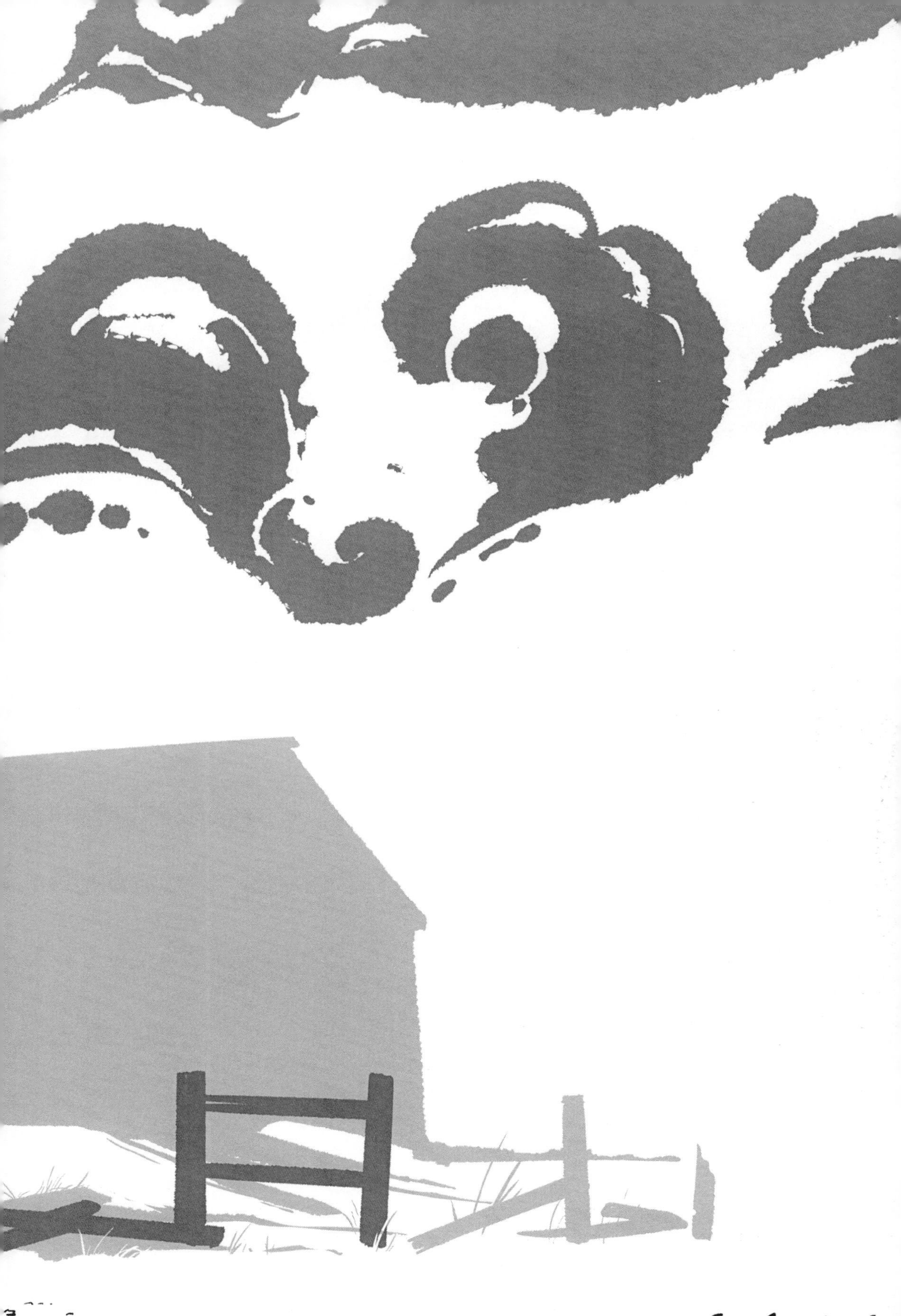

End Chapter 1.

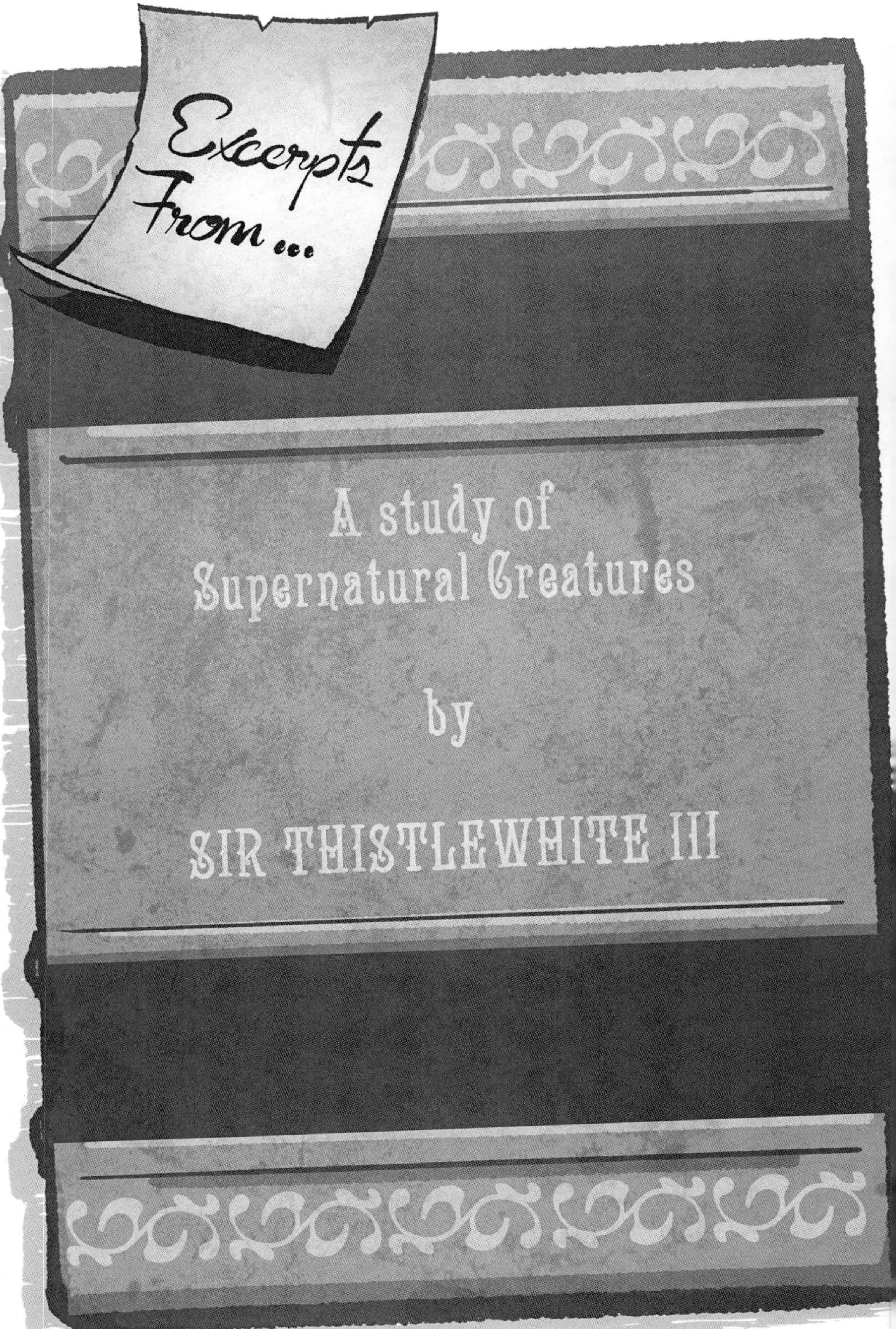
Excerpts From...
A study of
Supernatural Creatures
by
SIR THISTLEWHITE III

Preface

Dear reader, please note. The purpose of this journal is to catalogue demons and spirits that cross over into our world. My endeavor is strictly academic in nature and not intended as a guide for any of you wishing to go monster chasing. Monster chasing is an extremely dangerous activity that will most likely result in your death, and I cannot be held responsible for any foolish persons that choose to ignore my warning. In other words: Do not try this at home.

The vast majority of the creatures in this book are indiscriminately violent and will kill any human they come in contact with. I advise reading about them and not pursuing or confronting any demon, specter, ghost or other such supernatural creature that you may cross paths with. The best way to survive a demon encounter is to not have one in the first place.

While this journal is not affiliated with any specific Guardian or village, I do owe many of them a debt of gratitude for saving my hide on a few harrowing occasions. All observations, notes, and theories originate and belong to me alone, and cannot be recreated or redistributed without my prior written consent.

Lastly I'd like to dedicate this book to the brave bodyguards I hired to protect me while I did my research in the unpredictable and hazardous wilds. Without their help and fortuitous sacrifice, I could not have completed the journal you now hold in your hands. May their souls rest in peace.

– Sir Thistlewhite III

The Batmare

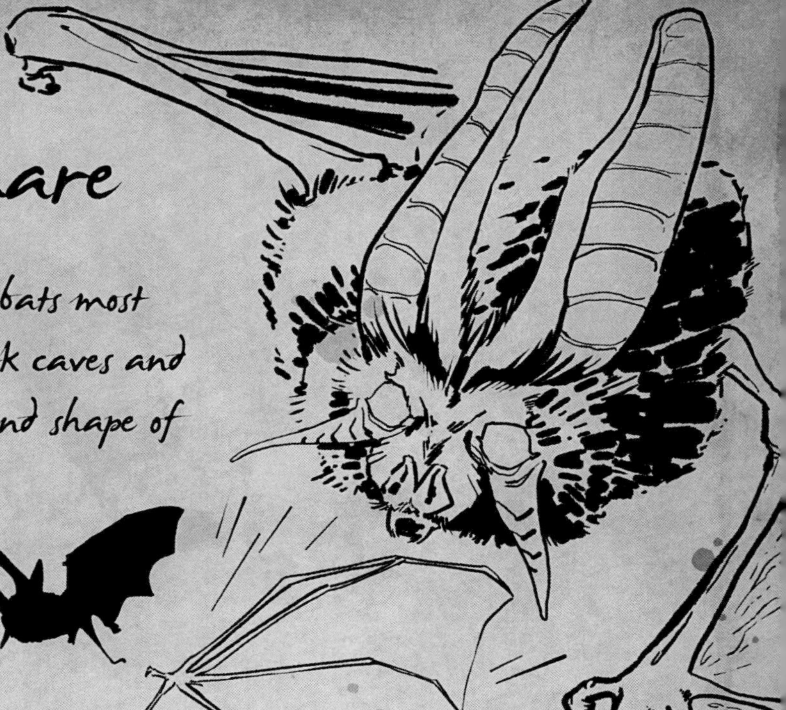

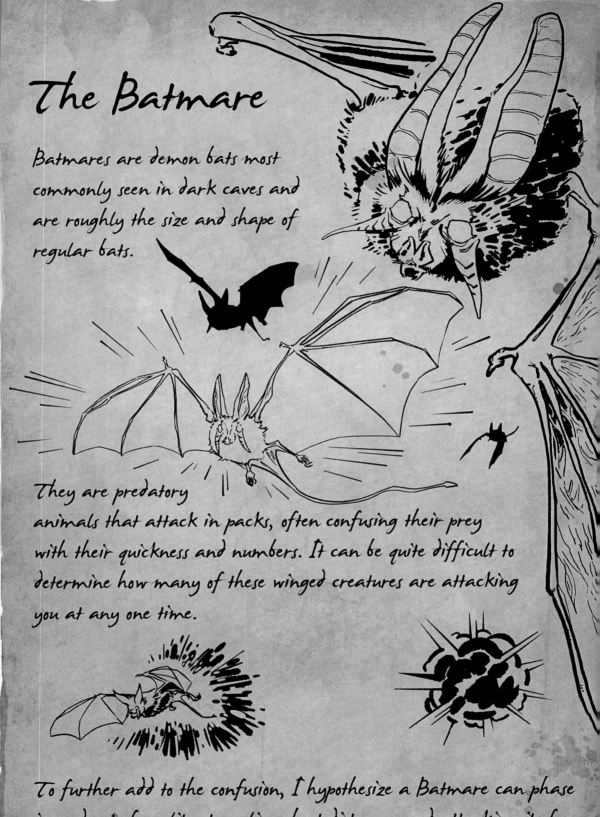

Batmares are demon bats most commonly seen in dark caves and are roughly the size and shape of regular bats.

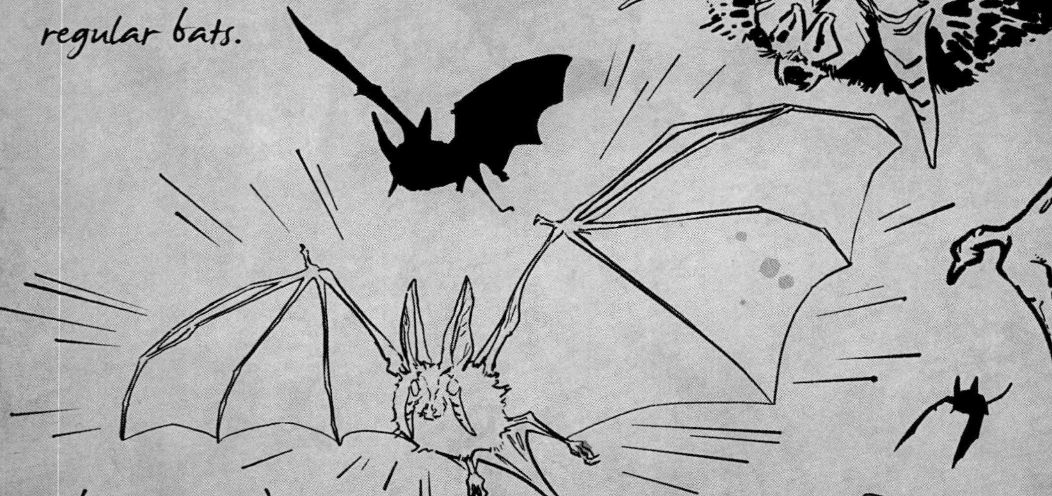

They are predatory animals that attack in packs, often confusing their prey with their quickness and numbers. It can be quite difficult to determine how many of these winged creatures are attacking you at any one time.

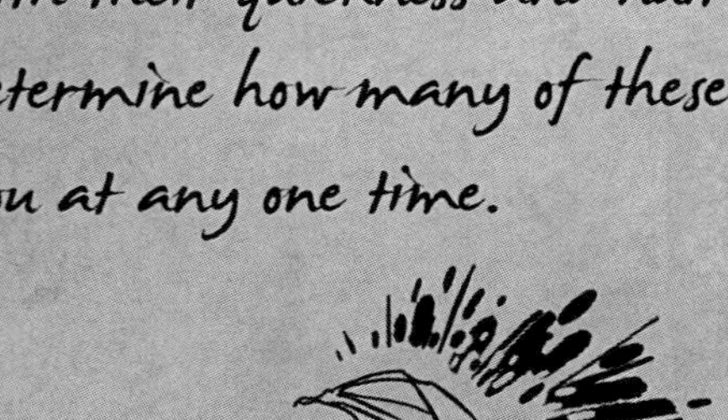

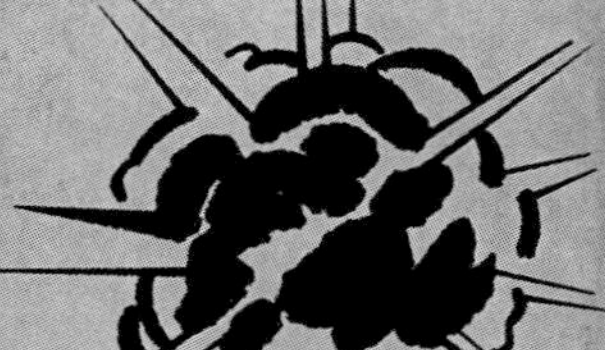

To further add to the confusion, I hypothesize a Batmare can phase in and out of reality, traveling short distances and attacking its foe from many angles. This makes a pack of five to six feel like fifteen or more.

The Slime Demon

Though not considered a major threat, don't underestimate a slime demon should you encounter one.

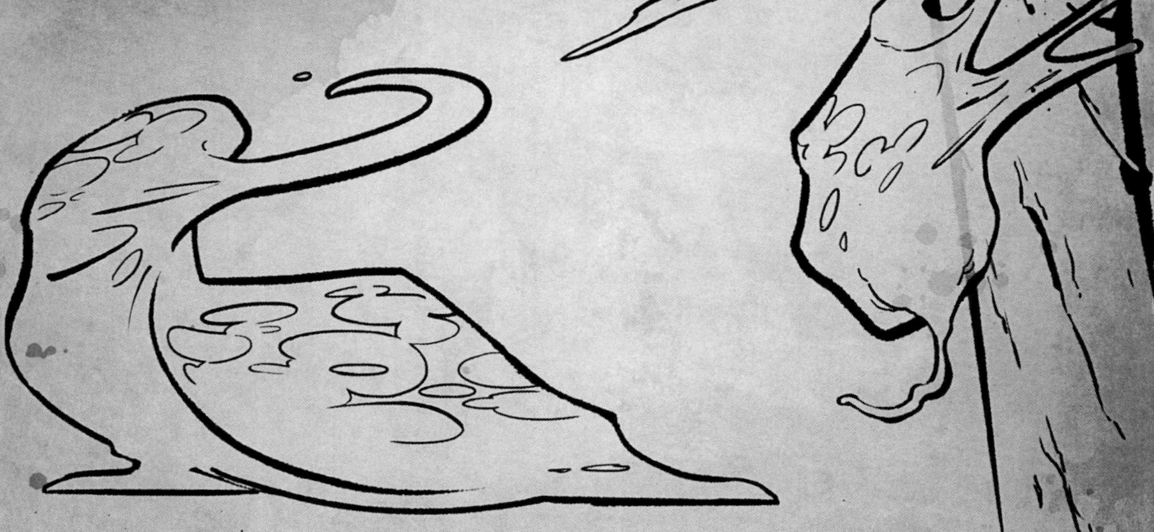

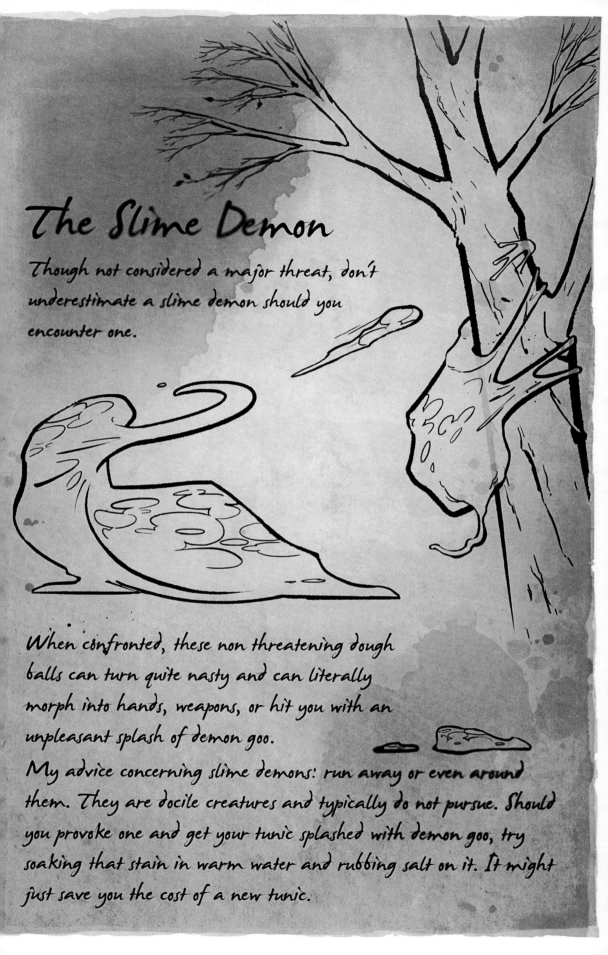

When confronted, these non threatening dough balls can turn quite nasty and can literally morph into hands, weapons, or hit you with an unpleasant splash of demon goo.

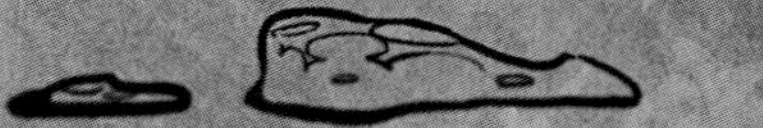

My advice concerning slime demons: run away or even around them. They are docile creatures and typically do not pursue. Should you provoke one and get your tunic splashed with demon goo, try soaking that stain in warm water and rubbing salt on it. It might just save you the cost of a new tunic.

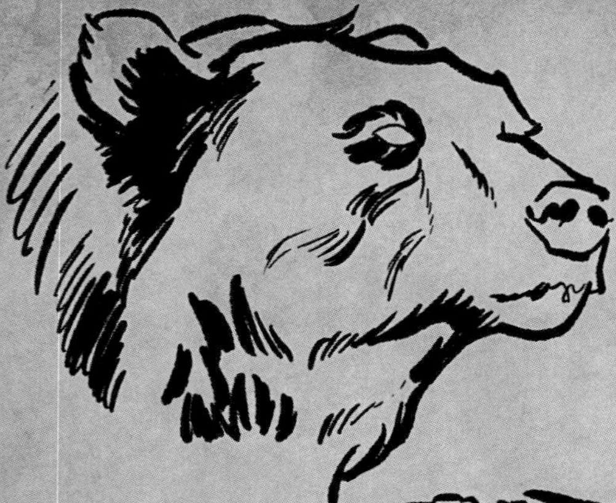

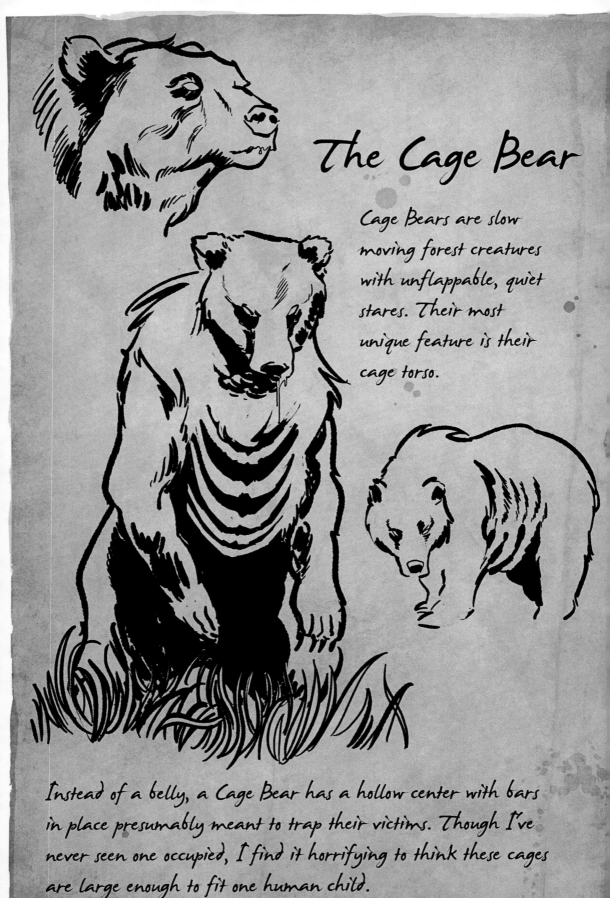

The Cage Bear

Cage Bears are slow moving forest creatures with unflappable, quiet stares. Their most unique feature is their cage torso.

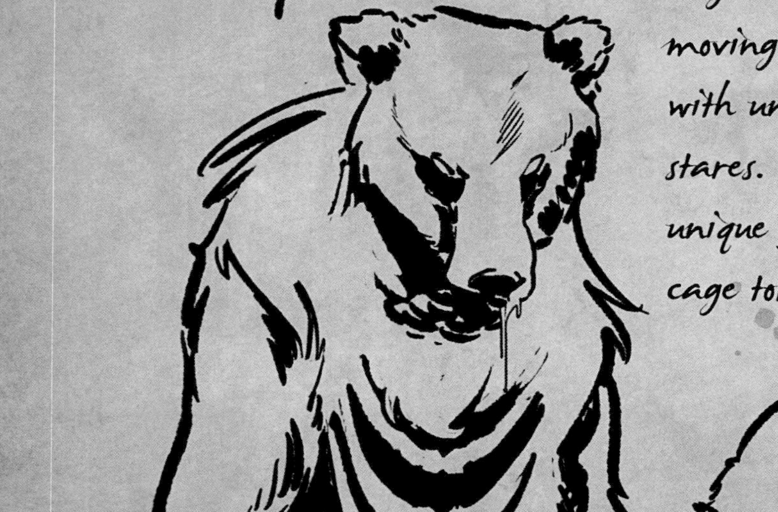

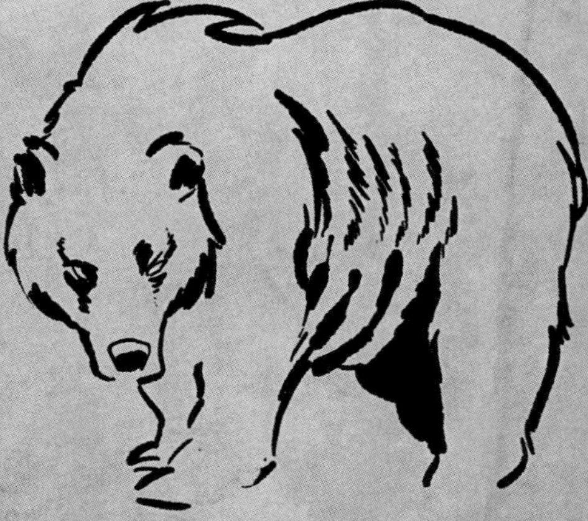

Instead of a belly, a Cage Bear has a hollow center with bars in place presumably meant to trap their victims. Though I've never seen one occupied, I find it horrifying to think these cages are large enough to fit one human child.

Tokari Demon

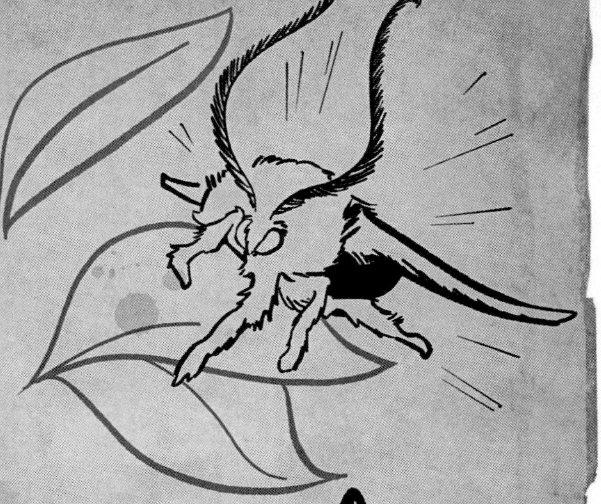

The Tokari Demon is commonly found in forested grasslands with an increase in activity around a full moon.

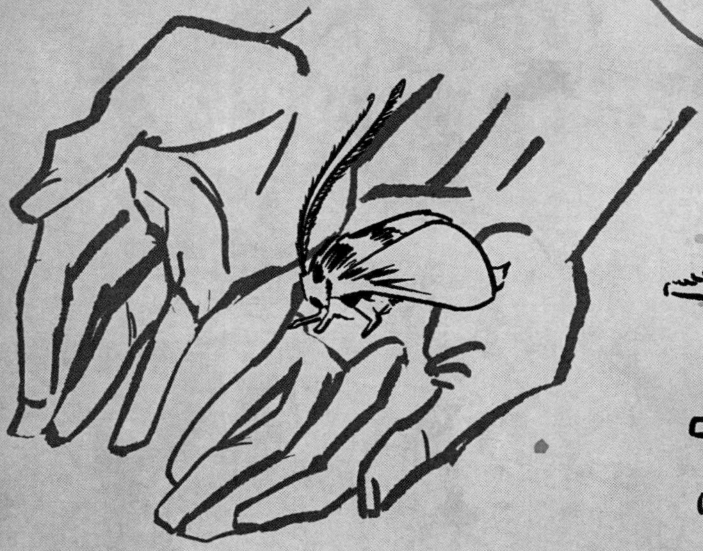

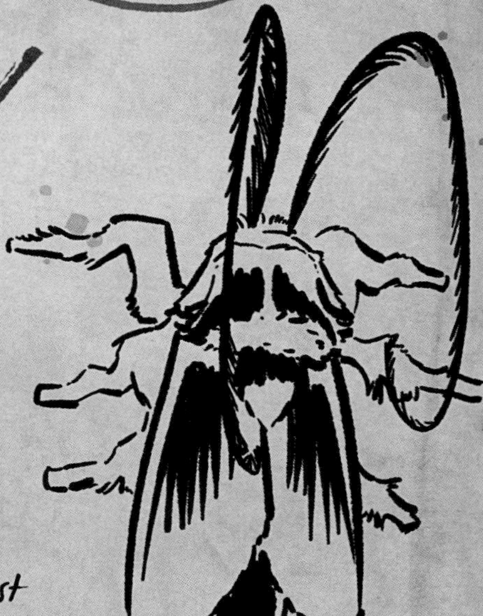

Tokari leave behind a shining trail of dust that causes an unnatural, deep sleep to befall any animal or human who breathes it in. The duration of the sleep varies widely with each case, but there is a report of one young woman's slumber so great that when she awoke she found herself transformed into an old lady.

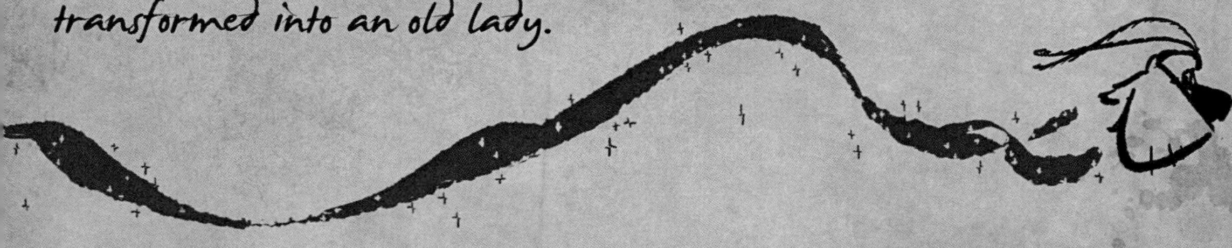

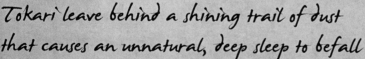

Thankfully, the woman's vigor and passion for life could not be defeated, and she lived everyday in an attempt to make up for the lifetime she had lost.

Chi-Yourn Demon

Known for its strength sapping
ability, the Chi-Yourn Demon
is a terrifying foe for anyone
foolish enough to do battle
against it. Believe me when
I say leave these to the
professionals. These horned
destroyers love to wreak havoc
on unsuspecting villages and
have an unquenchable taste
for livestock.

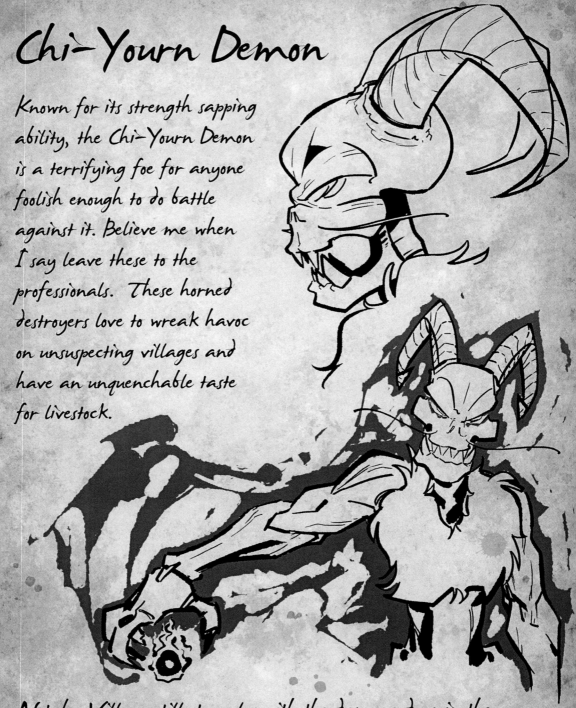

Netahn Village still struggles with the damage done in the
aftermath of their Chi-Yourn Demon encounter a year ago.
I'm proud to say I donated to their disaster relief fund, but I still
can't stand that wretchedly sappy song the bards wrote and sang over
and over again until they raised enough gold to rebuild the village.

The Four-armed Troll

The Four-Armed Troll is a barbaric brute that roams any densely forested area. The beast's extra set of hands allows it to climb and swing from the trees while still holding a pair of bludgeoning weapons. They are highly territorial so your best bet during an encounter is to run in a straight line and hope you escape quickly enough from their claimed territory.

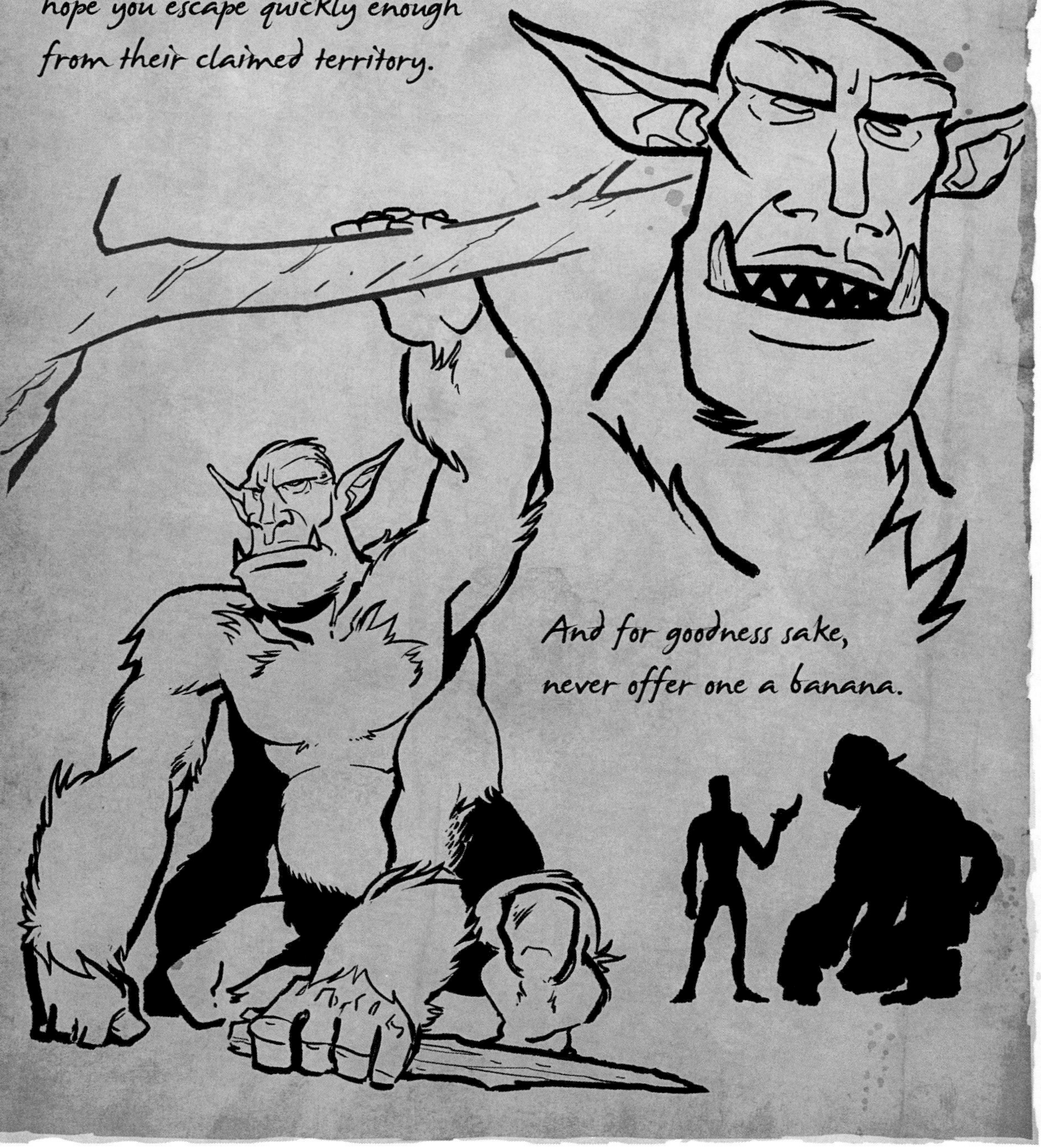

And for goodness sake, never offer one a banana.

The Pixie Rosa

I saw it!
Or at least I think I saw it.

The Pixie Rosa is a mythical spirit believed to roam the countryside, sprinkling good cheer amongst plants and vegetation. Some even say the first trees were planted by the Pixie Rosa, and the entire world is her garden. Legend also states if you catch this busy bee, she will grant you one wish in exchange for her release.

Of course I have no idea what device you would use to ensnare such a creature, or if I will be lucky enough to get another glimpse at this rare specimen. Needless to say I will keep my eyes and nets open.

Tapha Mushrooms

These dangerous fungi grow next to regular mushrooms in hopes to confuse the unobservant harvester. When ingested, these mushrooms from the spirit world cause permanent blindness, horrible indigestion, and in extreme cases, death.

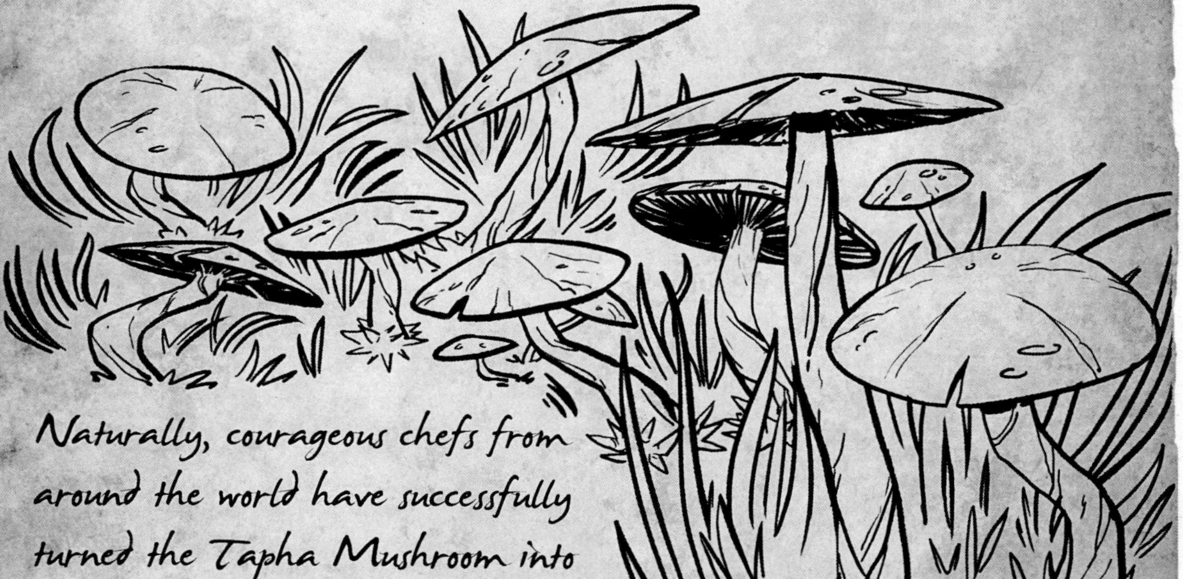

Naturally, courageous chefs from around the world have successfully turned the Tapha Mushroom into an expensive and exotic delicacy. If you boil and soak in vinegar, they can brighten any cream sauce or even be served on the side.

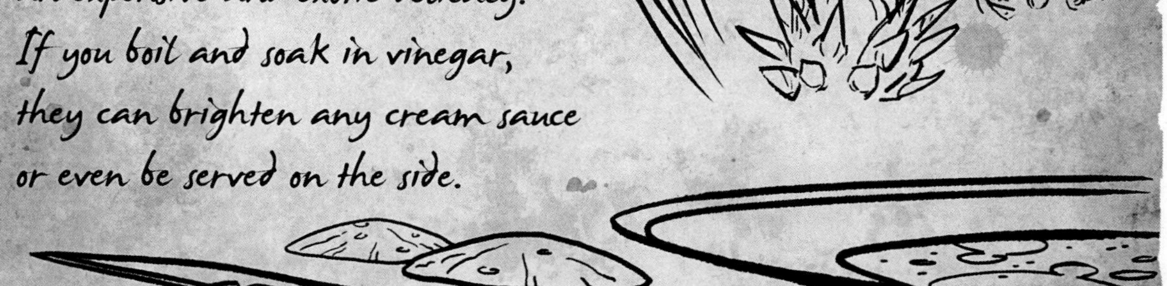

Tapha Mushrooms have a bold, tangy flavor and if prepared right may cause temporary spots to your vision, but if prepared wrong, which is the case more often than not, you may have just eaten your last meal.

Tornado Fist

The Tornado Fist, sometimes referred to as a Blur Fist or Tornado Hand, is a whirling demon comprised of powerful gusts of wind.

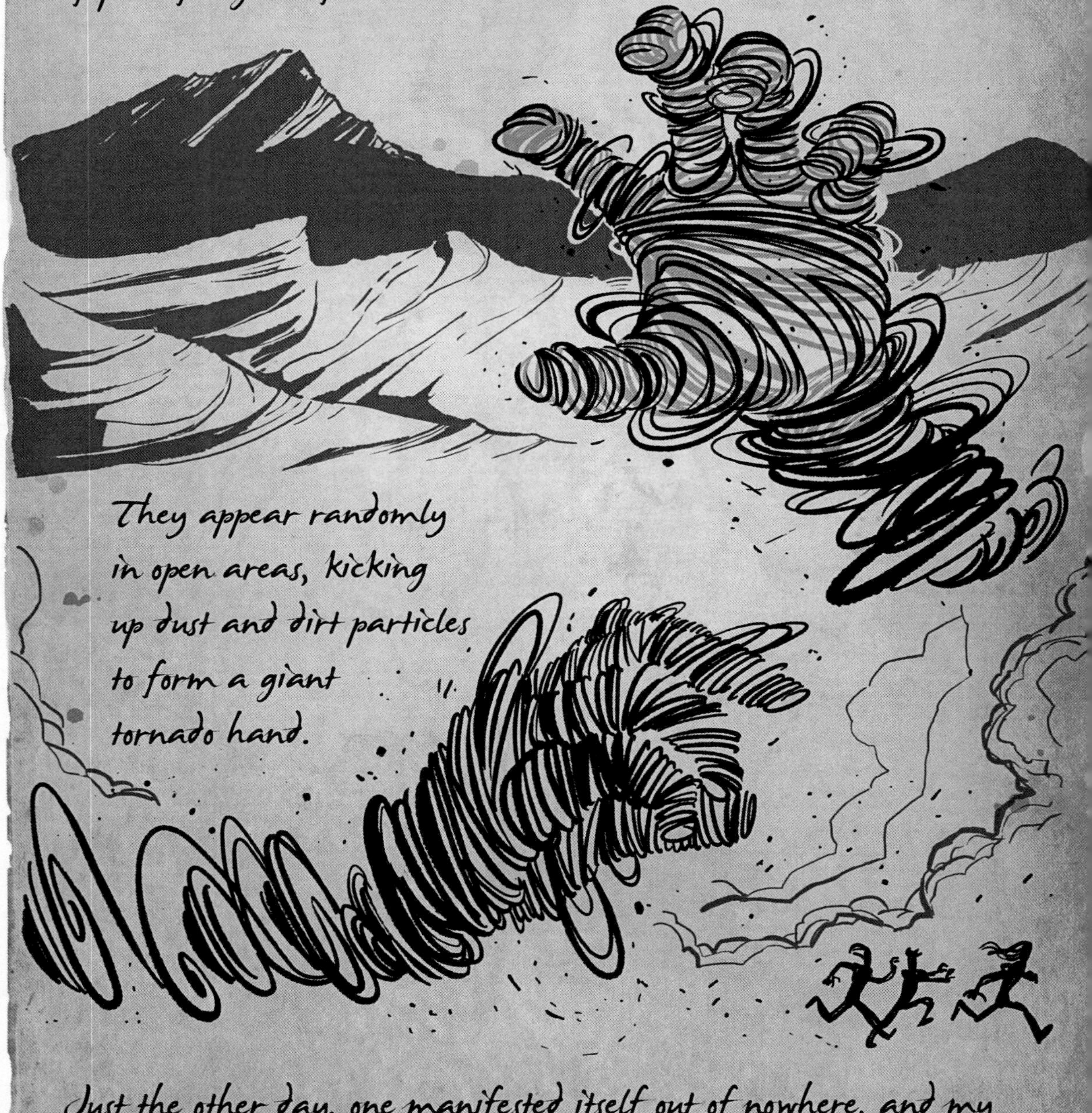

They appear randomly in open areas, kicking up dust and dirt particles to form a giant tornado hand.

Just the other day, one manifested itself out of nowhere, and my bodyguard was snatched up by it. When the dust finally settled my companion was nowhere to be found. I suppose it's time to head to the nearest town and look for a new bodyguard.

Mystery Egg

Traveling the countryside of this amazing land I constantly stumble across a great many curious things, but none more curious than the Demon Egg I found in the hallow of an ancient tree.

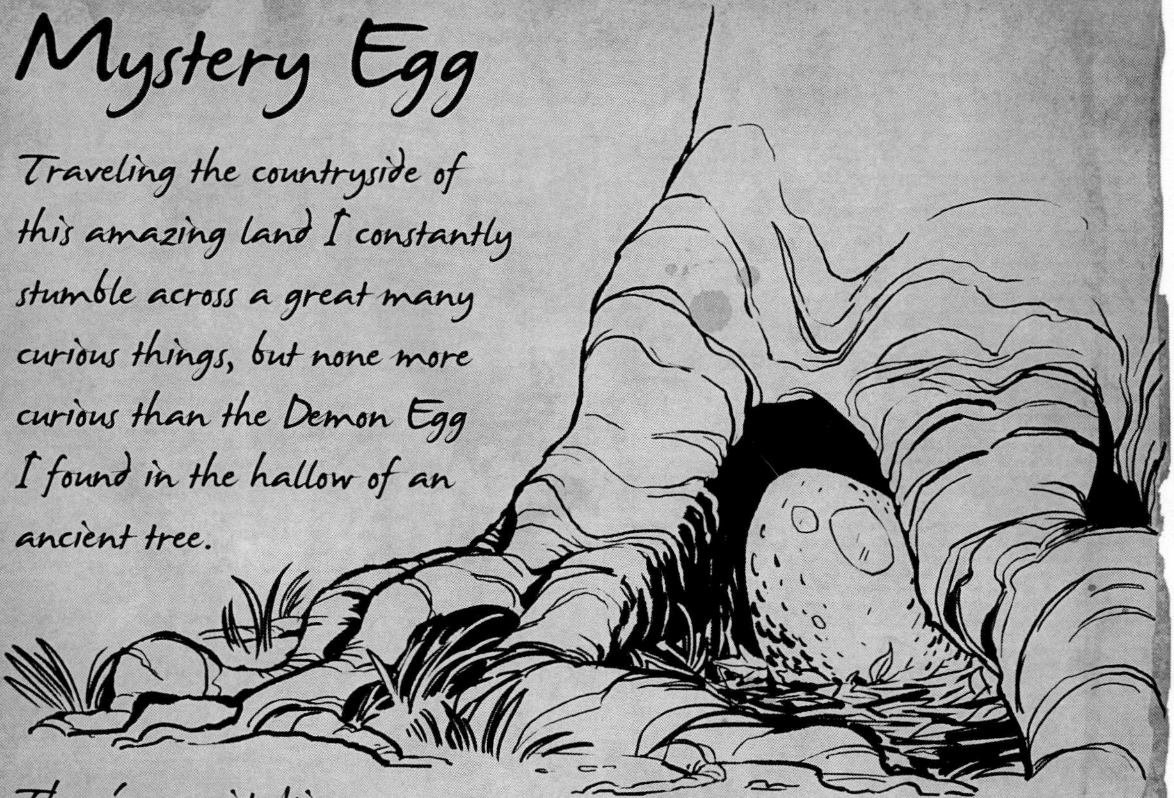

There's no mistaking the unearthly origin of the egg's glowing aura and unnaturaly large size and weight. My bodyguard begged me not to take it with us pleading, "What good could possibly come from taking a Demon Egg with us?"

When I refused to leave this precious artifact behind, he went so far as to try and smash it when I wasn't looking, but of course his man-made weapons had no effect on the impenetrable exterior of the mysterious Demon Egg.

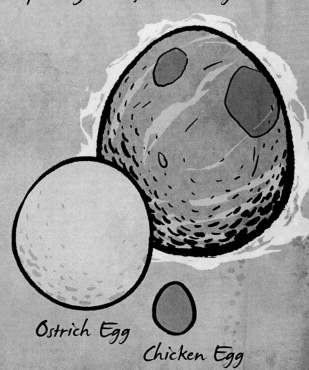

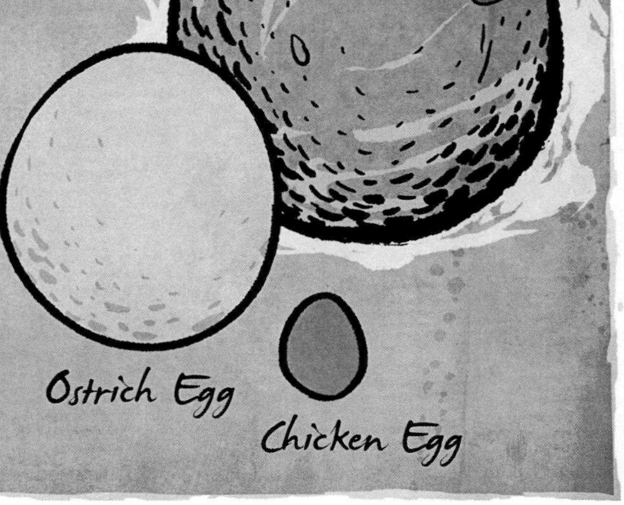
Ostrich Egg
Chicken Egg

Fear Mongrels

These slinky creatures of the night secrete a pheromone that cause paranoia and fear, usually resulting in any would be attacker fleeing in a wild panic. In reality these Fear Mongrels are quite harmless and surprisingly cute with their big eyes and small paws.

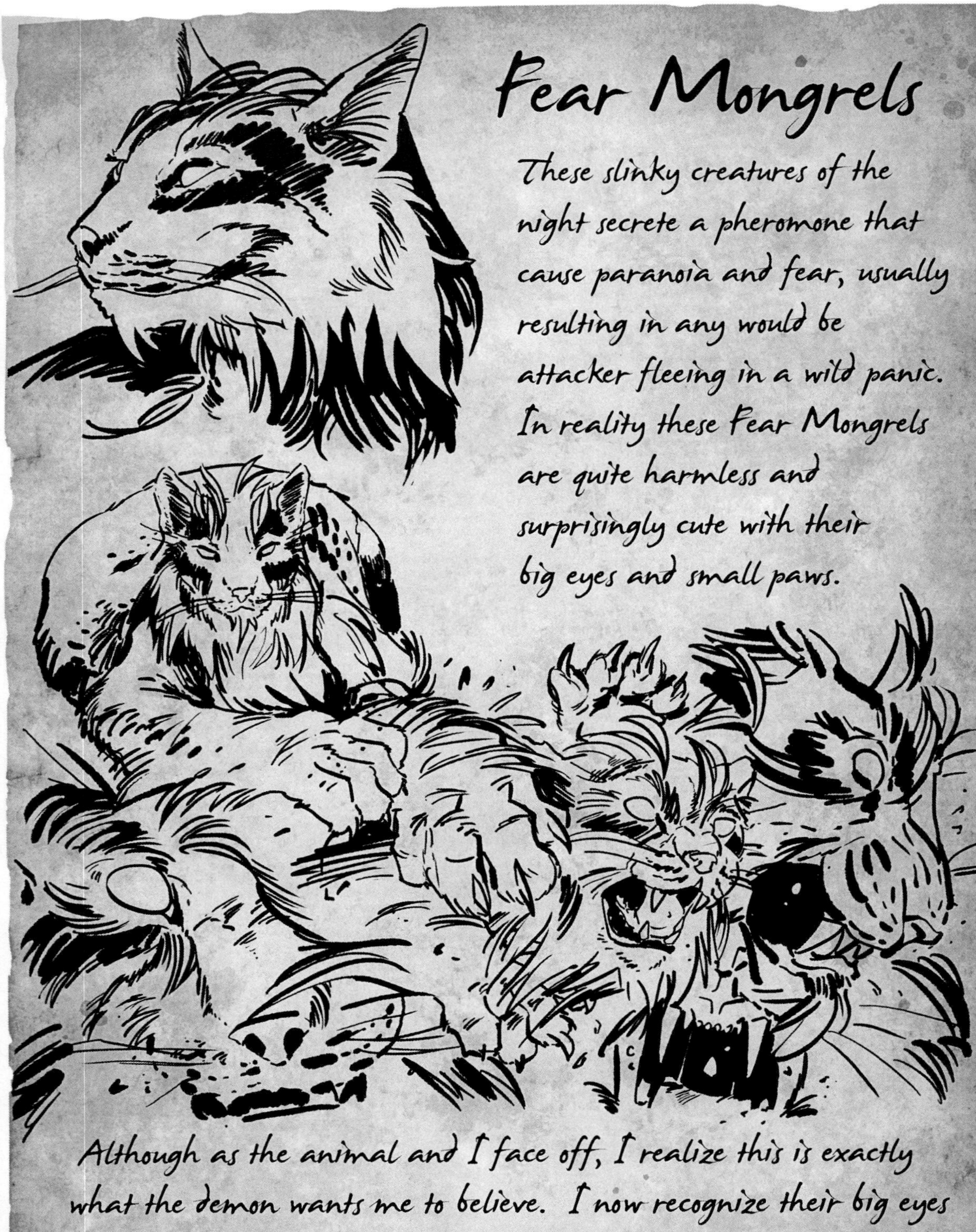

Although as the animal and I face off, I realize this is exactly what the demon wants me to believe. I now recognize their big eyes are sizing me up for the kill, and though their paws are small, they are well equipped with razor sharp claws. Wait. Could this be the effects of the pheromone? No. I am certain it could pounce and tear me to shreds at any moment. My only chance is to run and pray I am fast enough....

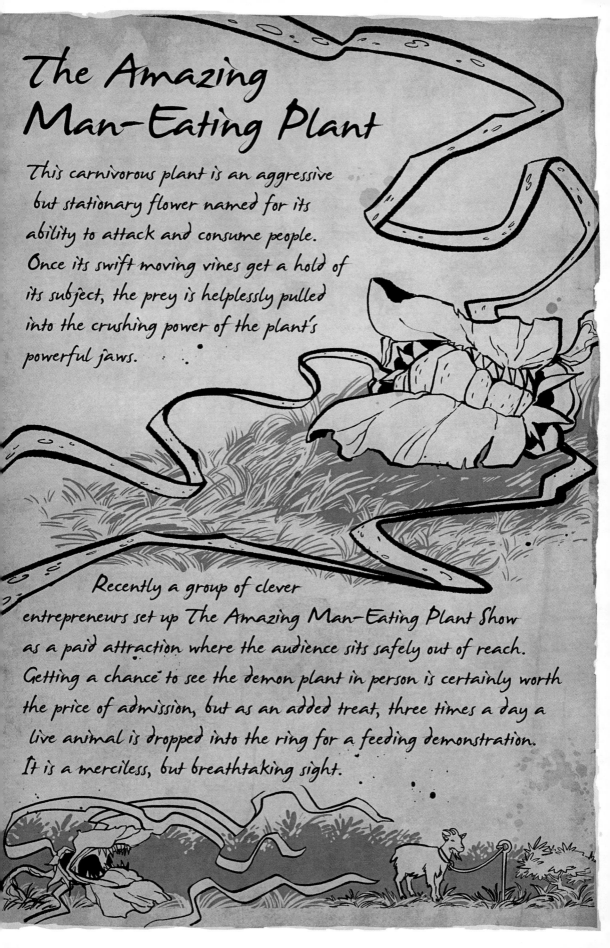

The Amazing Man-Eating Plant

This carnivorous plant is an aggressive but stationary flower named for its ability to attack and consume people. Once its swift moving vines get a hold of its subject, the prey is helplessly pulled into the crushing power of the plant's powerful jaws.

Recently a group of clever entrepreneurs set up The Amazing Man-Eating Plant Show as a paid attraction where the audience sits safely out of reach. Getting a chance to see the demon plant in person is certainly worth the price of admission, but as an added treat, three times a day a live animal is dropped into the ring for a feeding demonstration. It is a merciless, but breathtaking sight.

Ezou Monkey

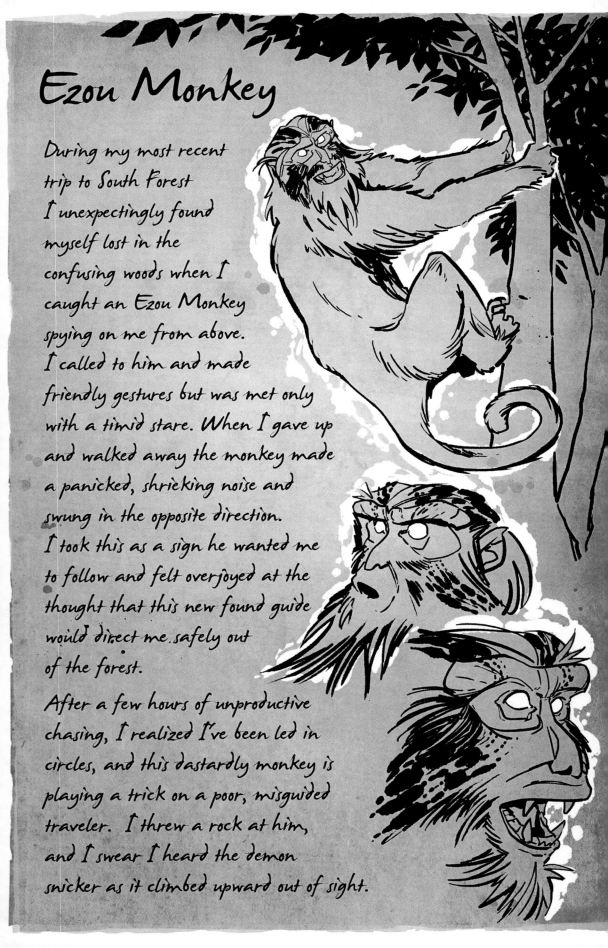

During my most recent trip to South Forest I unexpectingly found myself lost in the confusing woods when I caught an Ezou Monkey spying on me from above. I called to him and made friendly gestures but was met only with a timid stare. When I gave up and walked away the monkey made a panicked, shrieking noise and swung in the opposite direction. I took this as a sign he wanted me to follow and felt overjoyed at the thought that this new found guide would direct me safely out of the forest.

After a few hours of unproductive chasing, I realized I've been led in circles, and this dastardly monkey is playing a trick on a poor, misguided traveler. I threw a rock at him, and I swear I heard the demon snicker as it climbed upward out of sight.

The Pixie Rosa — Part II

Once again I am fortunate enough to
see the Pixie Rosa, the rarest of spirits.
After my unhelpful encounter
with the Ezou Monkey, I remained
lost in the dense South Forest, and
the Pixie Rosa must have taken
pity on my sorrowful predicament.
She appeared before me and
chanted these few words:

GOOD AND LOST

WOODS TOO DEEP

BAD AND FOUND

THEN FOLLOW ME

This cryptic verse proved most baffling. Was she trying to help me?
Was I an unwanted intruder in her forest?
She zipped off, and for better or for worse I followed.

The Elvidae

The Pixie Rosa seemed impatient as she guided me out of the forest. I was of course grateful for her kindness, but I couldn't understand what the rush was about. Then we came upon a small creek where a figure was trapped underneath a fallen tree trunk. I realized it was not me she was helping, but I that was to help her friend.

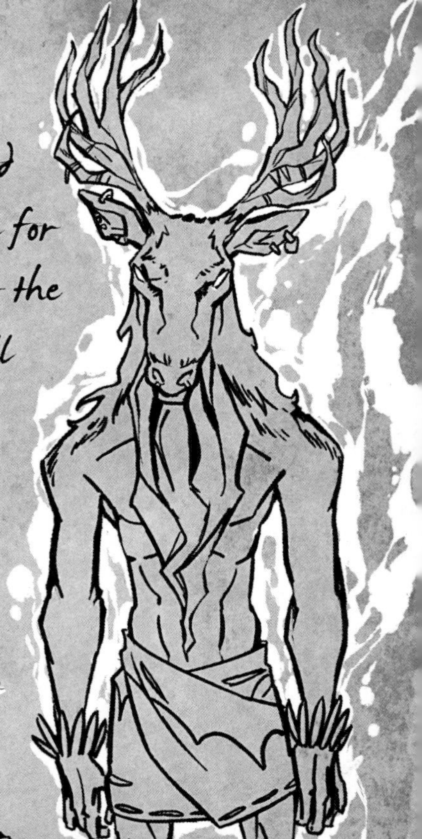

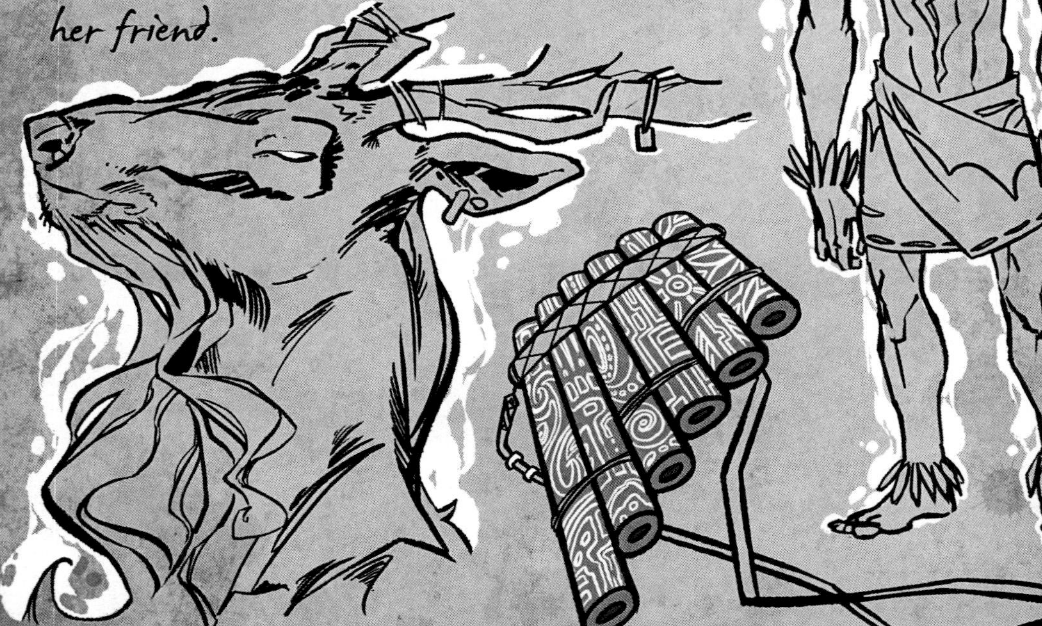

As I began pushing the log with all of my strength, I saw the figure was not a man at all, but a half man, half deer spirit called an Elvidae. Once freed, the creature stood on two legs and handed me a small pan flute. I gazed at the tiny instrument and marveled at the meticulously carved symbols engraved on it. When I looked up, both the Pixie Rosa and Elvidae had disappeared, leaving me alone and still lost in the woods of South Forest.

The Griffin

I blew into the Elvidae's flute as hard as my lungs could muster, and magically, a sparkling five note melody emerged. From above me descended a magnificent beast with the head of a lion and the wings and talons of an eagle. It grabbed me with its giant bird claws and flew me just above the forest trees.

When the exhilarating ride ended, I petted the Griffin and showed him the pan flute that would forever link us as friends. Unfortunately the beast did not see it that way. He instead batted the flute out of my hands and stomped it to pieces before he lifted off without even looking back at me. I later hypothesized the flute was most likely a single favor the winged lion owed to the Elividae, and the debt was repaid by depositing me out of South Forest